Praise for
Damn! Why Didn't I Write That?

"Demonstrating how lucrative the publis ... idea at the right time, McCutcheon describes ... query letters, and proposals to agents, contract ... each step, he offers insights from personal experience and shares the experiences of several well-known best-selling authors. Both upbeat and practical."
—*Library Journal*

"This book has everything you need to turn your ideas into cash. ...Don't delay, because the next bestseller you see on the shelf could have been yours."
—Book-of-the-Month Club

[McCutcheon] really does offer terrific advice."
—*The Tampa Tribune*

"McCutcheon shows you how to get in on the action by identifying lucrative publishing niches and filling them year after year."
—Quality Paperback Book Club

"...filled with the necessary details of not only writing a great nonfiction work, but also how to handle contract negotiations, why you need (or don't need) an agent, writing proposals, marketing and just about any other subject that the writer may need to know."
—*Midwest Book Review*

"Practical ideas for any who would not only get published, but make a living in the writing world."
—*The Bookwatch*

"Offers common sense advice for getting rich off writing a nonfiction book...Here's McCutcheon's big idea: Write a nonfiction book that doesn't already exist, one that will become a resource, and it will sell. It may sell slowly, but it will sell; and it will continue to sell and the royalty checks will continue to pour in."
—Samantha Puckett, *St. Petersburg Times*

"The title suggests how wonderfully simple ideas presented will can make for highly successful books. The reader is led logically through the process of finding, researching, and developing a market niche. [McCutcheon's] point is that nonfiction writers can score over and over again. This is a reference book for many writers' libraries. We give it five hearts."
— Bob Spear, The Book Barn

"This is a very different kind of writing book that is extraordinarily fun to read."
—*Writers Write, The Internet Writing Journal*

DAMN!

WHY DIDN'T I WRITE THAT?

How Ordinary People are Raking in

$100,000.00

...or more

Writing Nonfiction Books & How You Can Too!

New Updated Edition

by
Marc McCutcheon

Sanger, California

Printed in the United States of America.

Published by
Quill Driver Books/Word Dancer Press, Inc.,
1254 Commerece
Sanger, CA 93657
559-876-2170 / 800-497-4909

For a free e-mail newsletter on writing and getting published, please visit
QuillDriverBooks.com

Quill Driver Books/Word Dancer Press books may be purchased at special discounts for
educational, fund-raising, business or promotional use. Please contact Special Markets at
the above address or phone numbers.

ISBN 1-884956-55-6
To order a copy of this book, please call
1-800-497-4909.

2nd edition printing: 20 19 18 17 16 15 14 13 12 11 10 9 8 7 6 5 4 3 2
Quill Driver Books/Word Dancer Press Project Cadre:
Doris Hall, John David Marion, Stephen Blake Mettee, Linda Kay Weber

Cover image permissions
—From *Who Moved My Cheese?* by Spencer Johnson, copyright © 1998 by Spencer Johnson, M.D. Used by permission of G.P. Putnam's Sons, a division of Penquin Putnam Inc. —*Leadership Secrets of Attila the Hun* by Wess Roberts. Cover image reprinted with kind permission of Time Warner Trade Publishing, New York, New York. —*The Rules* by Ellen Fein and Sherrie Schneider. Cover image reprinted with kind permission of Time Warner Trade Publishing, New York, New York.—*Is There Life After Housework?* by Don Aslett. Cover image reprinted with kind permission of Writer's Digest Books, an imprint of F&W Publications, Inc., Cincinnati, Ohio. —*The Duct Tape Book* by Jim Berg and Tim Nyberg. Cover image reprinted with kind permission of Tim Nyberg. —*Gone With The Grits* by Diane Pfeifer. Cover image reprinted with kind permission of Diane Pfeifer. —*How To Keep Your Volkswagen Alive, 18ᵗʰ Edition* by John Muir, Tosh Gregg and Peter Aschwanden. Illustration copyright 1999 by Peter Aschwanden. Used by permission of Avalon Travel Publishing. All rights reserved. —*Roget's Super Thesaurus, Second Edition* by Marc McCutcheon. Cover image reprinted with kind permission of Writer's Digest Books, an imprint of F&W Publications, Inc., Cincinnati, Ohio. —*Don't Sweat The Small Stuff - And It's All Small Stuff* by Richard Carlson. Reprinted from *Don't Sweat The Small Stuff - And It's All Small Stuff* by Richard Carlson, Ph.D. Copyright (c) 1997, Richard Carlson, Ph.D. Published by Hyperion.—*Small Time Operator* by Bernard B. Kamoroff. Cover image reprinted with kind permission of Bell Springs Publishing, Willits, California.—*You've Earned It, Don't Lose It* by Suze Orman and Linda Mead. Cover image reprinted with kind permission of Newmarket Press, New York, New York. —*Random Acts of Kindness* by the Editors of Conari Press. Cover image reprinted with kind permission of Conari Press, Berkeley, California. —*Unbelievably Good Deals and Great Adventures That You Absolutely Can't Get Unless You're Over 50 (11ᵗʰ edition)* by Joan Rattner Heilman. Cover image reprinted with kind permission of The McGraw-Hill Companies, Inc., New York, New York.

Library of Congress Cataloging-in-Publication Data

McCutcheon, Marc.
    Damn! Why didn't I write that? : how ordinary people are raking in $100,000.00-- or more
writing nonfiction books & how you can too! / by March McCutcheon.
      p. cm.
    Includes bibliographical references and index.
    ISBN 1-884956-55-6
    1. Authorship--Marketing. I. Title.

PN161 .M39 2001
808'.02--dc21

2001019411

To all the kids on Hamilton Street who have drawn me away from the confines of my office to play whiffleball, break up fights, shoot hoops, check out salamanders, ants, and Pokemon cards, supply drinks and ice pops, apply bandages, build snow forts, scrounge up wood and nails for treehouses, set up lemonade stands, watch "off-Broadway" productions, witness rubber gloves bloat into the world's goofiest and most explosive water balloons, listen to gross jokes, marvel at marathon rounds of kick the can, and provide endless excuses not to work when I didn't want to anyway: Kara, Macky, Moira, Danny, Jake, Katie, Annie, Tom, Sam, Beth, James, Dominic, Derek, Matt, Coleman, Andrew, Adam, Alec, Kirsten, Jenny, Kelsey, Daniel J., Sam C., Tyler, and the Donahue girls.

To my Dad, too, whom I miss with all my heart and whose soul quietly reposes among the squeals and shouts of so many happy children, in the brown-eyed Susans of my backyard garden.

Acknowledgments

For their kind contributions, my sincerest thanks to Skip Barker of the Wilson Devereaux Co.; Dan Bial, literary agent; Nancy Baggett (The International Cookie Book); Vicki Cobb (Science Experiments You Can Eat); Diane Dreher (The Tao of Womanhood); Priscilla Huff (101 Best Home-Based Businesses for Women); Sharon Levy (National Association of Science Writers); Michael Larsen and Elizabeth Pomada, authors and literary agents; Jerry McTigue (Life's Little Frustration Book); Jean Amour Polly (The Internet Kids and Family Yellow Pages); Marilyn Ross (Jump Start Your Book Sales); and Dianne Schwartz (Whose Face Is in the Mirror?).

Above all, a giant thanks to Stephen Blake Mettee for all of his critical help in making this the best book it could be.

Contents

The
Don't Skip This Introduction
Introduction

*Some thoughts on the best home business anywhere…How much can
a modestly successful author make?…Fiction vs. Nonfiction…Do
you have to be a high school dropout to do this?*

Among all the home businesses touted these days, I can think of none that is easier to get into, cheaper to start, or offers more potential for recognition, respect, and reward than nonfiction book writing. It is, in my opinion, the ultimate dream job. Whether we write dictionaries, how-tos, personal experiences, in-depth guides or scandalous kiss-and-tells, nonfiction book writers today easily enjoy the most liberal of job environments with, possibly, more benefits than any other home-based business person.

Take a look at these advantages:

- No annoying employees or bosses

- No advertising costs

- No inventory

- No overhead

- No licenses, permits, or zoning allowances

- No three-piece suits or sensible dresses. (Your power jammies are fine.)

- Shaving, combed hair, and deodorant optional

- No alarm clocks

- No commute

- No feigning illness on Monday morning

- No meetings

- No ass-kissing

You can start this job *today* with no more than a rickety typewriter, a ream of paper, some postage, a kitchen table, a local public library, and a dream.

And, you can make a million bucks.

Or $1.95.

The beauty of nonfiction book writing is that the field truly is wide open to *anyone*, regardless of race, sex, age, education, financial background, or personal appearance. (In the corporate world, tall, beautiful people rule. In the writing world, even Yoda can climb to the top of the success ladder.) And talent? Talent is not only overrated but all too often used as an excuse for failing to *try:* "I have no inborn talent, alas, so why bother?" How much you succeed and how much you make depends almost entirely on your willingness to work hard and persevere.

> "How much you succeed and how much you make depends almost entirely on your willingness to work hard and persevere."

The downside of being a nonfiction book writer is the very same downside that every entrepreneur faces. If you don't follow the market, remain competitive, study trends, run an efficient, streamlined business, maintain your product (in this case your writing) at a high quality level, and promote your business and yourself with the fervor of a door-to-door Kirby vacuum salesman with seven hungry children and a new litter of St. Bernard puppies to feed, you will flop. Go belly-up. Go out of business. Choke. Suffer financial hardship. Blow it. Bomb. Lay an egg.

Yet, unlike other entrepreneurs, unless you do something exceedingly foolish, you will have very little money invested in your business—no employee payroll, no swank downtown office space, no six-figure equipment leases. You'll get in with minimum risk. In fact, it is likely to be the smallest financial risk of any entrepreneurial endeavor going today. And if you don't believe this, just try buying a Taco Bell franchise or opening even a closet-sized boutique for the price of a cheap computer.

Are you beginning to see just how exceptional this home business can be?

Indeed, the risks are as low as anyone could possibly ask for any business in light of the potential rewards. Your chief gamble is in the time and effort you invest, not hard cash. And that time, at least in the beginning, can be your spare time. In fact, easing into this business on a part-time basis is the wise strategy until you've reached a respectable perch on the learning curve. As accepting of beginners as this home business is, you can't learn it overnight. You also shouldn't roll the dice with your family's welfare until you know those dice are loaded in your favor.

It is my contention, however, that you can learn the trade and begin making a respectable income much faster than most people think possible—if you avoid the mistakes of others and stay away from both low-reward and super-high reward (but highly speculative) writing projects. (More on those later.)

I finished writing my first nonfiction book, *The Compass In Your Nose & Other Astonishing Facts About Humans*, in 1988. At the time, nothing else like it existed on the market, which was in itself astonishing. Here was a simple, universally interesting topic that could not only be serialized in scores of magazines, but one that would make a perfect fit at a book club, and could be marketed worldwide in virtually all of the major languages. That nobody had written a similar book appeared too good to be true. How could an inexperienced amateur—a *high school dropout*, no less—squirrel out such a potential-rich nut in such a fiercely competitive field?

Yet that's exactly what I did.

After an eleven-month effort, while working simultaneously at a full-time job and playing drums for a fully booked band on weekends, I sold the book.

The advance I received from my publisher, Jeremy Tarcher, was modest, just $5,000. By the time I paid my federal and state taxes, that would be whittled down to roughly $3,900. Hardly worthwhile compensation for eleven months' work, most folks would reckon, even if it was *part* part-time.

But to me it was a pure thrill. And, it was a thrill that was destined only to get better.

Because for nine years after I sold the book to Tarcher, every January and August, a check would mysteriously appear in my mailbox.

Not just any check. A *royalty* check. A check to compensate me for ongoing sales. And for serializations. And for second, third, and fourth printings. And for book club sales. And for overseas sales. And for foreign translations. And for fifth, sixth, and seventh printings…and for….

Oh joy!

Sometimes the royalty check was modest, and I would sock it away to save for a rainy day. Other times the check was big enough to buy a car. Or two.

In all my first nine years of royalty-collecting, I swear the only new work I put into the book was to sign my name on the checks.* Somewhere around $90,000 worth of checks all totaled.

Is this a great country or what?

On the Stephen King scale of royalties, of course, $90,000 weighs about as much as a gnat's left earlobe. King makes more than 100 times that figure in a single year. But he is, after all, the *king*.** To King, $90,000 is pocket change. Maybe even pocket *lint*.

But among commoners—we noncreative geniuses of the world—who

---

*That I haven't put in any additional work on my first book since it was published is a bit of a fib. About two years after the book's publication, *Reader's Digest* offered to buy some excerpts. But they wanted me to double-check a couple of facts first. So I went to the library, spent two hours, and got them what they wanted. For my efforts, and my excerpts, they paid me $4,000. That worked out to $4 per word. Yeah, I'll go to the library for $4,000. No problem!

**Actually, King isn't the king. His books have been eclipsed by the efforts of numerous nonfiction authors, whose names you probably wouldn't even recognize. More on these anonymous authors later. (By the way, it's Garfield who holds the record for most books on the best-seller lists at the same time, not King.)

wouldn't be satisfied with $90,000 of pocket change for less than a year of part-time work? For work we *enjoyed*? For work that brought recognition, respect, and a sense of accomplishment impossible to find anywhere else?

If you're like legions of hand-wringing mothers certain of the Dickensian poverty that awaits their children who choose to write for a career, you'll assume that my experience is the exception. Lucky breaks happen sometimes, but you can't count on them. Nor can you usually live off them for long.

If we were talking about fiction, despite what I just said about King, I might be inclined to agree. Fiction, as Mom rightly suspects, is indeed a difficult way to make a consistent living.

Let's look at facts.

Of the 50,000-plus commercial books published each year (180,000 if you count self-published and scholarly titles), only about 3,500 are novels (including genre titles), and poorly-paying, short-lived, paperback romances account for a whopping one third of the total. Not counting genre titles, only about 120 fiction releases each year are *first* novels, according to *Publishers Weekly*. Of these, three out of four will not earn out their meager advances of under $10,000.

New novelists fare poorly for one simple reason. Nobody knows them. With few exceptions (*Bridges of Madison County* and *Waiting to Exhale* among the most notable), big fiction sales only come about through recognition of an author's previous work. Thus, most authors must crank out several novels (in the same genre) before they become trusted by a large enough universe of book buyers to generate respectable word-of-mouth sales.

Not so in nonfiction, where an author's name recognition is less important. Although the very top spots on the nonfiction best-seller lists are almost always taken up by celebrities and people in the news, scores of unknowns and first-timers populate the hefty sales positions just under the lists' footlights. It is this small multitude of oh-so-interesting books just below bestsellerdom's glare that is so inspiring. Many of these books are written by teachers, small town reporters, housewives, out of work executives—and yes, even on occasion, *high school dropouts*.

I don't know how many people in the United States in any given year try to write and sell novels. Fifty thousand, I think, would be a conservative estimate, which would mean that only a fraction of one percent ultimately will meet with success this year.

Consider the figures again. *Annually, that's 46,500 nonfiction books vs. 3,500 novels.*

While you can't extrapolate from this figure and say your odds of selling are fifteen times greater writing nonfiction, you can be confident that the odds are, whatever the exact figure, *much* better. Not only are the odds of making a sale greater, but so is the likelihood that your book will stay in print and earn royalties for you longer. Why?

Because nonfiction has something going for it that fiction will never have.

In a word, *need.*

People *need* nonfiction books. They need reference books, how-to guides, self-help tomes, histories, directories, cookbooks, travelogues, chronicles, manuals....They need to know how to make more money. They need to know how to keep themselves healthy. They need to know more about current events and world affairs. They need to know how to run their computers, repair their leaky faucets, and trim their butts and bellies. They need to stay abreast of trends, ripoffs, corruption, scandals, politics, crime, education, careers, scientific breakthroughs...the list goes on and on. In short, they need a galaxy of useful, practical titles. Not only do they need these titles, they will often pay a premium for them if they think they can find the information no place else.

People do not, however, need the latest bodice ripper, mystery or thriller. As delightful as these books can be, we do not, as a whole, buy anywhere near as many of them as nonfiction books.

Lucky breaks? In nonfiction, lucky breaks await those who read the market wisely. And those lucky breaks can be mined. *Consistently.*

In my case, $90,000 *was* lucky. My second book, *Descriptionary*, earned only $39,000 in its first edition. But wait. After the book was in print for a few years, the publisher paid me an additional $10,000 advance to update the book for a second edition, and then three years later, paid another $10,000 advance to update it for a third. And, hey, *Descriptionary* only took *ten* months to write. Again, part-time.

And the updates? Six weeks each of embarrassingly simple labor.

But it gets better still. My third book took just seven months to write. To the uninitiated, it would appear to be the runt of the litter. How many people, after all, would buy an obscure title called *Writer's Guide to Everyday Life in the 1800s*? If you were an author writing about this time period, you would probably want a copy. But, realistically, how many writers work in this era? Five hundred? A thousand? To someone who is unfamiliar with the market, compiling such a book would appear a to be a goal worthy of a dunderhead.

But that is precisely why knowing the market is so crucial. Even this apparently obscure title—one that most others wouldn't dream of considering or perhaps even thinking of in the first place—has racked upwards of 40,000 hardcover sales to date and continues to sell steadily years after being released. (If you're unimpressed by 40,000 sales, do some quick math. Say, $19.95 times 10 percent royalty. Could you use an extra $80,000?) Because this is the *only* writer's guide of this historical period—and likely the *only* one that will ever be published—I have, in effect, cornered the market and will, undoubtedly, collect paychecks from it for some time to come. Possibly for another ten years. Possibly for the rest of my life. I can't tell you what a nice feeling that gives me.

What's even better, I've created a line that never existed before. With the success of an historical guide to the 1800s proven, my publisher could confidently launch a whole category of similar historical guides of different periods. And I was, of course, first in line to cash in on my publisher's new confidence. (Specifically, with the *Writer's Guide to Everyday Life from Prohibition Through World War II*.) Many writers have since followed my lead in this series with titles of their own.

It was only after thinking hard about these books that I began to learn something critical about publishing. I didn't know it, but I had stumbled onto the two crucial keys to making a secure living from nonfiction. These keys, these blatantly obvious yet surprisingly little-utilized keys, can be summed up in just two words: *Niche*. And *backlist*.

A *niche* is a small field or genre that an author gets to know better than his own child and succeeds in because of that knowledge. Finding or creating a niche that others have overlooked can open the door to sensational profits, especially if you get through the door first.

Backlist refers to a book or a line of books that stays in print for a very long time. Publishers love them. So do authors. Get three or four of these backlist titles working for you at the same time, and you've got the equivalent of a secure mutual fund or rental property paying dividends great enough to live off from year after year, with no risk of losing your initial investment money. (And no tenants demanding that you unclog their toilets for them!)

Unfortunately, most authors don't know the difference between a frontlist niche title and a backlist one. Thus, we'll be tackling this delicious topic in more detail in the pages ahead.

I stumbled onto my backlist niches completely by accident. But once I learned how important the distinction between front and back were, I wouldn't write another book until I was sure it had the legs to run a marathon. No sprinters. No middle-distance runners. No early retirements at the remainder table. Today, I won't write anything unless I think it can continue kicking for at least ten years.

Which is precisely why I compiled my next book, *Roget's Super Thesaurus*. Here's the kind of reference book that has the potential to stay in print for not just ten or twenty or thirty years, but possibly fifty years or longer! (But don't try this one at home. The market for thesauri has since grown horrifically glutted.) An update roughly every five years is all that is required of me to keep this oil well gushing. In between, I need only sign and cash the checks.

Which I've proven I can handle.

I started my career as a fiction writer. After collecting well over three hundred rejection slips, I, like thousands of others like me, became eligible for martyrdom. Was it really all that noble, I thought to myself as I gnawed out bits of kindling from my desk with my front teeth, to suffer for art's sake?

When I switched to nonfiction, my misery vanished with my first acceptance check. To my utter amazement, I started selling almost immediately. First short newsbreaks for magazines. Then longer articles. Then books. And the writing process, though hard work, did not make me miserable. It made me—dare I say it—content. Satisfied. *Happy.*

And well paid.

You'll find few in publishing who would argue the point: Among poetry, short stories, magazine articles, screenplays, novels, and nonfiction books, nonfiction books are the most likely to bring the largest rewards for the least amount of struggle and heartache. If your goal is to make a living writing, a secure living, it's that struggle-to-reward ratio that matters most, and nonfiction, and especially nonfiction *niche* writing, wins that ratio measure hands down.

If you're still doubtful, consider my final argument. It is, I think, as convincing a line of reasoning as a hit over the head with a carton full of rejection slips. To make sure nobody misses it, I'm going to set it off in bold print. Read it at least twice:

> **If you're an unpublished novelist, you must write an entire novel before anyone will even consider giving you a contract. If you're an unpublished nonfiction writer, on the other hand, you need only write the first *two or three chapters*. Most nonfiction books, whether written by veterans with long track records or neophytes without a single sale, are sold simply on the strength of those three sample chapters and a book proposal, *or less*.**

> "You'll find few in publishing who would argue the point: Among poetry, short stories, magazine articles, screenplays, novels, and nonfiction books, nonfiction books are the most likely to bring the largest rewards for the least amount of struggle and heartache."

Thus the nonfiction author's risk of time and effort is roughly one quarter that of a novelist!

If that didn't make a strong enough impression, consider this: You can find out if you have an unsalable nonfiction book idea just by reading editors' responses to an initial query letter. If nobody responds favorably, you save yourself from writing anything but the query letter. With fiction, you must write a query, a synopsis and at least three sample chapters just to get in the door. And, again, no editor buys a fiction manuscript from a newcomer on the strength of just three chapters.

If you're a fiction writer, you don't have to give up the dream. You can do what I do and have nonfiction as your major and fiction as your minor. Once you're up to speed with two or three nonfiction titles earning money for you, you can go into novels, screenplays, short stories, or even poetry, full-steam ahead. And with the pressure to earn a living relieved, you'll likely find the fiction writing/selling process much less miserable, if not occasionally tolerable and, perhaps, once in awhile, enjoyable!

Okay. I've preached my nonfiction sermon. With any luck, you've seen the light.

Now it's time to take a look at some of the faithful in the choir—that is, both those amateur and professional writers who have been born again through their own sensational book profits.

I want to prove to you that what I've done is no fluke. You really don't have to be a high school dropout to succeed at this.

Chapter One

Could You Have Written Any of These?

A select representation of the hundreds of titles that earn thousands and even millions of dollars for their authors every year

Sales figures given below were gathered from reports in *Publishers Weekly*, from publishers' catalogs, from book cover crowings (over 150,000 sold!), from book Web sites, or from the authors themselves.

Sales figures for many titles are for one year or less. Some are cumulative over several years. A few "copies in print" figures are also given, and actual sales are lower at press time but may exceed the number given in the near future. Some figures reflect sales of trade paperbacks, others hardcovers. Most are a combination. By the time you read this, the figures will, for most titles, be substantially higher.

These figures are accurate enough only to illustrate what kinds of books succeed in the nonfiction market. Due to the many variables involved, it's impossible to provide pinpoint accuracy for any book currently still in print.

This is only a skimming of the successful titles. Although I've included some books by famous authors, you'll notice far more from lesser known or unknown authors. I've left out many for space reasons.

You can search for the latest best-sellers by category (cookbook, religion, politics, self-help, etc.) at Amazon.com.

- *Celtic Needlepoint*, Alice Starmore, 50,000 copies sold.
- *Mark of the Grizzly*, Scott McMillion, 50,000 copies sold.
- *The Joy of Meditating*, Salle Redfield, 58,000 copies sold.
- *How to Live With a Neurotic Dog*, Stephen Baker, 60,000 copies sold.

- *Scrapbook Basics* (putting together your own scrapbooks), Michele Gerbrandt, 60,000 copies sold.
- *The Woodworker's Guide to Pricing Your Work*, Dan Ramsey, over 60,000 copies sold.
- *Surviving the Breakup* (effects of divorce on the family), Judith Wallerstein, 60,000 copies sold.
- *Miracles Happen When You Pray: True Stories of the Remarkable Power of Prayer*, Quin Sherrer, 61,400 copies sold.
- *Lies My Teacher Told Me: Everything Your American History Textbook Got Wrong*, James Loewen, 62,000 copies sold (one year's sales only.)
- *The Quotable Star Wars*, Stephen Sansweet, 63,000 copies sold.
- *Paint Your House With Powdered Milk, and Hundreds More Offbeat Uses for Brand-Name Products*, Joey Green, 63,000 copies sold.
- *Creative Wedding Florals You Can Make*, Terry Rye, 63,000 copies sold.
- *Fingerprints of the Gods* (evidence of a lost civilization), Graham Hancock, 65,000 copies sold.
- *You Mean I'm Not Lazy, Stupid, or Crazy?!: A Self-Help Book for Adults With Attention-Deficit Disorder*, Kate Kelly and Peggy Ramundo, 65,000 copies sold (one year's sales only).
- *101 Best Home-Based Businesses for Women*, Priscilla Huff, over 65,000 copies sold.
- *The Western Guide to Feng Shui*, Terah Collins, 66,000 copies sold.
- *Breaking the Rules: Last Ditch Tactics for Landing the Man of Your Dreams*, Laura Banks and Janette Barber, 67,200 copies sold.
- *Creating Your Own Heritage Album*, Bev Braun, 68,000 copies sold.
- *Raising a Daughter*, Jeanne and Don Elium, 69,000 copies sold.
- *Do What You Are: Discover the Perfect Career for You Through the Secrets of Personality Type*, 2nd ed., Paul Tieger and Barbara Barron-Tieger, 69,000 copies sold.
- *Almost Vegetarian* (cookbook), Diana Shaw, 70,000 copies sold.
- *199 Great Home Businesses You Can Start for Under $1000*, Tyler Hicks, 70,000 copies sold. This is one of many similar home business titles Hicks has written, with total sales in the millions.
- *The Bindi Body Art Kit* (instruction book, bindi paint, and removable,

self-stick jewels for 12, 13 and 14-year-olds), Beth Margetts, 70,000 copies sold.

- *The Patient's Guide to Prostate Cancer*, Marc Garnick, 70,000 copies sold.
- *From Panic to Power* (anxiety control), Lucinda Bassett, 72,000 copies sold.
- *Civil War Curiosities*, Webb Garrison, 74,000 copies sold.
- *A Woman's Guide to Tantra Yoga*, Vimala McClure, 75,000 copies sold.
- *Kids' Best Dog Book and Field Guide to Neighborhood Dogs*, Michael Rosen, 75,000 copies sold.
- *Smart Love: The Compassionate Alternative to Discipline That Will Make You a Better Parent and Your Child a Better Person*, William Pieper and Martha Heineman Pieper, 75,000 copies sold.
- *The World's Best-Kept Diet Secrets*, Diane Irons, 76,500 copies sold.
- *Wonderful Ways to Love a Child*, Judy Ford, 80,000 copies sold.
- *Quick and Easy Scrapbook Pages*, Memory Makers Books, 80,000 copies sold.
- *Starting on a Shoestring: Building a Business Without a Bankroll*, Arnold Goldstein, 80,000 copies sold.
- *Life's Little Frustration Book*, G. Gaynor McTigue, 80,000 copies sold.
- *The Next Place*, (a juvenile title on death and dying), Warren Hanson, 80,000 copies sold.
- *101 Things to Do With a Cake Mix*, Stephanie Ashcroft, 80,000 copies sold. (This book was followed by *101 More Things to Do With a Cake Mix*).
- *Getting the Words Right: 39 Ways to Improve Your Writing*, Theodore Cheney, over 80,000 copies sold.
- *97 Ways to Make Baby Laugh*, Jack Moore, 81,000 copies sold.
- *Polish Your Furniture With Pantyhose*, Joey Green, 85,000 copies sold.
- *Make Your Own Time Capsule*, Steven Caney, over 88,000 copies sold.
- *Keys to Drawing*, Bert Dodson, 95,000 copies sold.
- *Worms Eat My Garbage* (a self-published title on composting), Mary Appelhof, 100,000 copies sold.
- *The World's Dumbest Criminals*, Daniel Butler and Alan Ray, 100,000 copies sold.
- *101 Things to Do With a Slow Cooker*, Janet Eyring and Stephanie

Ashcroft, 100,000 copies sold. (This book was followed by *101 More Things to Do With a Slow Cooker*.)

- *What Color is Your Parachute?*, Richard Bolles. (A perennial bestseller for many, many years, with 100,000 copies sold in 2004 alone. See further down the list for more complete sales figures.)
- *How to Clean Practically Anything*, Edward Kippel, 100,000 copies sold.
- *All Fishermen Are Liars*, Linda Greenlaw, over 100,000 copies.
- *When Elephants Weep: The Emotional Life of Animals*, Susan McCarthy and Jeffrey Moussaieff-Masson, 100,000 copies sold.
- *The Bible Jesus Read*, Philip Yancey, over 100,000 copies sold.
- *Creative Cash: How to Profit from Your Special Artistry, Creativity, Hand Skills, and Related Know-How*, Barbara Brabec, over 100,000 copies sold.
- *Letters of the Century*, Lisa Grunwald and Stephen Adler, over 100,000 copies sold.
- *The New Drawing on the Right Side of the Brain*, Betty Edwards, over 100,000 copies sold.
- *Never Be Lied to Again*, David Lieberman, over 100,000 copies sold.
- *Dogs Never Lie About Love: Reflections on the Emotional World of Dogs*, Jeffrey Moussaieff-Masson, over 100,000 copies sold.
- *Baby Signs: How to Talk to Your Baby Before Your Baby Can Talk* (sign language for babies), Linda Acredolo and Susan Goodwyn, over 100,000 copies sold.
- *Simply Handmade, 365 Easy Gifts and Decorations You Can Make*, Carol Dahlstrom, over 100,000 copies sold.
- *35,000 Baby Names*, Bruce Lansky, over 100,000 copies sold.
- *The Straw Bale House*, Athena Steen, over 100,000 copies sold.
- *Homemade Money: How to Select, Start, Manage and Market and Multiply the Profits of a Home-Based Business*, Barbara Brabec, over 100,000 copies sold.
- *My Old Man and the Sea: A Father and Son Sail Around Cape Horn*, David and Daniel Hays, over 100,000 copies sold.

- *Surfing the Himalayas: a Spiritual Adventure*, Frederick Lenz, over 100,000 copies sold.
- *The Complete Book of Juicing*, Michael Murray, over 100,000 copies sold.
- *776 Stupidest Things Ever Said*, Kathryn and Ross Petras, over 100,000 copies sold.
- *Anatomy of the Spirit: The Seven Stages of Power and Healing*, Caroline Myss and Norman Shealy, over 100,000 copies sold.
- *Guide My Feet: Prayers and Meditations for Our Children*, Marian Edelman, over 100,000 copies sold.
- *The Complete Potter's Companion*, Tony Birks, over 100,000 sold.
- *Attention Deficit Disorder*, Thom Hartmann, over 100,000 copies sold.
- *Everything You Pretend to Know and Are Afraid Someone Will Ask*, Lynette Padwa, over 100,000 copies sold
- *Wine for Dummies*, Ed McCarthy and Mary Ewing-Mulligan, over 100,000 copies sold.
- *The Metrosexual Guide to Style*, Michael Flocker, over 100,000 copies sold.
- *The Darwin Awards*, Wendy Northcutt, over 100,000 copies sold. One year's sales only.
- *Beer Lover's Rating Guide*, Bob Klein, 102,000 copies sold.
- *Before You Were Born*, Jennifer Davis. (This is a lift-the-flap book about the inside of a pregnant woman's body), 102,000 copies sold.
- *Michelangelo and the Pope's Ceiling*, Ross King, 103,359 copies sold.
- *Love Coupons*, Gregory Godek, 104,000 copies sold.
- *A Hummingbird in My House* (hummingbirds and their behavior), Arnette Heidcamp, 105,000 copies sold.
- *The Ditches of Edison County* (parody), Ronald Roberts, 105,718 copies sold.
- *Totally Garlic Cookbook*, Helene Siegal and Karen Gillingham, 105,893 copies sold.
- *How to Draw Life-Like Portraits from Photographs*, Lee Hammond, 107,000 copies sold.
- *365 Outdoor Activities You Can Do With Your Child*, Steven and Ruth Bennett, 108,131 copies sold.

- *Yoga for Wimps: Poses for the Flexibly Impaired*, Miriam Austin, 110,000 copies sold.
- *Jesus CEO: Using Ancient Wisdom for Visionary Leadership*, Laurie Beth Jones, over 113,000 copies sold.
- *How You Can Make $25,000 a Year With Your Camera*, Larry Cribb, over 113,000 copies sold.
- *1001 Ways to Energize Employees*, Bob Nelson, 114,000 copies sold.
- *Don't Squat With Your Spurs On: A Cowboy's Guide to Life*, Texas Bix Bender, 114,945 copies sold.
- *Positive Discipline A to Z*, Jane Nelsen, 115,000 copies sold.
- *The Very Best Baby Name Book in the Whole Wide World*, Bruce Lansky, over 115,000 copies sold.
- *How to Make Clay Characters*, Maureen Carlson, 116,000 copies sold.
- *Will in the World* (biography of Shakespeare), Stephen Greenblatt, 117,000 copies sold.
- *The Tao of Inner Peace*, Diane Dreher, 118,000 copies sold.
- *Physics of Star Trek*, Lawrence Krauss, 120,000 copies sold.
- *Drinking: a Love Story*, Caroline Knapp, over 120,000 copies sold. (One year's sales only.)
- *The Complete Book of Essential Oils and Aromatherapy*, Valerie Ann Worwood, over 120,000 copies sold.
- *The Complete Book of Bread Machine Baking*, Lara Pizzorno, 125,000 copies sold.
- *The 21 Irrefutable Laws of Leadership*, John Maxwell and Zig Ziglar, 130,000 copies sold.
- *The Self Publishing Manual*, Dan Poynter, over 130,000 copies sold.
- *Bringing Tuscany Home*, Frances Mayes, 133,000 copies sold. (The latest of her bestselling *Tuscany* books.)
- *The Unofficial Guide to Walt Disney World*, Bob Sehlinger, over 130,000 copies sold.
- *How to Study*, Ron Fry, over 132,000 copies sold.
- *Overcoming Depression*, Demitri Papolos, 135,000 copies sold.
- *China Moon Cookbook*, Barbara Tropp, 135,000 copies sold.
- *What Would Jesus Do Today?* (children's edition), Helen Haidle, 139,000 copies sold.

- *The Baby Owner's Manual,* Joe Borgenicht, 140,000 copies sold.
- *How to Become a Successful Consultant in Your Own Field,* Hubert Bermont, 140,000 copies sold.
- *The Writer's Digest Handbook of Short Story Writing,* Frank Dickson and Sandra Smythe, 145,000 copies sold.
- *Oops! The Manners Guide for Girls,* Nancy Holyoke, 147,000 copies sold.
- *Fabric of the Cosmos,* Brian Greene, 148,486 copies sold. One year's sales only.
- *The Case for a Creator,* Lee Strobel, 150,000 copies sold. One year's sales only.
- *On Bullshit,* Harry Frankfurt, 150,000 copies. First two months' sales only.
- *Pasta Light,* Norman Kolpas, 150,000 copies sold.
- *A Practical Guide to the Runes,* Lisa Peschel, over 150,000 copies sold.
- *Looneyspoons* (a humorous cookbook featuring such dishes as *Jurassic Pork Roast* and *Yabba Dabba Stew*), Janet and Greta Podleski, over 150,000 copies sold.
- *The Rape of Nanking: The Forgotten Holocaust of World War II,* Iris Chang, over 150,000 copies sold.
- *Golf for Dummies,* Gary McCord, 150,000 copies sold.
- *Blackbird: A Childhood Lost and Found* (memoir of author from ages 5 to 12), Jennifer Lauck, 150,000 copies sold.
- *Organizing from the Inside Out,* Julie Morgenstern, 150,000 copies sold.
- *Buying Stocks Without a Broker,* Charles Carlson, 150,000 copies sold.
- *Bear Attacks: Their Causes and Avoidance,* Stephen Herrero, 150,000 copies sold.
- *Lawyers and Other Reptiles,* Jess Brallier, 150,000 copies sold.
- *Mrs. Witty's Monster Cookies,* Helen Witty, 150,000 copies sold.
- *My First Baking Book* (50 kid-tested recipes for children 6 and up), Rena Coyle, 152,000 copies sold.
- *Practical Feng Shui,* Simon Brown, over 155,000 copies sold.
- *The Internet for Dummies,* John Levine, 160,000 copies sold.
- *40 Common Errors in Golf and How to Correct Them,* Arthur Shay, over 160,000 copies sold.

- *Raising Self-Reliant Children in a Self-Indulgent World*, H. Stephen Glenn and Jane Nelsen, over 160,000 copies sold.
- *The Best Night Out With Dad*, Lisa McCourt and Bert Dodson, 165,000 copies sold.
- *Green River, Running Red*, Ann Rule, 167,500 copies sold.
- *Seven Things That Steal Your Joy*, Joyce Meyer, 168,000 copies sold.
- *The Book of Golf Disasters*, Peter Dobereiner, 170,000 copies sold.
- *The Seven Worst Things Parents Do*, John and Linda Friel, 170,000 copies sold.
- *Complete Home Bartender's Guide*, Salvatore Calabrese, 171,000 copies sold in 2003 alone.
- *Really Important Stuff My Kids Have Taught Me*, Cynthia Copeland, 172,000 copies sold.
- *Play Poker Like the Pros*, Phil Hellmuth, 174,000 copies sold.
- *Miracle Cures*, Jean Carper, 175,000 copies sold.
- *1001 Beauty Solutions*, Beth Barrick-Hickey, 175,000 copies sold.
- *Potpourri, Incense and Other Fragrant Concoctions*, Ann Fettner, 179,000 copies sold.
- *Why Cats Paint*, Heather Busch, 179,000 copies sold.
- *Farmhouse Cookbook*, Susan Loomis, 183,000 copies sold.
- *Jewish as a Second Language* (humor), Molly Katz, 186,000 copies sold.
- *The Beach Book and Beach Bucket*, Karen Dawe, illustrated with 40 species of saltwater plants and animals, 193,000 copies sold.
- *The Grand Tour*, Ron Miller (book of space for kids), 196,000 copies sold.
- *The Sibley Guide to Birds*, David Sibley, 200,000 copies sold.
- *Sinus Survival*, Robert Ivker, 200,000 copies sold.
- *Auto Repair for Dummies*, Deanna Sclar, 200,000 copies sold.
- *The Henna Body Art Kit* (body make-up and instruction book for 12-14-year-olds), Aileen Marron, 200,000 copies sold.
- *The Complete Guide to Foot Reflexology*, Kevin and Barbara Kunz, 200,000 copies sold.
- *101 Ways to Tell Your Child "I Love You,"* Vicki Lansky, 200,000 copies sold.
- *Away for the Weekend, New York* (travel within 200 miles of NYC), Eleanor Berman, over 200,000 copies sold.

- *Kids' Book of Fishing*, Michael Rosen, 200,000 copies sold.
- *Zlata's Diary* (13-year-old's war experience in Sarajevo), Zlata Filipovic, over 200,000 copies sold.
- *I Kissed Dating Goodbye* (Biblical approach to love and relationships), Joshua Harris, over 200,000 copies sold.
- *More Than a Carpenter*, Josh McDowell, over 200,000 copies sold. (One year's sales only.)
- *Backtalk: 4 Steps to Ending Rude Behavior in Your Kids*, Audrey Ricker, over 200,000 copies sold.
- *Book of Dreams*, Sylvia Browne, over 200,000 copies sold.
- *The Complete Guide to Offshore Money Havens*, Jerome Schneider, over 200,000 copies sold.
- *How to Regain Your Virginity and 99 Other Recent Discoveries About Sex* (humor), Patricia Marx, 203,000 copies sold.
- *Fat-Free Holiday Recipes*, Sandra Woodruff, 205,000 copies sold.
- *The Case for Faith*, Lee Strobel, 205,463 copies sold.
- *Anne Hooper's Pocket Sex Guide*, Anne Hooper, 210,000 copies sold.
- *How to Have a Big Wedding on a Small Budget*, Diane Warner, 213,000 copies sold.
- *Galileo's Daughter*, Dava Sobel, 213,287 copies sold. (One year's sales only.)
- *Wicked Spanish* (humor), Howard Tomb, 217,000 copies sold.
- *Founding Mothers*, Cokie Roberts, 220,000 copies sold.
- *The Book for People Who Do Too Much*, Bradley Greive, 222,000 copies sold.
- *Confessions of an Organized Homemaker*, Deniece Schofield, 233,000 copies sold.
- *Happy Endings: Finishing the Edges of Your Quilt*, Mimi Dietrich, 240,000 copies sold.
- *Low-Carb Cookbook*, Fran McCullough, 245,000 copies sold.
- *The Old Farmer's Almanac 2005*, 245,844 copies sold.
- *The Wonder of Boys: What Parents, Mentors and Educators Can Do to Shape Boys Into Exceptional Men*, Michael Gurian, 250,000 copies sold.
- *The Other Side and Back*, Sylvia Browne, 250,000 copies sold.

- *The 3-Hour Diet: How Low Carb Diets Make You Fat and Timing Makes You Thin*, Jorge Cruise, 250,000 copies sold. (One year's sales only.)
- *We Interrupt This Broadcast*, (historical news events), Joe Garner, 250,000 copies sold.
- *Money Doesn't Grow On Trees*, Neale Godfrey, 250,000 copies sold.
- *Earth Prayers from Around the World*, Elizabeth Roberts, 250,000 copies sold.
- *Nasty People: How to Stop Being Hurt by Them Wihout Becoming One of Them*, Jay Carter, 250,000 copies sold.
- *Crazy Time: Surviving Divorce and Building a New Life*, Abigail Trafford, 250,000 copies sold.
- *You've Earned It, Don't Lose It*, Suze Orman, 250,000 copies sold.
- *Backyard Explorer Kit*, Rona Beame, 256,000 copies sold.
- *Zip! Pop! Hop! and Other Fun Words to Say*, Michaela Muntean, 256,500 copies sold.
- *The Hungry Ocean*, Linda Greenlaw, 258,766 copies sold.
- *Gardening* (humor), Henry Beard, 259,000 copies sold.
- *Joe DiMaggio: the Hero's Life*, Richard Cramer, 259,000 copies sold.
- *Incredible Fishing Stories*, Shaun Morey, 260,000 copies sold.
- *500 Beauty Solutions*, Beth Barrick-Hickey, 261,674 copies sold.
- *A Short History of Nearly Everything*, Bill Bryson, 261,000 copies sold.
- *Wicked French* (humor), Howard Tomb, 266,000 copies sold.
- *Experiencing the Passion of Jesus*, Lee Strobel, 267,587 copies sold.
- *The Abs Diet*, David Zinczenko, 269,000 copies sold.
- *The Tightwad Gazette*, Amy Dacyczyn, 272,000 copies sold.
- *What Should I Do With My Life?*, Po Bronson, 274,000 copies sold. (One year's sales only.)
- *Tibetan Book of Living and Dying*, Sogyal Rinpoche, 275,000 copies sold.
- *Clutter's Last Stand* (housecleaning tips), Don Aslett, 275,000 copies sold.
- *You Can Do It*, Lauren Grandcolas, 275,000 copies sold.
- *The Incredible Truth About Motherhood*, Bradley Trevor Greive, 279,000 copies sold in 2003 alone.

- *Thin for Life,* Anne Fletcher, 300,000 copies sold.
- *The Jumbo Duct Tape Book,* Tim Nyberg and Jim Berg, over 300,000 copies sold in one year alone. (They have sold over 1,000,000 copies of all duct tape books in the series.)
- *Adventures of a Psychic,* Sylvia Browne, 300,000 copies sold.
- *Nice Couples Do,* Joan Lloyd, 300,000 copies sold.
- *Secret Language of Men* (humor), Sherrie Weaver, 300,000 copies sold.
- *The Nursing Mother's Companion,* Kathleen Huggins, 300,000 copies sold.
- *Random Acts of Kindness,* editors of Conari Press, over 300,000 copies sold.
- *Sweaty Palms: The Neglected Art of Being Interviewed,* Anthony Medley, 300,000 copies sold.
- *Meditations for New Mothers,* Beth Saavedra, 305,000 copies sold.
- *New Passages: Mapping Your Life Across Time,* Gail Sheehy, 306,661 copies sold. (A spinoff of *Passages,* which sold over 5 million copies.)
- *The Barbecue Bible,* Steven Raichlen, 310,000 copies sold.
- *Chili Madness,* Jane Butel, 312,000 copies sold.
- *Writing for Children and Teenagers,* Lee Wyndham and Arnold Madison, 321,000 copies sold.
- *Teen Love: On Relationships,* Kimberly Kirberger, 326,000 copies sold.
- *Take Time for Your Life,* Cheryl Richardson, 330,000 copies sold.
- *The World is Flat: A Brief History of the 21st Century,* Thomas Friedman and Oliver Wyman, 335,000 copies sold. One year's sales only.
- *Raising Your Spirited Child,* Mary Kurcinka, 350,000 copies sold.
- *My First Drawing Book,* Tedd Arnold, 356,000 copies sold.
- *Kids' Paper Airplane Book,* Ken Blackburn, 360,000 copies sold.
- *Chicken Soup for the Soul at Work,* Jack Canfield, 360,000 copies sold.
- *Leaders: Strategies for Taking Charge,* Warren Bennis and Burt Nanus, 370,000 copies sold.
- *Alexander Hamilton,* Ron Chernow, 375,000 copies sold.
- *The Bible Code,* Michael Drosnin, 400,000 copies sold.
- *Getting the Love You Want: A Guide for Couples,* Harville Hendrix, over 400,000 copies sold.

- *Woe Is I: The Grammarphobe's Guide to Better English in Plain English*, Patricia O'Conner, 400,000 copies sold.
- *Bad Cat*, Jim Edgar, 403,000 copies sold.
- *His Excellency: George Washington*, Joseph Ellis, 437,000 copies sold.
- *The Art of Cooking for the Diabetic*, Mary Hess, 450,000 copies sold.
- *How to Behave So Your Children Will, Too!*, Sal Severe, 450,000 copies sold. (Tim McCormick, the president of Greentree Publishing, told me that only 40,000 copies were sold to bookstores, while a whopping 335,000 more were peddled via a newsletter, Web site, workshops, door-to-door salespeople, and Book-of-the-Month Club, before a hugely impressed Viking/Penguin finally acquired the rights in 1999 for the highest advance ever paid for a parenting book.)
- *Birds of America*, Lorrie Moore, 451,000 copies sold.
- *Leadership Secrets of Attila the Hun*, Wess Roberts. Sold 485,000 copies by self-publishing, then was picked up by Warner Books.
- *How to Draw Pokemon*, Ron Zalme, 465,000 copies sold.
- *Fishing* (humor), Henry Beard and Roy McKie, 491,000 copies sold.
- *Is There Life After Housework?* Don Aslett and Craig Lagory, 500,000 copies sold.
- *Real Boys: Rescuing Our Sons From the Myths of Boyhood*, William Pollack and Mary Pipher, 500,000 copies sold.
- *The Case for Christ: A Journalist's Personal Investigation of the Evidence for Jesus*, Lee Strobel, 500,000 copies sold. (One year's sales only.)
- *The Damn Good Resume Guide*, Yana Parker, 500,000 copies sold.
- *Bread Machine Magic*, Lois Conway and Linda Rehberg, 500,000 copies sold.
- *And the Crowd Goes Wild* (historic sporting events), Joe Garner and Bob Costas, 500,000 copies sold.
- *Positive Discipline*, Jane Nelsen, 500,000 copies sold.
- *How to Get Happily Published* (originally self-published), Judith Appelbaum, 500,000 copies sold.
- *365 TV-Free Activities You Can Do With Your Child*, Steven and Ruth Bennett, 500,000 copies sold.

- *Into the Wild*, Jon Krakauer, 500,000 copies sold.
- *Leonardo DiCaprio: Modern Day Romeo*, Grace Catalano, 500,000 copies sold.
- *How to Make Money in Stocks*, William O'Neil, over 500,000 copies sold.
- *Inc. Yourself: How to Profit by Setting Up Your Own Corporation*, Judith McQuown, over 500,000 copies sold.
- *Bet You Can't! Science Impossibilities to Fool You*, Vicki Cobb, over 500,000 copies sold.
- *Don't Worry, Make Money*, Richard Carlson, over 500,000 copies sold.
- *The Seven Habits of Highly Effective Families*, Stephen Covey, over 500,000 copies sold.
- *Everyone Poops*, Taro Gomi and Amanda Stinchecum, over 500,000 copies sold. (Yes, this is about what the title says it is! Shinta Cho also had a great success with *The Gas We Pass: The Story of Farts*.)
- *Benjamin Franklin*, Walter Isaacson, over 500,000 copies sold in 2003 alone.
- *Blink: The Power of Thinking Without Thinking*, Malcolm Gladwell, 500,000 in 2005 alone.
- *Don't Sweat the Small Stuff for Teens*, Richard Carlson, 523,576 copies sold.
- *What to Expect: The Toddler Years*, Arlene Eisenberg, Heidi Murkoff, 520,837 copies sold.
- *Rich Dad, Poor Dad*, Robert Kiyosaki, 547,713 copies sold in 2001 alone, 512,464 copies sold in 2004 alone, a book with incredible legs! It's still on the bestseller list as of 2005.
- *Golfing* (humor), Henry Beard and Roy McKie, 525,000 copies sold.
- *101 Nights of Grrreat Sex* (self-published), Laura Corn, 525,000 copies sold.
- *Chocolate: The Consuming Passion* (humor), Sandra Boynton, 553,000 copies sold.
- *My World and Globe*, Ira Wolfman, a geography book and globe for kids, 558,000 copies sold.
- *Dress Your Family in Corduroy and Denim*, David Sedaris, 570,000 copies sold.

- *World Record Paper Airplane Book,* Ken Blackburn, 573,000 copies sold.
- *Kids' Book of Questions,* Gregory Stock, 582,000 copies sold.
- *Live and Learn and Pass It On,* H. Jackson Brown, 592,563 copies sold.
- *Liars Club* (memoir), Mary Karr, over 600,000 copies sold.
- *Unbelievably Good Deals and Great Adventures That You Absolutely Can't Get Unless You're Over 50,* Joan Heilman, 600,000 copies sold.
- *Small-Time Operator* (start your own business guide*),* Bernard Kamoriff, over 600,000 copies sold.
- *The Rules: Time Tested Secrets for Capturing the Heart of Mr. Right,* Ellen Fein, Sherrie Schneider, 605,000 copies sold.
- *The Devil in White City*, Erik Larson, 621,000 copies sold.
- *Good to Great*, Jim Collins, 654,000 copies sold.
- *Kids' Book of Chess,* Harvey Kidder, 619,000 copies sold.
- *Encyclopedia of Extremely Weird Animals* (kids' book of weird animals and bugs), Sarah Lovett, 700,000 copies sold.
- *Emotional Intelligence,* Daniel Goleman, 700,000 copies sold.
- *How the Irish Saved Civilization,* Thomas Cahill, 700,000 copies sold.
- *Sailing* (humor), Henry Beard and Roy McKie, 702,000 copies sold.
- *Under the Tuscan Sun: At Home in Italy*, Frances Mayes, 740,000 copies sold.
- *Wherever You Go, There You Are* (mindfulness and meditation), Jon Kabat-Zinn, 750,000 copies sold.
- *Let's Cook Microwave* (self-published), Barbara Harris, 750,000 copies sold.
- *The Handybook for Genealogists,* the editors at Everton Publishers, 770,000 copies sold.
- *Illustrated Dream Dictionary,* Russell Grant, 800,000 copies sold.
- *Beardstown Ladies' Common-Sense Investment Guide,* Leslie Whitaker, over 800,000 copies sold.
- *The Gentle Art of Verbal Self-Defense,* Suzette Elgen, 800,000 copies sold.
- *A Walk in the Woods,* Bill Bryson, over 900,000 copies sold.
- *Crossword Puzzle Dictionary,* Andrew Swanfeldt, over 900,000 copies sold. (In print for over 60 years!)

- *On Writing Well*, William Zinsser, over 900,000 copies sold.
- *The Dieter's Guide to Weight Loss During Sex*, Richard Smith, 935,000 copies sold.
- *14,000 Things to Be Happy About*, Barbara Kipfer, 950,000 copies sold.
- *Bird Book and the Bird Feeder*, Neil and Karen Dawe, field guide to 30 North American backyard species with feeder, 957,000 copies sold.
- *French Women Don't Get Fat*, Mireille Guiliano, 970,000 copies sold.
- *The Top 100 Pasta Sauces*, Diana Seed and Robert Budwig, 1,000,000 copies sold.
- *Science Experiments You Can Eat*, Vicki Cobb, 1,000,000 copies sold.
- *Eats, Shoots and Leaves*, Lynne Truss, over 1,000,000 copies sold.
- *The Tipping Point: How Little Things Can Make a Big Difference*, Malcolm Gladwell, 1,000,000 copies sold.
- *The Enchanted Broccoli Forest*, Mollie Katzen, 1,000,000 copies sold.
- *Having Our Say: The Delany Sisters' First 100 Years*, Annie Elizabeth Delany and Sarah Louise Delany, 1,000,000 copies sold.
- *Reviving Ophelia: Saving The Selves of Adolescent Girls*, Mary Pipher, over 1,000,000 copies sold.
- *How to Satisfy a Woman Every Time* (self-published), Naura Hayden, over 1,000,000 copies sold.
- *The Weigh Down Diet*, Gwen Shambin, over 1,000,000 copies sold.
- *Meditations for Women Who Do Too Much*, Anne Wilson Schaef, over 1,000,000 copies sold.
- *Chicken Soup for the Golfer's Soul*, Jack Canfield and Mark Victor Hansen, 1,000,000 copies sold.
- *Chicken Soup for the College Soul*, Canfield and Hansen, 1,000,000 copies sold.
- *Your Best Life Now*, Joel Osteen, over 1,000,000 copies sold.
- *Guns, Germs, and Steel*, Jared Diamond, over 1,000,000 copies sold.
- *Book of Cards for Kids*, Gail MacColl (mother of four), 1,100,000 copies sold.
- *1,000 Places to See Before You Die*, freelance travel writer Patricia Schultz, 1,135,000 copies sold.
- *He's Just Not That Into You*, Greg Behrendt and Liz Tucillo, 1,260,000 copies sold.

- *Bones Book and Skeleton*, Stephen Cumbaa, 1,655,000 copies sold.
- *Sugar Busters*, Leighton Steward, 1,201,000 copies sold.
- *Butter Busters*, Pam Mycoskie, 1,258,000 copies sold.
- *Chicken Soup for the Christian Soul*, Jack Canfield, 1,263,000 copies sold.
- *Life's Little Instruction Book II* (the first spinoff from the original), H. Jackson Brown, 1,483,573 copies sold.
- *1001 Ways To Be Romantic*, Gregory Godek, 1,500,000 copies sold.
- *The Perfect Storm*, Sebastian Junger, over 1,500,000 copies sold.
- *Nine Steps to Financial Freedom*, Suze Orman, over 1,500,000 copies sold.
- *How to Shit in the Woods*, Kathleen Meyer, over 1,500,000 copies sold.
- *All I Need to Know I Learned From My Cat*, Suzy Becker, 1,608,000 copies sold.
- *Prescription for Nutritional Healing*, James and Phyllis Balch, 1,657,000 copies sold.
- *Into Thin Air*, Jon Krakauer, 1,800,000 copies sold.
- *The Official Pokemon Handbook*, Maria Bobo, 1,800,000 copies sold.
- *The Book of Questions*, Gregory Stock, 1,985,000 copies sold.
- *The Moosewood Cookbook*, Mollie Katzen, 2,000,000 copies sold.
- *The Womanly Art of Breastfeeding*, authors from the La Leche League, 2,000,000 copies sold.
- *The New Router Handbook*, Patrick Spielman, over 2,000,000 copies sold.
- *How to Talk So Kids Will Listen and Listen So Kids Will Talk*, Adele Faber, 2,000,000 copies sold.
- *Juggling for the Complete Klutz* (originally self-published), John Cassidy, over 2,000,000 copies sold.
- *How To Keep Your Volkswagen Alive* (repair manual), John Muir, over 2,300,000 copies sold.
- *The Way Things Work*, David Macaulay, over 2,500,000 copies sold.
- *Creative Visualization*, Shakti Gawain, 2,500,000 copies sold.
- *The Five Love Languages*, Gary Chapman, 2,600,000 copies sold.
- *Beanie Baby Handbook*, Les and Sue Fox, 3,000,000 copies sold.
- *Each Day a New Beginning: Daily Meditations for Women*, Karen Casey, over 3,000,000 copies sold.

- *Codependent No More*, Melody Beattie, over 3,000,000 copies sold.
- *Chicken Soup for the Woman's Soul*, Jack Canfield, 3,297,000 copies sold.
- *Name Your Baby* (one of over 40 baby name books on the market), Lareina Rule, 3,500,000 copies sold.
- *The Power of Now*, Eckhart Tolle, 4,000,000 copies sold.
- *Angela's Ashes*, Frank McCourt, over 4,000,000 copies sold.
- *Embraced by the Light* (chronicle of near-death experience), Betty Eadie and Curtis Taylor, 4,500,000 copies sold.
- *50 Simple Things You Can Do to Save the Earth*, Earthworks Group, 4,500,000 copies sold.
- *Life's Little Instruction Book*, H. Jackson Brown, over 5,000,000 copies sold.
- *Men Are From Mars, Women Are From Venus*, John Gray, over 6,000,000 copies sold.
- *What Color is Your Parachute?* (originally self-published), Richard Bolles, over 6,000,000 copies sold.
- *The Simple Solution to Rubik's Cube*, James Nourse, 6,300,000 copies sold. This is an old title but I list it here to show how lucrative fad books can be. This was, by far, the bestselling title of all of 1981, despite the fact that there were two other Rubik's Cube solution books, also selling well, on the market!
- *Simple Abundance* (a daily inspirational guide), Sarah Ban Breath-nach, over 7,000,000, with numerous million-seller spin-offs.
- *South Beach Diet*, Arthur Agatston, 7,429,000 copies sold.
- *Tuesdays With Morrie*, Mitch Albom, 7,500,000 copies sold.
- *Feed Me, I'm Yours*, Vicki Lansky, 8,000,000 copies sold.
- *Who Moved My Cheese*, Spencer Johnson, over 8,000,000 copies sold.
- *Dr. Atkins New Diet Revolution*, Robert Atkins, 8,500,000 copies sold.
- *Don't Sweat the Small Stuff*, Richard Carlson, 8,500,000 copies sold.
- *The Prayer of Jabez*, Bruce Wilkinson, over 9,000,000 copies sold.
- *Elements of Style* (grammar), William Strunk and E. B. White, over 10,000,000 copies sold.
- *In Search of Excellence*, Thomas Peters, over 10,000,000 copies sold.
- *One Minute Manager*, Ken Blanchard and Spencer Johnson, 12,000,000

copies sold. (Originally self-published, then picked up by William Morrow.)

- *What to Expect When You're Expecting*, Arlene Eisenberg and Heidi Murkoff, over 12,000,000 copies sold.
- *Seven Habits of Highly Effective People,* Stephen Covey, 15,000,000 copies sold.
- *How to Win Friends and Influence People,* Dale Carnegie, over 15,000,000 copies sold. (Originally published in the 1930s and still going strong.)
- *Brain Quest* (a series of quizzing cards for children), Chris Feder, over 16,000,000 copies sold.
- *The Purpose-Driven Life*, Rick Warren, over 20,000,000 copies sold.
- *The Late Great Planet Earth*, Hal Lindsey, over 28,000,000 copies sold. The ultimate end-of-the-world book from the 1970s.
- *Guinness Book of World Records,* various authors. Since 1955, over 90,000,000 copies sold. Ironically, a world record!

Chapter Two

Nonfiction Success Stories

Make a sizable income writing nonfiction books...A score or more
best-selling titles you could have written

Each year, according to *Publishers Weekly*, roughly 130 new nonfiction hardcover books will exceed 100,000 sales in their first twelve months on the market.

Assuming an average cover price of $25 and a typical 10 percent royalty escalating to 15 percent after the first 10,000 copies, each of these books' lucky authors can expect to rake in at the very least $362,500 for first year royalties alone.

Of course, many of these books will break 200,000 or even 300,000 in sales. A few will shatter the 500,000 mark, and three or four, 1,000,000. One or two may even go to 2,000,000 or beyond. Keep in mind, these are *one-year* sales figures only.

Add paperback rights sales, book club sales, foreign sales, serialization sales, and second-, third-, fourth- and fifth-year sales, and an already impressive income jumps to a truly stratospheric level.

Throw into the mix the authors whose books were not released in hardcover but as trade paperbacks (the larger—often about 6" x 9"—paperback) and will surpass 100,000-copy sales, and the odds of making significant money begin to look considerably better than winning the state lottery.

Yes, it's still an elite group, but consider this: *You don't need to make anywhere near 100,000-copy sales to make a good living.*

The typical author, in fact, need make only 10,000 hardcover sales annually to produce a livable income. Judging by published sales figures in *Publishers Weekly* and elsewhere, it's clear that a small army of authors do just that and then some. Many will make that mark this year, next year, and the next year without even selling a new title, simply by relying on sales from previous books!

Yes, you can make a good living writing nonfiction books.

Ordinary writers have been doing it for years with a broad spectrum of titles. Some collect the proceeds from as many as a dozen modest-selling books, all earning royalties simultaneously. (Think how many checks a prolific author like Isaac Asimov, with 350-plus books to his credit, must have cashed before he died!) A few strike gold and retire with their very first book.

Many of the writers who do well have outstanding credentials; they are TV personalities, physicians, scientists and the like. But many have little or virtually no credentials.

Just consider the list below of credentialed and noncredentialed authors who have found success in the past few years. Could you have written any of these books?

$ In 1992, two sisters, Annie Elizabeth Delany, a former dentist, and Sarah Louise Delany, a former home economics schoolteacher, compiled their memoirs with the help of journalist Amy Hearth. The memoirs chronicled the sisters' experiences growing up in the South and, later, in New York City.

The Delanys were among the last living Americans to be born in the 1800s; their father had actually been a slave. That was all the hook most book buyers needed. *Having Our Say: The Delany Sisters' First 100 Years*, a rare "noncelebrity" biography, sold an astonishing one million copies.

$ Poet Mary Karr's biography, *The Liars' Club*, painted a painful portrait of childhood molestations, shootings, and dysfunctional, larger-than-life family members and earned the number two spot on the *New York Times* paperback best-seller list in 1996. Her publisher, pleasantly surprised at the success of a noncelebrity, quickly signed Karr to write *Cherry*, a follow-up title describing her teen years.

Karr's and the Delany sisters' ascent of the best-seller charts spawned a booming new market for soul-stirring memoirs, especially from unknowns. Now several years into the trend, noncelebrity memoirs remain a fabulous niche that shows little sign of fizzling out.

$ Among the many who have cashed in is a former air force crew member named Dave Pelzer, who wrote about his own abuse growing up under the hands of an alcoholic mother and neglectful father in a phenomenally hot-selling memoir called *A Child Called It*. He followed with other massive bestsellers, including, *The Lost Boy*, and *A Man Named Dave*.

$ Rosemary Green was another successful memoir writer. She had no rapes or shootings to write about but simply chronicled her battle with obesity in *Diary of a Fat Housewife*. The Beaverton, Oregon, housewife kept a diary about the travails of going from 320 pounds down to 135. Whether she said anything new about obesity or not wasn't relevant; her book plucked a resonant chord with thousands of overweight women and sales took off. In 1995, her publisher ordered new printings of the book every two weeks to keep up with the demand.

$ Caroline Knapp's *Drinking: A Love Story* describes a similar personal battle, this one with alcohol addiction. One of the few books on alcoholism written from a female perspective, her memoir sold over 120,000 copies in only its first five months on the market in 1996 and is, at this writing, still going strong. (Nothing breeds copycats better than success; in the fall of 1999, publishers released three "alcohol memoirs," *Where the Sky Ends: A Memoir of Alcohol and Family* by M. G. Stephens, *My Name is Izzy* by Isabel Covalt, and *Note Found in a Bottle: My Life as a Drinker* by Susan Cheever.)

$ Augusten Burroughs dropped out of school in the ninth grade. Yet by 2005, his memoir, *Running with Scissors*, had sold over 700,000 copies. His follow-up title, *"Dry,"* about his bout with alcoholism, sold an additional 240,000 copies. These were hardly flukes. An advertising writer turned author, Burroughs struck gold again with a collection of essays, *Magical Thinking*, which boasted a 200,000 copy first printing, and yet again when St. Martin's paid him a seven figure advance for three *additional* titles. (Incidentally, Burroughs reportedly wrote his first novel, *Sellervision*, in just seven, 18-hour days, which also sold to St.

DAMN! WHY DIDN'T I WRITE THAT?

Martins.) Lesson? Great writing always trumps lacks of a formal education.

💲 Lorenzo Carcaterra's coming-of-age memoir related a harrowing stay in the Wilkinson Home for Boys and the retribution he and his friends exacted on a guard for his brutality. His critically acclaimed *Sleepers*, a *New York Times* best-seller, has since been made into a movie.

💲 Yet another unknown, Andrew Pham, wowed bidding publishers with his memoir, *Catfish and Mandala*, in 1998. His story tells how his family fled from the Viet Cong to the United States. To succeed, his father had to escape from prison and his sister had to have surgery to transform herself into a boy.

💲 Journalist Gini Kopecky and law student Layli Bashir teamed up to chronicle the shocking true story of Fauziya Kasinga, a seventeen-year-old African girl sold by her aunt to be the fourth wife of an older man. Kasinga was scheduled to undergo ritual female genital mutilation when she fled to the United States and sought asylum. The book, *Freeing Fauziya: The Story of One Woman Who Defied Tribal Custom and Fought for Her Freedom in America,* earned a high six-figure advance from Delacorte in 1996.

💲 Three years later, another 17-year-old, Katie Tarbox, wrote a 75-page proposal for a book detailing how she was stalked by a man she met through the Internet. This one wasn't a memoir exactly, but more of a true crime chronicle. The proposal, called *Girl.com*, was sold for a sizable, albeit undisclosed, sum after a heated three-day auction. (In an auction, a number of publishers bid on a manuscript with the book's agent or other intermediary, phoning each bidder with news of the latest bid.)

Not every book requires harrowing experiences to succeed, though.

💲 Doris Grumbach experimented with the meditative side of life by spending fifty days alone in her coastal Maine home and wrote about the experience in *Fifty Days of Solitude*. The book tickled the imaginations of the *New York Times* and the public, went back to press five times between 1994 and 1995, and continues to sell.

$ David Borgenicht and Joshua Piven tapped national experts to compile a guide to escaping such unlikely emergencies as sinking in quicksand or plunging under water in your car. A huge bestseller, *Worst Case Scenario Survival Handbook* spawned numerous spin-offs, including *Worst Case Scenario: Travel* (771,785 copies sold in 2001 alone) and *Worst Case Scenario: Dating and Sex* (370,755 copies in 2001). It can't be stressed enough: the authors were authorities in *none* of the worst-case scenarios they described. They simply found the right professionals and asked for their tips and advice.

$ Businessman Donald Phillips was amazed that nobody had ever written a book on Abraham Lincoln's leadership skills. Seeing much in Lincoln's managerial style that could be applied to today's workplace, he wrote *Lincoln on Leadership: Executive Strategies for Tough Times*, which has gone back to press nine times since 1993.

$ Executive G. J. Meyer was fired from his job and became yet another victim of corporate downsizing. In a classic case of squeezing lemonade from a rotten lemon, Meyer wrote about his experience with joblessness in *Executive Blues*. His book, rejected sixteen times, finally landed a sale at a small publisher, who quickly turned around and sold paperback rights for $70,000.

$ Sixty-year-old historian Stephen Ambrose, delving into the Lewis and Clark expedition (he even walked every step of the famed trail himself), uncovered a facet of the explorers' story previous chroniclers overlooked: the very human, manic-depressive side of Meriwether Lewis. Lewis was a man who could not handle success, suffered a mental breakdown, and fell into a black hole of alcohol and opium addiction. The combination of exploration and human tragedy in *Undaunted Courage*: *Meriwether Lewis, Thomas Jefferson, and the Opening of the American West* so piqued readers' interest that the book remained on the best-seller lists for months and was optioned—for six figures—by *National Geographic Television* for a miniseries.

$ Seventy-five-year-old Harry Frankfurt wrote a book about bullshit in society and, in March of 2005, his academic treatise, *On Bullshit*, reached #11 at Amazon.com, selling over 100,000 copies in just one month! The Princeton philosopher knew how to slice through all the bull himself: The book is only 67 pages long.

$ Leo Marks, a seventy-something, first-time author, tapped into the public's fascination for historical secret codes when his *Between Silk and Cyanide: A Codemaker's War 1941–1945* was published by the Free Press in 1999. It was reviewed in the Sunday *New York Times* and *Washington Post Book World* and reached number five on Amazon.com's "Hot 100 Books" list.

$ In 1994, journalist Leslie Whitaker went to Beardstown, Illinois, to interview the members of a curious little investment club, who were earning the unheard-of return of 23 percent on their stocks. The investment club, comprised of elderly women, had figured out a method of outperforming even the sharpest Wall Street investment sharks. The result?—*The Beardstown Ladies' Common-Sense Investment Guide*, which sold 302,305 copies in hardcover in 1995 alone and was quickly followed by a spin-off volume. (In the publishing world, it hardly mattered that the ladies had inadvertently miscalculated their investment gains, as was later discovered. By the time they were found out, they had already made a very tidy sum from their books, none of which had to be given back.)

$ Former Oregon radio talk show host Neale Walsch asked God to answer some personal questions. God's purported "responses" are contained in Walsch's book, *Conversations With God*, which in 1996 won a seven-figure advance from Putnam-Berkley. At this writing, the publisher is projecting an estimated 5,000,000 copies in sales, with lots of spin-off volumes.

$ Ann Rule, a former Seattle police officer, began her book career by writing about shocking murder cases, starting in the '80s with *The Stranger Beside Me*, about serial killer Ted Bundy, and later with *Small Sacrifices*, about a mother convicted of killing her three children. Both of these titles were massive best-sellers. In 1992, Rule contracted for two new books, including *If You Really Loved Me*, with Simon and Schuster, for $3.2 million.

Rule reviews hundreds of murder cases to find the rare standout she can turn into a best-seller. The secret to success in the true crime genre, she says, is to find that case with a charismatic killer, a sympathetic victim, a sexual element, and brilliant detective work. Doing meticulous research like Rule does probably doesn't hurt either. As of 2005, she had authored no less than 22 *New York Times* best-sellers, including *Heart Full of Lies* and *Green River, Running Red*.

$ Ellen Fein and Sherrie Schneider came up with thirty-five tenets to follow in order to capture the love of a good man, including, *don't call him* and *rarely return his calls*. The rules, which include some clever bits of reverse psychology, have been found to be unusually effective among many single women, who, by word-of-mouth have helped to propel the book onto best-seller lists. At last count, *The Rules: Time-Tested Secrets for Capturing the Heart of Mr. Right* had sold over 750,000 copies. A follow-up title, *Rules II*, arrived on bookstore shelves in short order.

$ As a sort of reply to Fein and Schneider's books, Greg Behrendt and Liz Tucillo explained guys' dating behavior, including why they never call, in their smash hit, *He's Just Not That Into You*, which sold 1,260,000 copies in 2004 alone. The book struck a resonant chord with single women because of one vital factor: *it told the truth!*

$ One of the biggest successes of the '90s is H. Jackson Brown's *Life's Little Instruction Book*, a title originally written for Brown's son, who, in 1991, was going off to college for the first time. The book is a compilation of 511 nuggets of wisdom and advice, such as #123: *Learn to listen. Opportunity sometimes knocks very softly* or #173: *Be kinder than necessary.* Brown was fifty-one and worked as a creative director at an advertising firm when the book hit the big time. *Life's Little Instruction Book* tapped into the huge gift-book market and is, by far, the biggest-selling title in Rutledge Hill Press' history. It has sold more than 5,000,000 copies, and its spin-off titles have raced up bestseller lists again and again.

$ What do you get when you gather a collection of ugly and goofy cat photos and caption them with humorous quotes or descriptions? *Bad Cats, 244 Not-so-Pretty Kitties and Cats Gone Bad.* Author Jim Edgar was a code writer at Microsoft who reported that he was, in fact, allergic to cats and did not own one himself! Yet he devised what turned out to be the perfect gift or gag book for cat lovers. *Bad Cats* sold an astonishing 403,000 copies during the Christmas season of 2004 and remained on the best-seller list for months after. (Conversely, a less offensive book of photos of cats napping and reclining, entitled appropriately enough, *Cat Naps*, sold 60,000 copies in roughly a two-year span.)

$ Henry Beard and John Boswell made their mark by poking fun at the O. J. Simpson murder trial. Theirs was the clever but bizarre *O. J.'s Legal Pad*, a book made to look like the tablet O. J. Simpson took notes on during his murder trial. Trying to imagine what O. J. might be writing on the pad, the authors invented some thoroughly twisted notes and cartoons that some critics hailed as thoroughly "tasteless," a charge guaranteed to increase sales. And increase sales it did, to the tune of 322,747 copies.

$ Beard and Boswell knew a great opportunity when they saw one. They had previously collaborated on eight other humor books, including a title no sane person could possibly believe was a good book idea, *French for Cats*.

$ Another comedy pair is Tom Connor and Jim Downey, who are, at this writing, making a living spoofing Martha Stewart. Both of their titles, *Martha Stewart is Better Than You at Entertaining* and *Is Martha Stewart Living?* have climbed the bestseller charts. Their favorite subject shows no sign of being thoroughly milked, and so bet on more titles in the future.

$ Spoofs seem to do best of all when they concern cats. *A Cat's Little Instruction Book* by Leigh Rutledge offers bite-sized nuggets of advice from a mother cat to her kitten. Typical maxims include: *Forgive your enemies—but only after you've given them a couple of swats* and *Cuddle with someone you love on a snowy afternoon.* This slim but cute title has gone back to print six times since 1993.

$ If there is a humorous topic that sells as well as cats, it's Moms. One of the all-time greats in the humor category is *Momilies: As My Mother Used to Say* by Michele Slung. This author's idea was brilliantly simple; she listed every witty, funny, nagging thing her mother said, such as *It's only your mother who is going to tell you the truth* and *Oh, so it's the egg telling the chicken.* Twenty-four printings later, it's still going strong, as is the follow-up, *More Momilies.*

$ It might not seem possible to write anything humorous about duct tape, but the authors of *The Duct Tape Book*, Tim Nyberg and Jim Berg, did just that by telling readers all the clever and silly things they can do with the sticky stuff. It and its spin-offs have sold a combined 1,000,000 copies.

$ *Snaps* falls somewhere in the genre of joke and insult books. Snaps, for the uninitiated, are put-downs, such as "Your mother is so fat, she lives in two zip codes" and "Your mother is so ugly, she makes blind kids cry," aimed primarily at a victim's relatives—most often mothers. Trading snaps, or *play-*

ing the dozens, has long been a popular tradition among many African-American children and is—usually—done for fun. *Snaps* sold 200,000 copies in 1994. The publisher, of course, had authors Monteria Ivey, Stephen Dweck, and James Percelay do a snappy follow-up title in 1995 called *Double Snaps.*

$ It's not quite clear what category a book called *Grossology* falls into. Thirty-seven-year-old public school teacher Sylvia Branzei wrote this book in 1995, and little did she know what kind of juggernaut it would launch. (A raft of spinoff books, calendars, CDs, tattoos, t-shirts, traveling exhibits and a television show.)The book answers simply and straightforwardly those big, important questions we—and, of course, kids—have wanted to know for years, such as *Why do we puke? What makes feet stink? What exactly is a booger anyway?*

This 80-page guide to all things disgusting features an eye-catching and thoroughly stomach-turning representation of vomit on the front cover. I understand sex sells. But *puke* sells?

While we're on the topic, would you believe a book about *owl puke* could possibly have a market? *Owl Puke,* by Jane Hammerslough, is a book about owls that actually comes with a pellet of owl vomit for kids to study. What's so fascinating about owl vomit? It contains the undigested skeleton of their last meal!

$ Joanna Cole's *Magic School Bus* series for kids just keeps on rolling. Many of her educational, yet fun, titles, such as *The Magic School Bus in the Time of the Dinosaurs* and *The Magic School Bus Lost in the Solar System* have been selling over 100,000 copies *per year.* In fact, in 1996 she had ten titles all breaking the 100,000-copy sales mark simultaneously. The author of over ninety books for children, this former elementary school teacher calls writing "the greatest fun in the world." With those sales figures, it's easy to see why.

$ Another strong children's seller is *Dinosaur Days* by Joyce Milton. In print since 1985, it sold 146,468 copies in 1995 alone. *Where Did I Come From,* a children's facts-of-life book by Peter Mayle, has sold over 2 million copies and has become a backlist staple.

$ Care to guess how many copies of *The Beanie Baby Handbook* have sold? 3,000,000 at last check. All the more remarkable, authors Les and Sue Fox actually outfoxed the big houses in Manhattan and published this one themselves. Sharp!

$ Helen Witty found a way to delight kids and grown-ups alike with the huge but oh, so simple idea of giant cookies, and *Monster Cookies* is now at a delicious 150,000 copies and counting.

$ Cynthia Lewis got her material straight from her own children in *Really Important Stuff My Kids Have Taught Me,* with 172,000 copies in print.

$ Vicki Lansky struck a resonant chord among all parents (and grandparents) with her 200,000-copy selling *101 Ways to Tell Your Child "I Love You."* Vicki is no stranger to the best-seller lists. Her *Feed Me, I'm Yours,* which was originally self-published after being rejected by forty-nine different publishers, has sold a whopping 8,000,000 copies!

$ And, can you think of 365 activities to do with your kids that don't involve television? Steve and Ruth Bennett can; they described them all in brief, simple capsules in *365 TV-Free Activities You Can Do With Your Child.* Sales to date: 500,000 copies.

$ Being a tightwad pays. Big time. Maine resident Amy Dacyczyn gives all her money-saving household tips in a series of simple guidebooks, one of which, *The Tightwad Gazette,* has sold nearly 300,000 copies.

$ Kenneth Davis may score even bigger with his virtual publishing franchise known as the *Don't Know Much About* series (*Don't Know Much About the Bible, Don't Know Much About the Civil War,* etc.). During the '90s, Davis sold millions of copies of these "pop education" books and, in 1999, signed a contract to write twenty more for Harper Collins. Davis holds no special credentials to author these books, other than being a good writer and a thorough researcher.

$ Keeping it all in the family is the secret of the publishing phenomenon *What to Expect When You're Expecting.* The authors, Arlene Eisenberg, Heidi Murkoff, and Sandee Hathaway, are a mother and daughters writing team currently enjoying the ultimate publishing success story. Their extremely thorough and fascinating guide to pregnancy has sold nearly 9 million copies and continues to fly off bookstore shelves. It may well end up, in fact, the mother of all backlist titles. A lucrative spin-off franchise is churning out a steady flow of new best-sellers, including, *What to Expect: The First Year* and *What to Expect: The Toddler Years.* This book, too, was originally self-published!

$ Dan Gookin is the guy who wrote the book on how to write the computer book. When Gookin appeared on the scene in 1992, it was dry, technical text *out,* light, reader-friendly prose, *in.* His popular and very readable "Dummies" guides, including *DOS for Dummies, PCs for Dummies, WordPerfect for Dummies* and others have sold multiple millions of copies and helped launch a publishing empire of *Dummies* books. (More than 50 million *Dummies* books are in print at this writing.)

Ironically, many of the big bookstore chains originally refused to stock *Dummies* books, believing they were poorly titled. They have since changed their thinking.

$ Jack Canfield and Mark Victor Hansen have, on their own, eclipsed even the impressive sales record of the *Dummies* books. They collected simple, true stories of inspiration, love, and courage from people around the world and put them into a modest little book called *Chicken Soup for the Soul.* Little did they know that their book would usher in the beginning of the most successful series of the decade. At this writing, the *Chicken Soup* series is comprised of dozens of different titles, with a mind-boggling 40 million copies in print. The beauty of these books is they are largely written, not by the authors, but by contributors.

No doubt you've seen many of these books on the best-seller lists. Hundreds more like them exist that never quite reached best-seller status, but nonetheless earned sizable incomes for their authors.

Too often writers assume that books which are not best-sellers are disappointments in the profits department. It ain't necessarily so! When measured over the long haul of ten, fifteen, or even twenty years, strong sellers may actually outearn the more dazzling, flash-in-the-pan best-sellers. Some of the loudest, splashiest best-sellers, in fact, sometimes vanish from bookstores in as little as three years and are never seen again.

If you have average intelligence and a good work ethic, you could have created many of the above titles, formal education or not. As helpful as strong credentials may be, *the lack of them can often be overcome in the book world.* I'll show you exactly how to get around the "degree and authority barrier" in a later chapter.

Okay. Ordinary people *can* write extraordinary books. We've just seen a few examples to prove it. Are you inspired? Is your adrenaline flowing? Is your heart beating out a paradiddle in your chest?

If a little voice inside your head is shouting, "Good heavens, *I* could do this," run, don't walk, to the next chapter. The fact is, if you think you can, you *can*.

Chapter Three

What Kind of Nonfiction Book Should You Write?

Nonfiction's top-selling topics...A rundown of the basic nonfiction categories...A critical ingredient for author success

The choices of niche book categories to explore are as varied and as tantalizing as the bill of fare at Ben and Jerry's. Before winnowing those choices down, though, consider two hard-and-fast rules: You must pick a category (A) that you're passionate about and (B) in which you have or can achieve the most credibility or "authority."

Let's face the raw truth right up front: Writing a book can be the mental equivalent of clawing your way to the summit of Mount Everest and rappelling back down again, *alone*. It requires careful thought, preparation, and research, and it's all too easy, when the going gets tough, to lose your resolve. To fill all those blank pages with words, then to correct and rearrange those pages anywhere from three to six times or more, and then to market your work and face rejection after rejection is a task simply too daunting for some.

Thus, it is passion for your book's subject that is paramount. Passion will get you through the most trying of challenges. Passion will get you to the summit and back again when nothing else will.

In my twenty-three years in publishing, during which I built a 1,000-plus collection of rejection slips—admittedly a painful endeavor fit only for masochists—I've learned a lot about the market and what sells and what doesn't and why. Through trial and error, I've become acutely attuned to the top eleven nonfiction topics that can be counted on to appear on best-seller lists—with multiple titles—again and again, year after year, decade after decade. I list them here in no particular order.

- Dieting/Weight loss

- Relationships/Self-Help/Sex

- Parenting

- Health/Fitness

- Spiritual/Religious

- Business/Leadership/Career

- Money/Finances

- Cats

- Computer/Internet

Do any of these topics turn you on? If so, you're in luck. The highest odds of a sale are to be found within these categories, although best-sellers obviously show up in other categories as well. And, strong sellers—not necessarily best-sellers—can be found all over the board.

Computer and Internet books are obviously the newcomers to publishing success, but they are, without question, here to stay. Find a computer or Internet niche and your career as an author is as assured as one could possibly hope.

In recent years, natural healing books have mushroomed in popularity, but there is no telling if the trend will last. End-of-the-millennium or Y2K books had a great run in 1998 and 1999, but the brick wall of their market was well in sight. Nobody, obviously, would buy a *How to Survive the End of the World in the Year 2000* book in the year 2001 or after. Juicy scandal is a perennial favorite, but these days the scandal must be juicier than ever to attract interest away from TV. Feng shui, low-carb diet, and stock "day trading" are typical of fad book subjects that run hot for a few short years and then wither away.

Seventy to 85 percent of all book buyers are women. Need I say more? Well, maybe. Most editors today are also women. Anything oriented toward the female, then, will have an edge. On the other hand, men love true adventure, sports, business, and politics; authors have little trouble bringing men into the bookstores with these subjects.

Let's consider the basic nonfiction categories in more detail.

How-To

As I write this, scores of how-tos are racking up big sales, in topics largely overlooked by others. *101 Things to Do With a Cake Mix*, and *101 Things to Do With a Slow Cooker* (80,000 and 100,000 copies respectively), by Stephanie Ashcroft, are good examples. How about *Organizing from the Inside Out*, by Julie Morgenstern, with 150,000 sales?

How-to books teach readers how to do something or how to do something better, step-by-step. If you're an authority on your subject, you've got it made. If not, you can interview outside experts to help you. The how-to category offers a galaxy of possibilities, from *How to Grow Bigger Vegetables* to *How to Paint Your House Like a Pro*. Great ideas may be a lot closer than you think, so close, in fact, that you may overlook them. *Backtalk: 4 Steps to Ending Rude Behavior in Your Kids* by authors Audrey Ricker and Carolyn Crowder has sold nearly a quarter of a million copies. That's a book virtually any parent could have written with the right kind of research. And, how about *The Working Woman's Wedding Planner* by Susan Tatsui-D'arcy? It was specifically written for women who "already have too many demands on their time." In 1999, sales had surpassed the 300,000 mark.

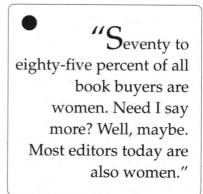

"Seventy to eighty-five percent of all book buyers are women. Need I say more? Well, maybe. Most editors today are also women."

In the '90s, everyone was looking for ways to simplify their lives. Thus the market for books showing readers how to embrace a "less is more" philosophy exploded, with several titles breaking the 100,000-copy sales mark. Typical of the group was *Simplify Your Christmas* by Elaine St. James. Virtually anyone could have written this book.

Look around you. The great ideas for how-to books are often so obvious that most people are blind to them.

Self-Help

Most self-help books fall under the "psychology" category. If you've been through a personal ordeal and have learned how to cope and can share that information lucidly, you may have a shot here. Dianne

Schwartz ingeniously combined a narrative of her own domestic abuse experiences with a self-help guide for abused women in *Whose Face Is in the Mirror?* It was so distinguished, its publisher decided to donate all of the profit from its sales to a women's charity. Previously, Dianne had virtually no writing experience.

Keep in mind, however, that editors and agents are deluged with manuscripts entitled *I Was Hideously Abused But Lived to Tell About It* or *My Secrets to Achieving Happiness*, and they look upon them with a jaundiced eye, to say the least. Thus, if yours is to have a ghost of a chance of even getting read, it must be "exceptional."

One of the most heartening self-help success stories that I know of from a "nonexpert" may be John Wiedman's *Desperately Seeking Snoozin'*. In a category glutted with competitors, his book stands out because he is not a physician or a psychologist, but an insomnia sufferer, and he writes of his own chronic sleeplessness, as well as the hellish experiences of other insomniacs (most of his interviewees were located over the Internet) and details not only the tips the experts advise, but the tips experts advise *that don't work*. He also provides some interesting food for thought by telling readers to not always trust "experts" in the field, because as well-intentioned as they may be, they may also be wrong. The book was so sincere and so helpful that even the *competing* author of the leading insomnia book on the market, a physician and international sleep authority, gave the book not only his blessings but a blurb for the jacket!

Can't think of a self-help book? Don't try too hard to be original. Merely look at what's already been done and try to come up with something better or a new slant. The walking wounded are everywhere: agoraphobia, alcoholism, anxiety, career dissatisfaction, compulsive gambling, divorce, depression, fear of public speaking, low self-esteem, loneliness, marriage survival, obsessive-compulsive disorder, post traumatic stress syndrome, rape victimization, seasonal affective disorder, sexual addiction, shyness, substance abuse, and the list goes on.

Biography

No "credentials" necessary here in most cases. Simply find a celebrity or historical figure who hasn't already been done to death, research his or her life thoroughly, and start writing. The ideal is to write what is called an "authorized" biography, which is a bio that is given the blessings of the subject, and who, in fact, may actively participate in the compilation of the book by providing interviews and research materials. However, "unauthorized" biographies are published all the time. If you can't interview your subject (because he or she refuses or is, in fact, dead), you'll need to interview secondary or related sources and delve into all the news stories generated by the celebrity. When it comes to famous people, usually a great deal of material is available in the public record, through newspaper and magazine stories and interviews, through other books, through friends and acquaintances, and so on.

Leonardo Di Caprio: Modern-Day Romeo and a second title, *Leonardo: A Scrapbook in Words and Pictures*, sold 500,000 copies each in just their first year of release. *Hanson: An Unauthorized Biography* sold 785,000 copies within months of its release. A spin-off, *Totally Taylor! Hanson's Heartthrob* almost instantly sold 335,000 copies. Heartthrobs are always big in publishing. Keep a keen eye open for the flavor of the month and move quickly.

One would assume that an author writing a biography on a subject that has already been covered would be foolhardy. Not always so. A new biography on Joe Namath, for example, was released in 2005, decades after his stardom faded. When the Leonardo and Hanson bios were published, they competed head to head with a dozen other titles.

Any pop icon is likely to have several biographies. Frank Sinatra has had as many as twenty-five in print at any one time. Gloria Steinem has had half a dozen. Albert Einstein had more than a dozen written about him in the 1990s alone. A biography of John F. Kennedy, one of a long line, actually made the best-seller lists in 1999. Victoria Woodhull, the first woman to run for president, is the subject of no less than five biographies currently in print, so even historical figures from over a century ago or more are fair game. I counted more than seventy new biographies released by publishers in the fall of 1999 alone, and more than half of their subjects had already been done before.

Be wary, however, of "minor" celebrities, celebrities whose careers are on the wane, and little-known historical figures. These are tough sells.

Cookbook

Several hundred new cookbooks will enter the market this year. According to *Publishers Weekly*, at least ten of these will break 100,000 in first year sales. Will yours be among them?

Like every other category, the cookbook market is sometimes propelled by fads and trends. "Low-fat" and "no fat" were big for several years and then were eclipsed by low-carb tomes, crowned by *Atkins* and *The South Beach Diet*. "Quick and easy" is a perennial favorite. A popular trend for several years has been "grilling." *The Barbecue Bible* by Steven Raichlen, for example, has sold over 310,000 copies. When bread machines came onto the market, bread machine cookbooks quickly became all the rage, some selling over 500,000 copies.

The competition is intense, and to have a chance, you'll either need to write a highly distinguished book, with a theme that captures the imagination of the public, or be a highly accomplished or esteemed cook (recognized with awards or degrees in the culinary arts or similar achievement) or at least be able to promote your title heavily. The ideal is a mix of all three. Dozens of niche cookbook categories exist. Try to find a fresh one or at least one that hasn't been thoroughly covered.

Some titles that performed well at the turn of the century included *Top Secret Restaurant Recipes* by Todd Wilbur, with 130,000 sold; *Pasta Light* by Norman Kolpas, with 150,000; *The Farmhouse Cookbook* by Susan Loomis, with 183,000; *Chili Madness* by Jane Butel, with 312,000; and *The Top 100 Pasta Sauces* by Diane Seed, with 1,000,000 copies sold. Cookbooks with medical or health tie-ins can sometimes do spectacularly well, too. *The Art of Cooking for the Diabetic* by Mary Hess, for example, has sold over 450,000 copies.

"I can think of several ways a (cookbook) novice without formal training might compete and succeed," says best-selling cookbook author (*The International Cookie Book*) Nancy Baggett. "One way is by working with a brand-new product or piece of equipment (for example, a bread machine) and developing an expertise that no one else has had time to develop. There is also opportunity with a quirky, funny topic or humorous approach. If you can make people laugh, you have a chance.

"That one isn't formally trained doesn't mean one can't develop a valuable expertise," Baggett says. "If there is interest in the subject, a novice can sell to a publisher and ultimately to the public."

History

You don't have to be a history professor to write a history book. (Although admittedly, you're way ahead of the competition if you are.) But you do need to be a thorough and scholarly researcher and you need to avoid rehashing what's already been done.

Contrary to what most laymen believe, all the history books have *not* already been written. There are always new slants, newly discovered information, and fresh ways of looking at things.

If I told you to write a book on the history of Ireland, for example, you'd think I was daft. Surely Irish history has been done ad nauseam, with virtually zero potential for anything new to be written or said. Not quite. Find a new angle, sensationalize just a bit and, presto! We have *How the Irish Saved Civilization* by Thomas Cahill. It has sold over 700,000 copies. Not bad for a history book, eh? Cahill used the same formula to liven up the history of the Jews with *The*

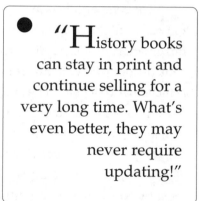

"History books can stay in print and continue selling for a very long time. What's even better, they may never require updating!"

Gifts of the Jews: How a Tribe of Desert Nomads Changed the Way Everyone Thinks and Feels, which at last check was following the same stellar sales course as Cahill's Irish book.

In 2001, Laura Hillenbrand's race horse story *Seabiscuit* became a *New York Times* #1 best-seller, as well as a hit movie. A chronic fatigue sufferer, Hillenbrand wrote most of the book while in bed. Laurence Bergreen plumbed onboard diaries and other publicly-available documents to chronicle Ferdinand Magellan's first circumnavigation of the earth in *Over the Edge of the World*, a bestseller in 2004. Richard Shenkman created a runaway hit with *Legends, Lies and Cherished Myths of American History*, still cruising along after seventeen years in print.

The smashing success of *The Perfect Storm* opened the floodgates to all kinds of historical storm and disaster-related titles, including *Isaac's Storm: A Man, a Time and the Deadliest Hurricane in History* by Erik Larson in 1999. A big best-selling title always spawns copycats, so a niche author must be alert for opportunities. If you want to get in with a copy-cat book of your own, get in *within a year* of the vanguard book because the market will likely be saturated with imitators after that.

History books can stay in print and continue selling for a very long time. What's even better, they may never require updating!

True Adventure/True Narrative

The remarkable thing about the *New York Times* best-seller, *The Perfect Storm*, is that the true adventure it chronicles was *not* experienced by the author, Sebastian Junger. Those who suffered through the ordeal, in fact, died and could share none of the horrible details. What the author did was play investigative journalist and piece together bits and pieces from interviews of surviving friends, relatives, and coworkers and meld them with a description of the monster storm that would doom a group of fishermen too far out to sea to save themselves. Adding nitty-gritty details about commercial fishing, rescue operations, the ocean, and little known horrors about drowning from a medical standpoint added to the terror and fascination.

This bears repeating. Junger had *no* experience as a professional fisherman. He was *not* a meteorologist. He did *not* experience the 100-foot waves of the storm he writes about himself. He could interview *none* of the eyewitnesses. Yet he is able to make the reader feel as if he is *there* among the crew of the doomed fishing vessel. A terrifying, harrowing ordeal brought to life through carefully chosen words and research. Somerset Maugham sums up this magic nicely:

> **"There is no need for the writer to eat a whole sheep to be able to tell what mutton tastes like. It's enough if he eats a cutlet."**

Of course, if you *have* lived through an adventure yourself, all the better. Middle-aged Bill Bryson walked almost all of the Appalachian

Trail with his buddy and wrote about in *Into the Woods*, a huge best-seller in 1999. Jon Krakauer is another "I was there" author. His personal account of the Mount Everest disaster, *Into Thin Air*, rode best-seller lists in 1998 and 1999 for months.

Have you survived a catastrophe? Your story might make for great reading. The market is always receptive to harrowing stories.

If, however, you're like me—more of an armchair adventurer who wouldn't dream of going too far afield without a twenty-seven-inch TV and a satellite dish—take heart. Even milder experiences can captivate readers, assuming you're an exceptionally talented ink-slinger. Tracy Kidder had two big successes with *Home Town*, a real-life portrayal of small town Northhampton, Massachusetts, and *House*, a chronicle of, yes, incredibly, *the building of a house*.

Personal Memoirs

"Hey," you say, "I can't write a memoir, nothing interesting has happened to me." Try telling that to Amy Rosenthal, whose *Encyclopedia of an Ordinary Life* reached #13 on Amazon.com nonfiction best-seller list in March 2005. Rosenthal reveals the very minutiae of her ordinary life, including the act of pumping gas. Her front cover blurbs say it all:

> I have not survived against great odds.
> I have not lived to tell.
> I have not witnessed the extraordinary.
> This is my story.

But it just so happens that Rosenthal knows how to write, and so should you before trying a memoir like hers.

Of course, if you have stories to tell like those of Sanyika Shakur, whose book, *Monster: The Autobiography of an L.A. Gang Member*, sold over 200,000 copies, publishers will be more than happy to help you beef up a bit of weak writing here and there.

The market for personal memoirs, as I've profiled, took off during the second half of the 1990s and has yet to show signs of slowing. Unknowns have found surprisingly great success here. Frank McCourt's

Angela's Ashes, with four million copies sold, stands as a testament to the public's fascination for life stories, especially tragic ones. (His book sold so well, the publisher asked his *brother* to write one, too, and for a very large advance, no less.) But a caveat: Amateurs ply publishers with stacks of "My Life" manuscripts every day, and I would wager that far less than one in a hundred reaches publishable standards. Memoir authors must not only have a great life story to tell, they must also be great writers. (McCourt, incidentally, was a writing teacher when he wrote his book.) Here are six ingredients found in successful memoirs:

- *History.* Your memoir doesn't necessarily have to be historically significant, but if you fought in a war or took part in other historical events or at least witnessed them firsthand and can describe them in a colorful way, you'll be ahead of the pack. It's not enough to write about what you did in the past. You must also illuminate the period you write about with everyday life, you-are-there details.

- *Glamour.* If you hobnobbed with celebrities and have interesting anecdotes to share, that's a big plus.

- *Sin.* Sex and violence sells. That's no different for memoirs. Readers want to be titillated. So do editors.

- *Deep, personal details.* You can't be superficial in a memoir. If you want an audience, you literally have to tell all, and that includes revealing less appealing aspects of yourself. One night stands. Suicide attempts. Drunken stupors. Shoplifting. Racism. Heartbreaks. If you've got dirt, dish it up.

- *Tragedy.* The more horrible and wretched, the better.

- *Exemplary writing.* If you're a noncelebrity with little history or glamour to report, your writing will be tantamount. A talented writer can make the ordinary seem extraordinary. Check out *All Creatures Great and Small* by James Herriot to see how a pro weaves delightfully fascinating character portraits and everyday vignettes of veterinary life into a rich tapestry beloved by readers everywhere. Herriot's are among the most popular memoirs of all time, and for good reason. If nothing else, studying his books will teach you how deceptively difficult good writing is. Even if you don't master it, you'll hardly waste your time with such pleasurable reading.

Humor

After receiving a copy of S. J. Perelman's new book, Groucho Marx told the humorist author, "From the moment I picked up your book until I laid it down, I was convulsed with laughter. Someday I intend reading it."

Writers are attracted to humor books because of their length: They are often short. But what humor books lack in girth, they make up for in sheer difficulty of writing. Humor writing isn't funny or easy.

"It's a tough market to crack," says Jerry McTigue, author of *Life's Little Frustration Book* and other successful humor titles. "Editors are very finicky."

Editors must have a clear sense of market before they'll bite, even if your book is riotously funny. Market considerations are more crucial than usual with humor because, McTigue says, "humor books are usually paperbacks sold at the back of the store," and they can be difficult to promote.

Humor books are often given as gifts. Some of the hottest humor books revolve around cats. No wonder. With a market of over fifty million cat owners, only a tiny fraction of 1 percent of this population need to be convinced to buy a copy. (A tiny sampling of recent humorous cat titles: *Diary of a Cat*; *The Kama Sutra for Cats*; *Listening to Catnip—Stories from a Cat Analyst's Couch*; *Women Who Love Cats Too Much*; and *101 Reasons Why Cats Make Great Kids*.)

Parodies can do well if they're published fast on the heels of the subject they're parodying. Ronald Roberts' *The Ditches of Edison County*, a parody of *The Bridges of Madison County*, sold over 100,000 copies in its first year alone.

That men are humorously skewered in print more often than women testifies to the dominant female buying profile. *How to Make*

Your Man Behave in 21 Days or Less Using the Secrets of Professional Dog Trainers by Karen Salmansohn, sold 147,000 copies in one year alone.

On the other hand, I'd bet my next royalty check that the biggest population of buyers of *The Duct Tape Book* (a best-seller illustrating all of the humorous things to do with duct tape) were guys.

Other popular humor categories: golf, fishing, marriage, sex, dating, lampoons, dirty jokes, gross jokes.

Warning: I once had as clients two popular stand-up comics who made regular appearances on all of the major comedy shows and tried to write a couple of humor books and sell them. As you would expect from nationally respected professionals, both attempts were laugh-out-loud funny, yet editors turned down both of their books. "No market," they said. "Funny, even very funny, but no market," they told me again and again. And so it was that far less funny books appeared in print, while my two comedian clients scratched their heads in frustration. Your book must, absolutely *must,* have an identifiable market. Fishermen. Cat owners. Women frustrated by their men. Exactly *who* will buy your book? Can't answer that question? Then take heed: Funny alone is not enough!

Reference

If this category seems dull to you, think again. While its lack of pizzazz may turn off a large segment of writers, long-term profits can be dazzling. A good reference book never goes out of print. The author simply updates it roughly every one to eight years and continues to collect royalties year after year after year, decade after decade after decade.

Computer and Internet books, for example, frequently sell in the hundreds of thousands and sometimes millions, and they must be updated at least every couple of years, generating that revenue all over again! Elizabeth Crowe's *Genealogy Online* has sold 100,000 copies. Harley Hahn's *Internet and Web Yellow Pages* has sold more than two million copies.

Can a book about proper punctuation make the grade? In 2004,

Eats, Shoots and Leaves, by journalist Lynne Truss, topped bestseller lists in the U.S. and U.K. For months.

Periods and commas as best-seller material? A once-in-a-lifetime phenomenon, right? Wrong. Another grammar book, *Between You and I: A Little Book of Bad English,* by James Cochran, became the number one best-selling nonfiction book on Amazon.com in March of 2005, at the same time *Eats, Shoots and Leaves* was still in the top 25. But don't miss this. *Eats, Shoots and Leaves* was published just a short time after another grammar bestseller, *Woe Is I* (400,000 copies sold, its author tells me), which in turn nipped at the heels of the greatest-selling grammar guide of all time, *The Elements of Style*, which has been a perennial backlist bestseller for decades.

To round out the reference possibilities, consider a lucrative subcategory: directories. Directories may appear about as exciting as watching rust form, but they can generate great income, which is replenished every year with updated editions. According to Gale Research, there are currently over 15,500 directories in print!

I once self-published a directory called *Dial-an-Expert*, which was basically a telephone directory for writers and reporters. Writer's Digest Book Club made a bulk purchase before I even finished compiling it!

Travel Guide

This can be a wonderful category once you become established. With the credibility of a couple of travel books under your belt, you'll be invited to stay for free at all kinds of resorts and hotels. Your writing can literally pay for all of your vacations and then some. A great way to make your vacation become a vocation.

Traveling on the cheap has always been a hit with book buyers. *Europe on $50 a Day* by Beth Reiber sold 55,000 copies in 1998 alone. *Away for the Weekend, New York* by Eleanor Berman captured a huge niche market by showing New Yorkers where they could have a good time within two hundred miles of their city on a weekend, netting more than 200,000 sales. Two of the most popular travel books of 1999, according to Ingram Book Company, the nation's largest book wholesaler, were *Pay Nothing to Travel Anywhere You Like* by Eric Gershman and *The Penny Pincher's Passport to Luxury Travel* by Joel Widzer.

Would it surprise you to learn that the *World Guide to Nude Beaches and Resorts* also made behemoth book wholesaler Ingram's list of best-selling travel books?

Be careful with some of those "franchise" travel books; they may pay only a flat fee for your book. I was once offered such a fee ($6,000) to write a travel book about southern Maine. By the time I had personally visited, researched, and written about all the restaurants, museums, amusements parks, shopping meccas and natural attractions the publisher required, I figured that my net pay would work out to somewhere around four dollars an hour. Not a good deal, and thus I left this project for someone hungrier than I was.

Flat-fee travel books are attractive only when you have nothing else in the offing or if you're trying to build your publishing resume for something better. Always work with publishers who pay an advance and royalties unless you have no other choice.

Children's

This is a difficult market for nonfiction writers. The big sellers almost always have TV or movie tie-ins, and fiction clearly dominates. Still, *a new crop* of dinosaur, space, and shark books will be sold this year, as they are every year and, because of their lengths, they can often be written in as little as a month. But a warning: Competition is intense. Authors everywhere assume the children's market is easy pickings, and often, when a writer has poor luck with the adult market, he turns here. This creates overcrowding and lowers the odds of a sale. If you're an unknown, your book must clearly shine.

If you've got kids of your own, you've got a big advantage. You've seen what they and their friends like firsthand. Tune in. Listen. Watch. Aileen Marron did and hit a home run with *The Henna Body Art Kit*, an instruction book with body makeup for girls aged twelve, thirteen and fourteen, with sales to date of 200,000 copies. She naturally followed her success with a spin-off book on Indian jewelry, which at this writing is performing equally well.

It's a no-brainer: Kids love gross and weird. Thus, the *Extremely Weird* series (weird animals and bugs) by Sarah Lovett continues to pile up sales, with more than 700,000 copies in print. Ditto *Grossology*. (See description in chapter two.) Among kids, poop and puke sells! And, how can you lose with a title like *Science Experiments You Can Eat*? The book's author, Vicki Cobb, tells me it has sold around 1,000,000 copies since 1972. Talk about having a long shelf life!

Finally, in the ultimate, *Damn! Why Didn't I Write That!* category is *Brain Quest* by Chris Feder. This series of quizzing cards designed for kids proves that the biggest ideas are sometimes the simplest: Provide some questions, which anyone from the age of twelve on could have compiled, and have kids give the answers to test their knowledge. Sales of the entire *Brain Quest* series to date: *Over 14,000,000!*

Damn!

Medicine

This category is always hot. Think of the thousands of illnesses and disorders that plague human beings. Every one of those ailments is a potential market for a book. No medical degree is required, but it sure helps. If you're not an medical professional, there are a number of ways to gain the credibility of one without spending a single minute inside a medical school. In chapter five, I outline how to write authoritative books by either liberally quoting experts and expert studies or by collaborating with one or more experts.

If you worry your lack of professional education precludes you from delving into this category, consider one of the biggest smash hits of 2005, *French Women Don't Get Fat*, by Mireille Guiliano. Guiliano had no health credentials other than her experience of losing 20 pounds upon returning to France after being an exchange student in America. Nothing succeeds like success, of course, so publishers were quick to jump on success, notably with *The French Diet: The Secrets of Why French Women Don't Get Fat*, by Michel Montignac, with a 100,000 first printing, and, in the humor department, *French Cats Don't Get Fat*, by Henry Beard.

Sports

Not all sports books do well in the market. Baseball titles, for example, almost always outperform football titles. Why? Nobody knows. In 2005, Mathew McGough's *Bat Boy*, a coming of age chronicle of a New York Yankees bat boy, was launched with a 60,000-copy first printing. *Coach: Lessons on the Game of Life*, by Michael Lewis, showcases the influence of a high school baseball coach on a young player; it was launched in the same year with a 300,000-copy first printing.

But less popular sports can do well. *Swimming to Antarctica, Tales of a Long Distance Swimmer*, by Lynne Cox, boasted a 75,000 first printing in 2005. For the first time ever, girl's surfing became a mini trend, with no less than four books on the topic published in the spring of 2005.

As for instructional guides, golf titles rank high, and no wonder; hitting a tiny ball where you want it to go is a lot harder than it looks. Beginners richly embarrass themselves in front of strangers on hole after hole, a discomfort that publishers exploit to the fullest by promising miraculous improvements in their games. *Golf for Dummies*, by Gary McCord has sold over 200,000 copies, as has *40 Common Errors in Golf and How to Correct Them*, by Arthur Shay.

You don't necessarily need to be a sports pro to write one of these books—although that's an obvious advantage. Many nonpros simply collaborate with one or more experts in the field.

Occult/Paranormal

Psychics. Life after death. The "other side." UFO kidnappings. Bible codes. Channeling. Past-life experiences. Ghosts. Some of the biggest selling books of the 1990s fell squarely into this category, while others straddled an amorphous category falling somewhere between religious and the occult.

Adventures of a Psychic by Sylvia Browne sold over 300,000 copies, as did her follow-up, *The Other Side and Back*. Never mind what scientific investigators and critics say about her credibility and that of other humans with self-professed super powers. In the book business, people buy books about what they *want* to believe, not necessarily what's true.

(Books debunking psychics and the paranormal far undersell their more colorful rivals with their outrageous and untested claims.) For these books, there is a sucker born every minute, and publishers feel little remorse exploiting our national naivete.

Publishers will happily invite you to the dance if you can present your paranormal claims on TV and radio with a straight face. It helps if you strongly believe in it yourself.

Religious/Spiritual

In 1992, Bret Nicholaus and Paul Lowrie teamed up to write a book comprised mostly of questions "aimed to spur discussion" around spirituality and values. Their book, *The Conversation Piece*, was originally self-published and sold 20,000 copies before it was picked up by Random House, which sold over 100,000 more.

Around the time of the Millennium, books concerning the soul were all the rage. So were individual books of prayer. Bruce Wilkinson's 96-page *Prayer of Jabez* , which borrows from an actual prayer in the Bible, sold an astonishing 9,000,000 copies. A child's version became the bestselling kids' hardcover of 2002.

You can take this fact to the bank: People are always looking for meaning in their lives. Consequently spiritual books are perennially high on the list of publishers' must-haves. (According to *Publishers Weekly*, romance is the best-selling book category, followed by business, and then religion/spirituality.)

One author who hit a grand slam by tapping into our yearning for deeper meaning is Pastor Rick Warren. He enlisted the help of over 1,500 churches in 50 states and nine countries to promote *The Purpose Driven Life*. At this writing, sales have exceeded 20,000,000, with an additional 6,500,000 gift and audio book versions! Warren does just what he touts in his book. He donated 90 percent of his profits to charitable causes.

People never tire of reading new books about Jesus, of course. *The Case for Christ: A Journalist's Personal Investigation of the Evidence of Jesus*, by Lee Sobel, has visited and revisited bestseller lists several times, as has a kids' book called, *What Would Jesus Do?*

And need anything be said about the multimillion selling series, *Conversations With God*?

God sells!

True Crime

True crime books can sometimes generate millions of dollars, not only with book rights, but with motion picture and TV rights. These books require lots of face-to-face interviews and often lots of reading of court transcripts, not to mention thoroughly screening hundreds of potential crimes for that rare gem that can be turned into a book that people will want to read.

Ann Rule is the undisputed queen of this genre. She's been churning out best-seller after best-seller since the 1980s. Check out a few of her titles to see how a true master writes true crime.

Science

This was a category long ignored by many writers, under the assumption that there was little money it. One particular literary agent who specializes in science titles, however, changed all that in the '90s following the dazzling success of Stephen Hawking's *A Brief History of Time*, by demanding six figure advances for certain high-profile science books.

Who would have dreamed that *The Physics of Star Trek* could sell over 100,000 copies? (Why, *Star Trek* fans, of course!) *Chaos: Making a New Science* by James Gleick sold 500,000 copies, proving that the reading public doesn't even need to have a clear idea of what the book's science is exactly about in order to sell! Gleick followed with another nontraditional science subject—speed—in a book called *Faster*, chronicling how society and technology are forever speeding up.

And, would you bet that a book on something as dry and esoteric as *longitude* could ever catch on with a general reading audience? Yet that's exactly what Dava Sobel's slim chronicle about clockmaker John Harrison's forty-year quest to provide a means of accurate ocean navigation—a problem that stumped even Newton and Galileo—did with *Longitude: The True Story of a Lone Genius Who Solved the Greatest Scientific Problem of His Time*, a big best-seller in the 1990s.

I would be severely remiss if I didn't mention Hannah Holmes, the science writer who laid down in the grass of her tiny, South Portland, Maine backyard for months and watched the goings on among the ants, slugs, crows, and squirrels and then wrote a critically acclaimed book, *Suburban Safari*, about what she witnessed. Previously, she tackled another topic few would consider book-worthy: dust. *Her Secret Life of Dust: From the Cosmos to the Kitchen Counter*, in fact, was chosen among the best books of 2001 by the editors at Amazon.com. Look hard. Focus. Sometimes great science ideas are right in front of your nose.

"The best trade science books are only peripherally about science, maybe science is the backdrop to a story about exploration and the scientists themselves," says Skip Barker, of the Wilson Devereaux Company, a literary agency specializing in science titles. "They're written in an engaging narrative style and they tell a story and make the reader feel a part of that story."

❧ *Note:* To stay abreast of what's on the cutting edge of scientific research, subscribe to *Science News, Scientific American, Discover*, and other science-oriented magazines. As you'll learn later in this book, you can go one step further and be placed on the mailing list for science news from all of the major universities in the United States, a great way to stay ahead of your competition!

Business

Business books are a big and booming category. At this writing, readers are snapping up copies of *Customers.Com: How to Create a Profitable Business Strategy for the Internet and Beyond* by Patricia Seybold. According to Ingram, top-selling business titles include *Who Moved My Cheese: An Amazing Way to Deal With Change in Your Work and in Your Life* by Spencer Johnson; *The Millionaire Next Door: The Surprising Secrets of America's Wealthy* by Thomas Stanley; *Rich Dad, Poor Dad: What the Rich Teach Their Kids About Money—That the Poor and Middle Class Don't* by Robert Kiyosaki; *First, Break All the Rules: What the World's Greatest Managers Do Differently* by Marcus Buckingham; *E-Business: Roadmap for Success* by Ravi Kalakota; and *The 21 Irrefutable Laws of Leadership: Follow Them and People Will Follow You* by John Maxwell. See any patterns there? Money and leadership are the themes that rise to the top of this category again and again.

Most veteran authors would agree that the greatest predictor of success in publishing is neither high IQ nor the number of degrees one holds, but the discipline to sit down at the word processor every day, to carry out research tasks thoroughly, and to laugh off—yet learn—from rejections.

A little luck never hurts, either. But experienced writers know better than to wait for serendipity. Sorry to trot out a tired cliche, but successful authors make their own luck, or they at least actively *look* for it. They watch for trends. They read the news. They make lists of what sells and what doesn't. They study the market's changing landscape as acutely as soldiers on picket duty. When they see an opening, they launch their own quiet reconnaissance mission at the library or on the Net.

That reconnaissance involves a hunt for the second most important ingredient, after self-discipline, in publishing success. Without it, all the blood, sweat, and toil mean nothing. It is the one ingredient that all of the authors profiled above possessed and profited from. It is the ingredient many new authors will profit from next year and the year after and the year after that.

Without this critical ingredient you will go nowhere.

That critical ingredient is— a great idea.

Have you got an idea? Have you got a *great* idea? How do you know it's great? How can you prove to an editor it's great?

Read on.

How to Know
if Your Book Idea Will Fly

Avoid listening to family and friends…Testing your idea…
The Great Book Idea checklist

Okay. You've thought about it. You've lain in bed at night and stared at the cracks in the ceiling for hours. You've wandered for days through the labyrinthine corridors of your mind, zombie like, utterly preoccupied by it.

And now, you think you have finally got it.

A great idea.

At last, heady with dreams and hot with adrenaline, you're ready to motor to the stars. Best-seller list, here you come!

Stop. Before you rush out and buy a single piece of paper, before you type a single word, before you book a cruise in anticipation of the royalty checks rolling in, do yourself a favor and ask yourself one critical question:

How can I prove to an editor that this is a good idea?

Of all the research you will do, answering this question in detail is the most critical. Simply because you think it's a good idea, and your spouse and your children and your neighbor think it's a good idea, and you're excited by the idea, does not necessarily make it a good idea—at least to an editor's way of thinking. An editor is going to have to ask his publishing company to plunk down slightly more than the equivalent of the average wage-earner's salary for an entire year to launch even the slimmest of volumes into print and onto the market. You, therefore, must convince him that the company's investment will pay off.

In the first rush of excitement, our emotions almost invariably eclipse our more rational thinking processes. And, as every veteran writer knows, feedback from friends and relatives is unreliable. For starters, they don't know the market. Sure, your Uncle Joe heard about a certain book on macrobiotics that sold 500,000 copies some years back. So why shouldn't yours sell equally well?

What your Uncle Joe may have no concept of is that topics wax and wane in popularity. A book that may have hit a home run last year may completely whiff this year. What was hot and fresh in one decade may go completely stale in the following decade. Sometimes topics vanish from store shelves entirely and are never heard from again. Others remain stable, but competing titles so thoroughly glut the market that newcomers are effectively shut out. Ask Uncle Joe to answer this question: Do you know how many books lost money last year and which titles they were? Odds are he won't have a clue.

And let's face it. Most family members and friends don't want to hurt your feelings. They'll tell you your idea is good even when it probably should be put on ice and buried with a strong deodorant. Beware of well-intentioned encouragement. You could, propelled by the good words of family, invest months of your time and effort only to be told by thirty different editors that your book completely lacks a market.

Here's the golden rule of evaluating book ideas: Never trust your feelings or the advice of family and friends.

It is my experience that most ideas, at least at first, are best kept to oneself. Not only for the reasons stated but because most "hot" ideas cool off after a week or two and end up being replaced with something better. Get all in a lather by a new book idea every week and you'll lose credibility with everyone around you. They'll simply think you're fickle.

But, you ask, if you can't go to your friends and family for feedback, what do you do?

Fortunately, a method exists for testing the soundness of new book ideas. But it requires doing some legwork and a little research. Rest assured, it will be time wisely spent.

Answer the questions below as honestly and in as much detail as you can. They're the same questions veteran book authors ask themselves before starting any new project. They're the same questions editors will be trying to find the answers to in your book proposal. If your concept passes this test, you have very likely got a sound idea. A sound idea that, if executed well, will have a strong chance of selling and making a decent profit. Knowing your idea is good, not just guessing, will give you the confidence you'll need to get the project rolling and keep it rolling.

Follow the checklist carefully. You're building a business from the ground up and this, your first big investment, requires careful evaluation. Do it right and your profits could start rolling in in as little as a year. Do it wrong and you may be so discouraged with the results that you give up in disgust and never come back.

The Great Book Idea Checklist

✔ *Is your idea "big" enough?*

As an agent, I received an astonishing number of proposals for books which would have had potential audiences ranging from less than a thousand to exactly two (the author and his mother). I got proposals for books on "Packing With Mules," books on "Teaching Boyfriends What To Buy Girlfriends For Gifts," books on "My Experiences in a Mental Institution," and many others which few people in the real world would actually shell out money to buy. Because publishers spend over $30,000 to launch even a small book into print, they must be assured they can sell from 5,000 to 10,000 copies to recoup their investment and make a small profit. Most large publishers, in fact, won't even touch a book unless they think they can sell at least 15,000 copies, preferably in the first year. Small-market book ideas won't cut it in Manhattan.

Of course, exceptions exist for every rule. Anthony Guglielmo, a massage therapist who massages animals—including walruses—for a living, proposed a book on his work in 1999. Ludicrous, you say? Certainly a small-market subject if there ever was one, right?

The book was put up for auction, with several publishers bidding. It ended up earning a *six-figure advance* from St. Martin's Press.

Explanation? The editors knew it would be a highly promotable book, which is part of the reason they bent over backward to get it. Reportedly, the media was clamoring for author appearances (with his animal patients) before the book was even written.

Yes, anomalies exist. But try hard to avoid being one. The odds are stacked higher than the Sears Tower against you.

✔ *Is there space for your book among the competing titles?*

The first thing you can do is go to the library and consult *Books in Print*. This is a multi-volume set of reference books that lists all of the books currently on the market by author, subject, and title. By checking here first, you'll get a comprehensive picture of the competition.

Increasingly, though, I skip *Books in Print* and go directly to Amazon.com. Enter your idea's subject matter and Amazon's search engine will give you an near-instant rundown of current books on your topic. The books may be listed by author, by order of sales rank, or by other useful criteria.

Most books Amazon lists are fully described, with publisher name, number of pages, price, ISBNs (the book industry's identification number assigned to each title), date of publication, and so on. Most are also fully reviewed by professionals as well as amateurs, and given an overall star rating—one star being worst and five being stellar—(the book you now hold has a five-star rating at this writing, my ego hastens to add). Many books include excerpts you can read. And to make things really easy, many titles are accompanied by a list of very similar or related books.

If your book idea is a good one, chances are you will see a lot of competing titles already out there.

Don't let that throw you.

You can find more than five hundred books on cats in print at any one time. Does that mean no one should write a new book on cats?

Of course not. What it means is, to be successful, a new book must be better than those already in existence, present the subject from a different angle, or include updated information.

Let's assume you want to write a cat book. Your first task, as with any other book, would be to narrow down the listings in Books in Print or at Amazon.com to identify which books are true competitors to yours. This is actually a much easier job than you might think.

By carefully examining the listings, you'll be able to eliminate a sizable number of apparent rivals, first by simply separating the aca-

Don't spin your wheels needlessly

"*K*nowing the market is extremely important unless you're willing to take a gamble on wasting your time. If the topic you propose has been covered before, probably the only way you will sell your idea to a publisher is to find a new slant or twist. One of the key questions you must satisfactorily answer is, how would this book be different from those that are out there already?

"When I proposed to do a cookie book years ago, my agent's immediate response was, 'There are already lots of cookie books. Why do we need another one?' My answer, based on knowing the market, was that nobody had done a cookie book of recipes from all around the world. *The International Cookie Cookbook* was not only published, but has now sold more than 100,000 copies."

—*Cookbook author, Nancy Baggett*

demic titles from the lay titles, which don't normally compete with one another. Academic books typically have dry, serious titles, such as *Effect of Neutering on Two Groups of Feral Cats*, while the lay titles are more colloquial, such as *The Complete Guide to Understanding Your Cat*.

Occasionally, it may be unclear if a book is for an academic or lay readership. In those cases, it helps to know publishers. Some publishers publish strictly for academia, while others focus solely on the popular market. You can familiarize yourself with who publishes what by studying the company profiles in the latest editions of *Literary Market Place*, *The American Directory of Writer's Guidelines*, *Writer's Market* or *The Insider's Guide to Book Editors, Publishers and Literary Agents*. (See page 233 for a list of helpful books.)

It's usually quite easy to differentiate between humor books and serious works, by title alone. The how-tos and care guides are almost always obvious by their titles as well, as are big, expensive pictorial works. Too, the listings always give a notation (juv.) when a book is a juvenile title, that is, for kids, so these books can easily be eliminated from the field of competing adult books.

A close reading also flushes out any unusually long (over 500 pages) or short (under 100 pages) books. The long books may be too pricey for a large section of the population, while the small may not be comprehensive enough to attract the serious cat lover. Thus it might be possible to discover a niche just by understanding the importance of length, price, and so forth.

Once you've winnowed the listings down in this fashion, you might find that there are, in reality, only a dozen or so books that would directly compete with the book you'd like to write. Is a dozen too many? That depends on the market. In most cases, a dozen would be considered formidable. In the case of cat lovers, a truly lionesque market, a dozen competitors may not be unreasonable. With some subjects, of course, just one or two competitors may be too much because the universe of potential buyers is simply too small.

One key to your assessment may be how recently those close competitors were published. Take note of their copyright dates. If a litter of *very* similar titles to yours has been released in the last two or three years, you'll want to think seriously about considering another topic, changing your approach to this topic, or at least putting this topic off for a few years.

There are, of course, exceptions. These exceptions all depend on how big and how hot the market is for your topic. More than fifty books on the O.J. Simpson trial were released in 1995 and 1996 alone, and were still being released years after the fact. Ditto, terrorism books after the 911 disaster. Debacles and disasters can create huge markets. Not only huge, but hot and, in publishing, that's a winning combination. Huge, hot markets (think of the death of Princess Diana, the low-carb diet fad, or the recent resurgence in interest in spirituality/purpose of life) will easily support several titles on the same topic, even when they're released in the same year. A cold or small market obviously would not.

Hot markets can be lucrative if you and your publisher get in early enough. Jump in at the cooling end, however, and the results can be, well, chilling.

The most important thing you'll learn from *Books in Print* or Amazon.com is whether a book nearly identical to the book you want to write already exists. If you're unsure by title and brief description alone, you may want to check it out at your local library or order it from a retailer. A quick examination of the competitor's content and style will tell you if your idea is too similar or if you have a chance of writing a better book or one with a substantially different slant or angle. Think you can do better or differently? Super.

Competing books, incidentally, can sometimes be used to supplement your own research, and they may cover things that may never have occurred to you that you may wish to cover. At the very least, they may list resources for you to explore.

> ● "**H**ot markets can be lucrative if you and your publisher get in early enough. Jump in at the cooling end, however, and the results can be, well, chilling."

No check of the competition is complete without consulting the companion volume to *Books in Print*, called *Forthcoming Books*. This lists books scheduled to be released in the next six months. Libraries usually shelve *Forthcoming Books* next to *Books in Print*.

Hold on to your *Books in Print* list. If you decide to write your book, you'll need to order at least some of the competing books, not only to check out their content but to see how they handle various components of the subject and to supplement your research. Competing books, after all, are among the easiest and quickest medium to tap for information.

❦ *Note:* The Internet and the word processor are to the author what the hammer and saw are to the carpenter. If you are not using a computer to write, or if you're not yet online, jump in. If it's money that's holding you back, you should be able to buy a discarded computer complete with modem for $200 or less. And, as of this writing, free Internet access is available from a number of Internet service providers—you just have to put up with banner advertising at the top of your screen. In fact, while inexpensive word processing programs abound, after you get online, you can download one of the "shareware" word processor programs from the Internet for free. (If you find you like the program, you are morally obligated to send the author a small payment.)

After I've scanned the titles in *Books in Print* and Amazon.com, I visit my local superstore bookstore, which can almost always be counted on to stock the top competing titles. There's nothing quite like sizing up your competition by holding them in your hands and perusing the dust jacket copy and the book's content. Quite often, I'll buy the two or three leading competitors in order to study them in detail and uncover weaknesses. Even if you must drive 300 miles to the nearest superstore for such a reconnaissance mission, do it.

Having said all this, it may be that yours is truly a unique idea, never having been done before by any author in any fashion. (Think of *Zen and the Art of Motorcycle Maintenance*.) In this case, you won't find competing titles in *Books in Print* or anywhere else, which is, at the same time, good and bad. It is good in that your title may attract a lot of attention due solely to its uniqueness; bad that the idea has never been tested before and therefore may make your editor leery about offering a contract for it. This was obviously the case with the unique *Chicken Soup for the Soul*, which was originally rejected scores of times. Still, most editors are sharp enough to recognize the potential of a title like *Life's Little Instruction Book*. Editors and publishers will and do take risks with unique books if the profit potential is sufficient to warrant it.

✔ *Are you blatantly copying a recent best-seller?*

Many new authors do this, and the funny thing is, they're blissfully in denial about it. After Neale Walsch's *Conversations With God* books came out, my literary agency received no less than a half a dozen nearly exact imitations from people all claiming to have talked to God and gotten the answers to all our philosophical questions. I continued to receive *Life's Little Instruction Book* and *Don't Sweat the Small Stuff* copycats years after these winners ran their courses and ran out of gas. Agents turn these copycat books away by the carload.

While it's true that getting in on a market trend or fad can be hugely

Read all about it!

If you plan on writing for a career, one of the wisest invest-ments you can make is a subscription to *Publishers Weekly*. (You can read decades worth of back copies in any large library.) Its articles, lists, and ads often reveal which books are selling well and which are not. Sometimes actual sales figures are provided. These numbers alone are worth the price of the subscription. A single sentence I read in *Publishers Weekly* a few years ago led me into a project that has already brought in over $100,000 in royalties and will continue to do so for years to come. I never would have considered such a book if I hadn't read what I did in *Publishers Weekly*.

profitable, you shouldn't copy someone else's idea exactly. Exact cop-ies are unlikely to be picked up by reputable publishers. And, if you're trying to cash in by doing something similar, better do so quickly, be-cause everyone and his brother-in-law and second cousin copies suc-cess. A general rule of thumb: If the big vanguard book you'll be imitat-ing has been out for over a year, it's too late. Editors will already be swamped by similar wannabes.

✔ *Can you find strong sales figures for books like yours that were published in the past?*

How many copies your book can reasonably be expected to sell is the question your editor will want to answer more than any other. There are several ways to evaluate your book's sales potential, although none of them offers any guarantees of real-world accuracy.

Much of the time, sales figures are impossible to find, especially when those figures are less than spectacular. But, if a title has sold well, chances are *Publishers Weekly* will have provided sales information for it either in its weekly bestseller update or, more likely, in its annual March rundown of the previous year's winners and losers.

Occasionally you can find sales figures—although sometimes in-flated—in a publisher's book catalog or on the cover of the book itself.

General magazine and newspaper profiles on books and authors sometimes give figures, too, but usually only if sales are extraordinary.

If your subject is unique—if it truly has never been done before in any fashion—you'll obviously find no comparative sales figures to share with your editor. This makes it doubly important to closely identify the book's potential buyers.

✔ *Can you identify a large, specific group of people who would be interested in buying your book?*

Exactly *who* would be interested in your book's topic? If you can describe a large, specific market of people who will not only want the book but, even better, *need* the book, you're in luck. In the case of cats, a lot of people obviously want and need to know more. Supply some hard numbers on a large group of people who are interested in your topic and would benefit from reading your book and you will get an editor's attention.

Make it a priority to find some concrete numbers. If you're doing a book on Persian cats, for example, look up recent articles (check your library's periodical index) to find statistics on how many people own one and whether or not the breed is growing in popularity. If you can't find any stats in recent articles, contact a cat enthusiasts' association.

⋙ *Note*: One great source for information and numbers is *The Encyclopedia of Associations,* a huge volume that lists and describes virtually every organization, association, and interest group in North America and elsewhere. In it, you'll find associations of environmentalists, disease sufferers, cat breeders, UFOologists, balloonists, farmers, Trekkies, hobbyists, professionals, tradespeople, and groups of every imaginable description. From these listings, you'll learn how many people belong to a given association—which in itself is often a valuable number—and where to write, call, or fax for more information. Ask to see a copy at your library.

Be forewarned that identifying your potential market as *everybody* will not sit well with publishers. *Every woman* is probably still too vague. *Every woman over thirty who identifies herself as a feminist* is better. *Every woman over thirty who identifies herself as a feminist and loves Persian cats* is getting down to the kind of core identification that editors like to see.

✔ *Is your book likely to attract free publicity?*

Perhaps as important as compiling hard figures and a list of competing titles for your editor is realistically assessing the potential for free publicity and promotion. With the exception of reference books and a very few others, promotion and publicity are extremely important to a book's success. (A single appearance by an author on *Oprah*, for example, can increase a book's sales by tens of thousands of copies overnight.)

Does your book have a promotable topic? Does it have a *hook*?

If your book is going to do more than sell a mediocre number of copies, if it's going to earn the big, long-paying royalties, if it's going to approach anywhere near a best-seller list, it must have a compelling hook.

A hook is a component of the book's appeal that makes it stand out from others. Sex is a classic hook. So is shock value. Escapism, voyeurism, adventure are all hooks for potential book buyers. Need is the most powerful hook of all. People will always buy if they need what a book has to offer. Sometimes, of course, the hook is the author. A book by football star Reggie White on his controversial life views is compelling. Madonna on sex is irresistible.

A hook gives book publicists something to attract the attention of book reviewers, magazine editors, and radio and TV talk shows. Without this free media exposure, most books drown in a sea of anonymity.

With thousands of book titles competing for media attention, yours must stand out. The sharper your book's hook, the easier the publicist's job will be. If your book is controversial or if it contains information a lot of people want, you've likely got a winner.

❧ *Note:* As a general rule, money spent on advertising a book is wasted. Why? Who knows? Maybe the selection of a book is too personal or maybe readers are too cynical to turn to paid advertisements for advice. For whatever reason, money spent on ads is normally money wasted. This makes your publicity hook all the more important.

✔ *Is your book timely?*

For some titles, the question is irrelevant. For others, it is crucial. A book written about Jack the Ripper, for example, would obviously benefit from being released a year or two before a big anniversary date for the murders attributed to this killer.

A book on the first moon landing would garner more attention if it is released just prior to that event's tenth, twentieth, twenty-fifth, or fiftieth anniversary, when the media is much more likely to do commemorative pieces. A book on campaign politics would attract much more attention when released in an election year.

☞ *Note*: If the timeliness of your subject is important, you must make an accurate calculation of how long the book will take not only to research and write, but to market to a publisher, allow for multiple rejections, to be contracted for, to be copyedited and finally, printed. The best-case scenario, from the first word you type to the time your finished book appears in print, is typically eighteen to twenty-four months, although in unusual cases publisher and author may work together to crank out a title within as little as ninety days. However, these cases are exceedingly rare and you shouldn't count on such exceptional effort from a publisher.

A book that is released after an important tie-in event or anniversary is likely to lose money. And publishers hate to lose money! If you don't think you can churn out your timely book quickly enough to take advantage of an important tie-in event or anniversary, move on to something else.

If one cliche rings true in publishing, it is this: *You snooze, you lose.* Great ideas are often generated by things we've been exposed to on television or radio or through magazines or newspapers, and the obvious problem with that is that thousands of competing writers—all hungry for ideas—are exposed to that same media. If you've been inspired by something on the news, make no mistake: That same *aha!* moment will strike other potential authors. From that moment on, a race will be on to get proposals out to publishers. Wait too long to get yours started, and you'll be left holding a worthless manuscript.

Think ahead. Your editor and your competitors, keenly sensitive to timing issues, most certainly will.

✔ *Is this a book that will likely stay in print for several years?*
Part of succeeding in the nonfiction book business is choosing book

projects that won't fizzle out after just a year on a bookstore's shelves. Reference books usually have a long shelf life, although they may require updates or revisions every few years. History books may stay in print for decades with *no revisions or updates of any kind*. Humor books spoofing a timely event (the O.J. trial) may make a big splash initially but then quickly vanish when the event is over. A humor book poking fun at stable subjects (moms, cats, etc.) will have much longer shelf life.

Books that stand out from their competitors—those that are unusually well written or are the most comprehensive or garner the best reviews—usually enjoy remarkable longevity, even as several new titles try to knock them off their thrones. If you don't make your book better than ordinary, its shelf life will almost certainly be fleeting.

What to Expect When You're Expecting faced a formidable line of competing pregnancy books when it was first released. But the book's superior organization, thoroughness, and sheer readability made it a standout that today eclipses all competitors. Odds are, this title will outlive virtually all of its rivals.

Should you *always* limit yourself to writing books with a potentially long backlist life? Most of the time, yes. But there are, as always, exceptions. Fad books, for example. These books may make a bundle of money up front and then completely vanish from print by their second or third year. As I mentioned, Les and Sue Fox self-published *The Beanie Baby Handbook* and sold 3,000,000 copies. Several years ago, a book offering the solution to the Rubik's Cube sold six million copies in one year. With these kinds of opportunities, you'd be foolish to worry about the backlist potential.

✔ *Will your book take less than a year to write?*

If a book that is only going to end up selling 10,000 copies takes you three years to research and write, is it worthwhile? If you're absolutely passionate about your subject and you don't care much about making a living writing, then the answer may be yes. However, I'm assuming your priority is to make a livable income. Therefore, a three-year project of any kind should give you pause.

When the author is writing full-time, most nonfiction books can be compiled in six months or less. Normally, I stick with these more typical six-month projects because the risk is obviously smaller. In this instance, six of these books could be cranked out in that same three-year span. *Six books to one.*

Which scenario is likely to earn you more money? In the majority of cases, the more titles you have in print, the better. You could labor for three years only to have your one big project go out of print after a year. Even if three of your six books go out of print quickly, you've still got three pulling in income.

On the other hand, I wouldn't eliminate entirely the possibility of a three-year project. If the potential for big profit were there, I would have to consider it. If you're new at book writing, however, save these big projects until later in your career, when you can more accurately assess the risk to reward ratio.

✔ *Is there enough material on your subject to flesh out a full-length book?*
This is an easy one to overlook. But if you aren't careful, you may work for months compiling material only to find that the finished book is only seventy pages long. Even padding won't rescue a book that short.

Most nonfiction titles are at least 60,000 words in length, and probably average around 70-75,000 words. Typically, a full-length book has roughly a dozen chapters, with each chapter comprised of approximately 5,000 words or, depending on the size of your type, fifteen to twenty manuscript pages, for a total of at least 200 manuscript pages. The finished, published book of this length will be roughly 160-170 pages. This is usually the minimum acceptable length for most subjects, although your editor may require twice or even three times that length.

Normally, the only types of books that can get by with less are humor books and juveniles, which may be as short as 1,500 words.

Gauging length is one reason it is always wise to draw up a detailed table of contents, estimating chapter by chapter the number of pages, according to the research material you have on hand or know is available.

✔ *Could your book be turned into a series? Does the book lend itself to spin-offs?*
The *Chicken Soup* series has generated over twenty-five titles. The

author of the *Don't Know Much About...*series signed a contract in 1999 for twenty more titles. Rest assured, new authors, publishers *will* milk every cash cow as dry as, well, powdered milk!

It isn't necessary, of course, to write a book with a series in mind, but having that potential obviously makes the idea that much more valuable to you and your publisher. A life's career can be made out of spin-offs, buying a wonderful sense of security for the author. What's more, the need to do tiring and time-consuming marketing is eliminated. If your book sells well, be prepared: Your publisher will be thinking of creating a series of related titles, if at all possible.

✔ *Would your book have national or, even better, international appeal?*

A book with only regional interest is unlikely to make much money for its author, although a few exceptions exist. For gargantuan sales, try to slant your book to appeal to all of North America as well as Australia, Europe, and even Asia. While still a small slice of the pie, United States publishers are selling more book and translation rights into these foreign markets than ever before.

A gardening book featuring plants that can only be grown in the American Southwest obviously has limited appeal. A gardening book featuring plants that can be grown in virtually any region of most countries would have a much larger potential audience. A book on American football would probably do poorly in most nations outside of North America. A book on the human body, however, would have universal appeal and could conceivably be sold in virtually every country with a viable book market. For the largest potential sales, think globally.

✔ *Can you write this book?*

Library and online research is all that is necessary to flesh out many books, but some others clearly require travel and in-depth interviews with experts. Are you able to travel if your subject demands it?

If research tasks come easy, your writing tasks might not. Some books, such as reference titles or how-to books, require basic, brown-bag writing skills, skills anyone can master with a reasonable amount of study and time. Other books, such as literary memoirs, require a high degree of proficiency. Slice-of-life biographies, such as James

Herriot's *All Creatures Great and Small*, again, appear deceptively simple, but are in reality quite difficult.

You may be tempted to write humor, but remember, this category is notoriously difficult. It is one thing to be funny. Quite another to write funny.

Be certain your research and writing skills fit the book you're thinking of writing.

✔ *Have you let the idea cool off?*

Letting an idea sit and steep for awhile is more important than you might think. As I noted earlier, most hot ideas cool off considerably with time. In two or three weeks, you may feel very differently about the idea than you do now. You may decide that you don't have sufficient passion to write such a book. Once the initial excitement has died down, you may find you're discouraged by the sheer amount of research that would be involved. You are also likely to be more realistic about potential sales figures after time passes.

If a month goes by and you still feel the idea has sufficient heat, by all means continue to the next stage.

How did you do?

If you answered no to one or more of the above checkpoints, it's time to rethink your idea.

If you're a risk taker, you may be tempted to go through with your project anyway. Don't. As a beginner, the smart choice is to save the risky projects for later in your career, when a letdown is unlikely to scare you away from the writing business permanently. Find another idea or modify this one. Then go through the checklist again.

If you answered yes to all of these questions, you have, in all probability, a first-class, rip-snortin', blue ribbon *great* idea. Congratulations. Truly great ideas are not easy to find.

But now the real challenge begins.

How? Who? What? Where? When?

Read on.

Why You Don't Need a College Degree

*Establishing credibility...Where to find expert information...
Contacting experts...Collaborating...*"With a foreword by..."

At about this time, you may be having self-doubts about your qualifications to write the book you've chosen for yourself. You may not have graduated from college. You may not have even gone to college. You may not have graduated from high school.

Does a lack of education automatically disqualify you?

Yes and no.

You need an education to write most nonfiction books. But you don't necessarily need a college degree or a high school diploma. You can, like Mark Twain, be an autodidact. That is, one who is self-schooled.

Perhaps you already know a lot about your topic but if you don't, you can learn by doing research, interviewing experts, or by working in the field to gain personal experience.

You may have scored last in your entire school as far as grades go but your book's readers don't have to know that, nor will they care, assuming you've done your homework and your writing is authoritative.

The key word is *authoritative.*

Readers and editors demand authority. In fact, you can't make a book sale without it.

If you're not a noted expert on a subject, how do you convince editors and readers that you can write your book? How will you give your writing that ring of truth and authority so vital for success?

There are, in fact, several ways.

If you have no personal experience with your book's topic and you're writing something other than humor, you will need to cite university studies or other credible sources and interview outside experts, including people who do have personal experience with your topic. You can contact these experts in person, over the phone, through the Internet, or by mail. Finding experts is easy and quick once you know the various sources available to you.

Let's assume you want to write a fitness book on flattening your belly (a perennial favorite). Let's also assume worst-case scenario: You know nothing about fitness and your own blubbery gut shows it.

Obviously, this would be a big credibility problem to overcome. But it's not impossible.

You could handle this problem several ways:

• Use yourself as a human guinea pig. Contact a fitness expert and ask if she would like to participate in a book project, using your body as the main subject.

If you've been published anywhere before, but especially nationally, most people will be thrilled to help you out, especially if they think they're going to be credited in the finished book. If you've never been published, it might be more difficult to get an expert to participate, but many will still be happy to work with you. You can often transcend this problem by offering to pay a reasonable amount for the expert's time. If you're really charming, you might be able to convince the expert to accept a small percentage of your book's royalties in lieu of immediate cash.

Once you've convinced the fitness expert to participate, you could have her demonstrate her most effective abdominal exercises. With a few basic (they don't need to be artsy by any means) illustrative photos, along with the expert's tips, plus citations of a few national studies on reducing fat, a credible book proposal is born. Suggesting you'll include a series of before, during, and after shots as your belly transforms to a rock-hard washboard would add a super touch.

• You might locate one particularly photogenic or charismatic fitness expert and offer to do all the writing while he or

How I Bought Instant Credibility

I once proposed a book called *Building Believable Characters* to one of my publishers, Writer's Digest Books. The book would, quite simply, show writers how to create great characters for their short stories and novels. Only one serious credibility problem stood in the way: I had no published novels or short stories to my credit.

Without any real authority, who, I wondered, would believe that I knew what I was talking about?

Answer: Nobody.

Did that stop me? Hardly. I simply contacted six well-known novelists and offered them $100 each to supply me with in-depth interview material on how they created their own characters. The end result was a unique "roundtable discussion" which served as my opening chapter and which ultimately brought the rest of my book all the credibility it needed.

Yes, I spent $600 out of pocket. But the book has earned all of it back, more than twenty-five times over, in fact. And it recently went into an additional printing, promising several more years of royalties. Quite a good return on investment, I would say.

When it comes to establishing your book's authority, don't be afraid to spend a little money.

she supplies the information and shares the promotional duties. This strategy offers the editor a two-for-one deal. Two people to help promote the one book. Usually, in this case, you would share the royalties and the byline with the expert.

• You could opt to act as a behind-the-scenes health reporter writing about the various methods of reducing flab. You would propose to poll fitness experts across the country and ask them about their most effective abdominal exercises. If you can brag in your proposal that you will interview more than two dozen fitness experts, you've got instant credibility.

As long as you've got experts and expert studies to cite and quote, you will have little problem establishing credibility, even with medical books. Robert Kowalski looked up all the studies on how oat bran lowers cholesterol and assembled *The 8-Week Cholesterol Cure*, which not only ended up a massive best-seller but spawned numerous spin-off books and helped millions of people lower their heart attack risk.

Was this valuable medical literature that Kowalski cited hidden away in a hospital vault somewhere? Was it available only to those with medical degrees? Not at all. *Anyone* could have found the same studies in his local public library. In fact, the studies Kowalski cited could have been gathered in less than a week's time and possibly even in a day's time by anyone familiar enough with the research materials.

Let me make this plain: *There is absolutely no law stating that one must be an industry professional in order to collect and use the information from medical studies in a book, and this is true in nearly any field.*

To demonstrate to yourself how easy it is to find medical studies, go to your local library and ask to see their periodical article index. The librarian will point you to a computer database that holds an index to thousands of magazine articles, including those from the *Journal of the American Medical Association, New England Journal of Medicine, Scientific American, Science News* and many others. Simply punch in the word *cholesterol,* and the computer will run down a long list of cholesterol article citations, which you can then look up right there in the library. Those articles will in turn lead you to additional sources of information and so on. This kind of research can now even be performed online from home if you know where to look. (More on that later.)

Savvy writers have followed Kowalski's path, cashing in on books on everything from the melatonin craze to St. John's Wort, writing books based on no more than a handful of scientific studies available for anyone to read and ultimately exploit.

In the manuscript for my first book, *The Compass in Your Nose & Other Astonishing Facts About Humans,* I carefully cited every source for each of my facts. My editor, however, cut every one of them, because he was convinced of the accuracy of my information and knew readers would be, too. "Your facts have a ring of truth about them, so you don't need the citations," he told me.

If you do your homework before you start your proposal, it will show in your writing. It will have that *ring of truth* editors require.

Perhaps the ultimate example of not needing to be an expert on a book's topic is the book *How to Make Love to a Woman*, a big, best-selling how-to originally published in 1984.

What exactly was the credibility problem?

Both authors were gay.

In fact, they eventually admitted in a *People* magazine interview that "we obviously didn't have that much experience making love to women."

The book's authors got around this serious credibility problem by some clever subterfuge. They enlisted the help of a friend to serve as a kind of surrogate author to do all the publicity appearances. These authors, by the way, went on to win a Pulitzer Prize for their biography of artist Jackson Pollock.

Writing a book with an expert on your subject as a collaborator is perhaps the easiest way to buy credibility with editors. Carol Colman collaborated with a medical doctor and a Ph.D. to write *Stop Depression Now: Sam-E, The Breakthrough Supplement*. Colman boasts her own franchise of similar collaborations with doctors, including *The Melatonin Miracle, Dr. Scott's Knee Book, The Female Heart, Shed Ten Years in Ten Weeks, The Lupus Handbook for Women*, and many more.

Sometimes the expert will start with a rough draft and approach a writer to clean the manuscript up, but typically the author approaches the expert, does the lion's share or even all of the actual writing, and the collaborating expert supplies facts, research materials, and credibility.

Another method of gaining credibility is to have a doctor, CEO, scientist, or any other famous or credible person write a foreword to your book. The foreword lends credibility to the book's content because consumers assume that the expert would not write a foreword to a book that was inaccurate.

> ### Question:
>
> "*I've written a book showing people how to achieve happiness. Everyone who has seen the manuscript says my ideas are excellent. What are my chances of selling such a book?*"
>
> Indeed, if there is anything agents and editors groan at it's the "personal theory" book. Reading a personal theory book is like listening to somebody in a bar try to solve the world's problems.
>
> *How to Be Happy* or *How to Succeed* or *How to Cure Alcoholism* or *How to Save the World* and similar books by first-time authors arrive at agents' and publishers' doorsteps every day. For this type of book to have any chance with a publisher, there has to be something highly unusual about the project. This could be your own credentials (Are you a Tibetan monk?) or the fact that you have accomplished something truly remarkable (Are you the founder of a Fortune 500 corporation?).

The expert is often paid a sum, but not always. If the person is a good friend, has something to gain by his contribution, or is just a good guy, payment may be unnecessary. In any case, the expert's name appears on the front cover as "with a foreword by Dr...." In this arrangement, the expert doesn't actually collaborate in the writing of the book. Nor does he share in the book's advance or royalties. Even if you have to pay $500 or $1,000 to get someone in authority to write a foreword, the respect it buys is usually worth it.

If you're writing a book on evolution, think of the credibility a foreword by the head of the National Center for Science Education can buy. Or a book on space travel introduced by a former NASA astronaut. Or a cookbook with a foreword by the prestigious head of a culinary arts school.

Because a foreword can be as brief as a page or two, an expert might be able to dash one off in as little as two hours. The writer, as part of the deal, can offer to clean up his prose afterward. Sometimes the author may actually ghostwrite the entire foreword himself and simply have the authority give his approval. Convincing an authority to write one (or have one written in his name) is not as hard as you might think; they are often anxious to see their name on the cover of a book.

As literary agent Michael Larsen points out in his book *How to Write a Book Proposal*, "The less qualified you are to write your book, the more you need experts to vouch for you."

Approaching and talking to experts

Don't be intimidated. Remember, the publicity they will garner from the book helps experts and/or their institutions in myriad ways. For most, granting interviews and fielding media questions come with the job. More often than not, heads of organizations are eager to share their expertise, not only to champion their causes, but as a way to draw more attention to their groups. Authors equally welcome new opportunities to promote their books. Professors routinely make themselves available, for any numbers of reasons, through their university's public relations departments.

Be professional. In most cases, yes, the director of the Kinsey Institute would be *happy* to give you a quote. So would the world's leading authority on insomnia, and the top expert on headaches, and the world's most vocal advocate for a manned spaceflight to Mars, and the guru on maintaining a happy marriage...if approached professionally.

Many directories provide the office numbers of the experts you need. With a personal office number, you can contact your expert directly. But sometimes experts are best contacted through their institution's public affairs office. The staff in these offices are there precisely to help you find the information and the expert you need. Take advantage of their services.

From time to time you'll have trouble with "gatekeepers." Most receptionists don't screen calls, but if your expert is exceptionally popular with the press, you may have to pass muster in order to make a connection. Describe your book project and maintain a friendly attitude. If you're calling from a distant city, mention it; sometimes this is enough to get you through. Don't be overly forceful or rude; you want the receptionist as an ally, not an enemy. Most people like to help book authors get what they need.

Be prepared just in case the expert has time to talk to you immediately, but usually the best policy is to ask when a convenient time might be to call back with a few questions.

Talk to the expert in the most professional manner possible. That means, know something about your topic before you place the call. Also, have questions ready on a sheet of paper in front of you and have your tape recorder set up and ready to go.

One fear experts often share is the fear of being misquoted. They might be concerned about this possibility if you plan to take only written notes. Get an inexpensive telephone microphone, the kind that is available at Radio Shack. Tell the expert you'd like to tape the interview and ask if he or she has any objections.

When the interview is finished, ask if you may call or e-mail back in case you have further questions or need to clarify something. Also be sure to ask if the expert would like a copy of your book when published. Rarely will the answer will be "No."

Speaking of e-mail, it's fabulous. Often, you can skip awkward telephone interviews and write experts directly. Many busy people prefer to provide answers by e-mail because it gives them more time to consider their answers and to even change them completely before sending them. If you can't find your expert's e-mail address in a directory, pick up the phone and ask his or her secretary for it.

"It works well to e-mail the person you want to interview, list your main questions, and give that person the option of an e-mail or phone interview," says veteran science writer Sharon Levy. "If the person is willing to do e-mail, it can be great—no transcribing. (But) it all depends on the person. Some just don't have the time to write a long e-mail, but are willing to chat on the phone. In a few cases I've had people who gave very minimalist answers via e-mail, so that I had to follow up by phone anyway."

Locating experts and expert information

So where can you find experts and expert information quickly and easily?

The Internet has now become the author's most vital information resource. Incredible as it sounds, it's now possible to write an entire

book without ever once visiting a public library in person! Most of the
sources cited below are easily exploited over the Internet, although a
few of the classic standby reference tomes are still best consulted at the
library. And yet even this may change soon, as virtually everything is
being offered online nowadays.

Get to know the resources below. They are virtually all you need
to flush out any sort of information or experts you need.

• **www1.ProfNet.com** One of the premier online sources
for experts. ProfNet is comprised of 6,000 public relations professionals, including news and information officers at colleges,
universities, corporations, national laboratories, medical centers, and think tanks, plus an up-to-date database of 2,000 leading experts on a wide variety of topics, from archeology to zoology, all connected via the Internet for easy access. If you can't
find the expert you want in the ProfNet database, you can send
a general query and ProfNet's army of public information officers will bend over backward to find an appropriate connection for you. I've queried this wonderful resource several times
and have been amazed at how many leads I received within a
matter of hours.

If this isn't enough, the site also offers a service called ProfNet
Briefs, which are tip sheets of breaking news to alert reporters on
new developments in health, science, technology, business, etc.
All you have to do is ask to be put on the mailing list.

• **National Press Club's Directory of News Sources**
(http:\\npc.press.org/). This prestigious organization not only
offers a directory of experts, but an online library that provides
authors with an astonishing array of useful resources and websites, including college telephone directories, worldwide telephone books, news search engines, and much more. To get a
taste of some of its resources, consider the online biographical
dictionary: It features information on 27,000 notable men and
women, and it can be searched by names, birth or death years,
positions held, professions, or achievements.

The staff at the online library is available to find facts, statistics, articles, and software for members, too.

• *The Address Book: How to Reach Anyone Who is Anyone* by Michael Levine. An inexpensive and frequently updated directory of over 4,000 celebrities, corporate executives, and other VIPS, with snail mail and e-mail addresses. Available at your public library, or order it through Amazon.com.

• **Switchboard.com** Find the telephone numbers and websites of more than 10 million businesses and organizations nationwide. I entered the word "gardening" in this site's search feature and in less than ten seconds was supplied with a huge listing of resource links. This is a mere fraction of what popped up:

Botany at the University of Georgia
Daylilies: the American Hemerocallis Society
Eclectic Rose Page
Garden Gate: Roots of Botanical Names
Garden Guides
Howard Garrett's Basic Organic Program
National Gardening Association Home Page
Ponds and Aquatic Plants Forum
Rosehelper Home Page
Rose Society
Xeriscape Garden Club

• **AOL E-mail Finder** (aol.com/netfind/emailfinder.adp). America Online's e-mail address search service. Simply enter the name of the person you're looking for and you'll have his or her e-mail address in seconds.

• **AOL Government Representative Finder** (government.aol.com). America Online's search service will help you quickly find the e-mail addresses and websites of any member of any branch of local, state, or federal government, including congress and the president of the United States. Looking to query someone in the federal court system? The Department of Agriculture? The Department of Defense? Your regional representative? This service will even locate the most recent news stories about the representative you're looking for.

• **lawyers.findlaw.com.** The Internet's largest collection of lawyers, over one million of them, in fact. This site offers not only connections to legal experts and lawyers in every area of expertise, but a database of more than 400 legal topics, from bankruptcy to sexual harassment. Excellent.

• **Medscape.com.** Search for medical articles dating as far back as 1966. Receive free medical news via e-mail. Medscape's huge database is expanded and updated daily. You may search abstracts free of charge, but a nominal fee is charged for copies of full-text articles.

• **NYTimes.com.** Here you can access an index to over 16 million articles published in the *New York Times,* and the articles themselves, dating back to 1851. You can also access NY Times articles in The New York Times Index, in your local public library. Recent articles are a good place to look for experts on your topic. In most cases, articles will include clues to where you can find quoted experts ("Dr. Smith, a professor in the physics department at MIT,…") so you can contact them for your own interviews.

• *Reader's Guide to Periodical Literature,* H. W. Wilson Co. A multivolume index of articles from 250 popular magazines, such as *Time, Newsweek, Discover, Psychology Today, Sports Illustrated,* etc. Use it as you would the *New York Times* Index. Available at your local public library.

• *Yearbook of Experts, Authorities & Spokespersons* (yearbook.com/search.html). A directory of nearly 1500 experts and organizations on hundreds of topics. The listings are actually paid advertisements from the experts themselves.

• *The Encyclopedia of Associations,* Gale Research Company. Thousands of associations on virtually every imaginable topic from barbed wire collectors to UFO enthusiasts. Often the directors or heads of associations offer themselves to writers for interviews, or they may help you connect with someone else within the organization. Great not only for finding experts, but for gathering statistics and other information. Available at public libraries.

• *Research Centers Directory*, Gale Research Company. This annual directory lists the addresses of over 13,000 university, government, and nonprofit research laboratories and organizations. You can find the directory in any large public library or at academic libraries.

• *Who's Who* series. This is a directory of prominent people, with brief bios of their accomplishments, degrees, etc., along with their addresses. There are several books in the series which is available at public libraries.

• **Mad Scientist Network** (madsci.org). A global network of scientists maintained by the Washington University Medical School. The scientists in the network are available to field questions in twenty-six areas of science. They've supplied information on everything from how a cat purrs to why the moon always appears larger when it is low on the horizon. This site also has some great links to other science sources. One of many similar "Ask a scientist" sites on the Web.

• *Directories in Print*, Gale Research Company. An annual directory listing more than 15,000 directories covering who's who and who's where in everything from agriculture to zoology. Available at your public library.

• **Amazon.com** This monster online bookstore boasts three million titles to choose from. An excellent research tool for checking out not only competing books, but how well those books are selling (they give sales rankings) and for learning who publishes what. If you want to write a book about rose gardening for Simon and Schuster, for example, you could check the listings (under rose gardening) and see if it already publishes a similar book. Checking the field beforehand saves a lot of useless submissions.

☙ *Note*: Buying the books you need for research, as opposed to borrowing them, appears at first glance to be wasteful, but unless you live in a large metropolitan area, your local library's collection may be lacking or its titles may be outdated. You might also be put on a waiting list. You can keep your purchased books as long as you want without the hassle of renewing. You can also mark them up with notes and dog ears, which saves you from endlessly transcribing notes onto paper.

• **Barnesandnoble.com** The online medium of the world's largest bookstore chain. What you can't find at Amazon.com, you'll probably find here.

• **OneLook Dictionaries** (onelook.com/). Can't find the word you want in your desktop dictionary? This is the place to turn. At last check, it boasted entries for 7,613,432 words indexed in hundreds of different dictionaries. You can either enter the word you want for a quick search or browse the individual dictionary and glossary lists. Here you'll find thematic dictionaries on art, automobiles, ballet, book collecting, British-American words, British and Aussie slang, castles, cats, computing, cooking, dogs, the environment, finance, golf, the Internet, Irish slang, law, magic, music, meteorology, the military, the paranormal, politics, rap slang, real estate, religion, Shakespearean words and phrases, skateboarding, snowboarding, street slang, Yiddish expressions, and much, much more. A tremendous resource and, in the aggregate, far more comprehensive than any single desktop dictionary.

• **Britannica.com** Yes, the entire set of encyclopedias, constantly updated, is available here. A superb resource.

• **Refdesk.com** There is only one appropriate word for this site: awesome. The BBC calls it "A trusted friend to baffled surfers everywhere." CNN calls it the "reference guide to all things Internet." It is, without exaggeration, a reference resource for darn near *everything*. Consider a partial listing of Refdesk's instant links: U.S. statistics, 50 States.com, Acronym Finder, Address Server, Ask Jeeves, Ask the Experts, Bartlett's Quotations, Biography.com, Chiefs of State, Consumer Law, Currency Converter, Dictionaries, Encyclopedias (search your subject), Do-It-Yourself, Family Search, Find a Doctor, Find a Lawyer, Health A to Z, Human Anatomy, How Stuff Works, How Far Is It?, Holidays, Language Translator, Learn to Do Anything, Look Up Foreign Words, Map Collection, National Hurricane Center, Nobel Prize Winners, World Newspapers, Magazines (*Time*, *Newsweek*, *People*, etc.), People Finder, Robert's Rules of Order, Yellow Pages, Zip Code Finder...and this just scratches the surface! They even give you directions on how to make the site your start-up or home page on your computer.

• **The Electric Library** (www.elibrary.com). This site's encyclopedia.com is a free database of 17,000 searchable articles, a great starting place for any research project. I found twenty articles here under "evolution." To delve deeper, these articles contained links to related or more specific articles (Cro-Magnon Man, Neanderthal Man, etc.), which I could access instantly. To go still deeper, there are also exhaustive listings of newspaper and magazine articles to tap.

The Electric Library, in fact, boasts a truly monstrous database of over six million newspaper articles, 760,000 magazine articles, 500,000 book chapters, and over 150,000 transcripts from TV and radio shows. Its resources include 150 full-text newspapers, hundreds of full-text magazines, plus national and international news wires, and scores of radio and TV programs.

• *The World Fact Book* (odci.gov/cia/publications/factbook/index.html). Compiled by the Central Intelligence Agency, this is a compendium of useful facts, from population to exports, on virtually every nation on earth.

• **Internet Public Library** (ipl.org). Sponsored by the University of Michigan. The reference library here is almost as good as the real thing.

• **The Library of Congress** (loc.gov/?clkd=iwm). The biggest library in the world.

• **The Polling Report** (pollingreport.com). Based in Washington, D.C., this is an independent, nonpartisan resource on American opinion; it conducts polls on politics, business, sports, Hollywood, work, health, current events, and more.

• **Newsgroups** A newsgroup is a global bulletin board. Newsgroups exist on every imaginable topic. Tap into any newsgroup with your online service and you'll be connected instantly to people who are intensely interested in that newsgroup's topic. Newsgroups are great places to ask questions and to find people or even experts to quote. I logged on to one discussing evolution and encountered a lively debate about how people can or cannot believe in God and evolution at the same time. Talk about getting multiple viewpoints!

• **Magazines and newspapers** Recent articles are a great place to find experts. Nowadays you can find all of the biggies online. Log on to Yahoo.com or one of the other major search engines and type in the periodical's name.

• **University news & public information offices** Public information offices are the media's links to a vast array of university specialists, including scientists, physicians, psychologists, sociologists, researchers, etc. Contact these offices when you need an expert or when you need more information on a breaking news story. The public affairs officers will be more than happy to help you find the expert or information you need. Many universities offer journalists media directories, with telephone and e-mail listings of dozens and sometimes even hundreds of professors and other faculty members available for interviews. Identify yourself as a professional writer working on a book project, and you may be given one of these directories free of charge. Simply enter the university you're looking for in any search engine and then go directly to that university's public relations page for contact information.

In the old days, they called it legwork. In the high-tech age, it's the fingertips that do most of the walking. Conducting solid, reliable research has never been easier or faster.

Hit the books. Hit the computer. Hit the Internet. You now have a start on the resources you need to frame out your idea and lay the foundation for a book as authoritative as any on the market today.

Chapter Six

Do You Need an Agent?

Fees...Duties and responsibilities...Representing yourself...
Sample agent/author contract...Choosing an agent

Sooner or later every writer wrestles with this fundamental question: Do I need an agent? Certainly every author who wants to maximize his profits ought to have one, right? Not necessarily.

Unfortunately, there is no one-size-fits-all answer. For some, the 15 percent commission most agents charge is a bargain. To others, it's tantamount to throwing money down a woodchuck hole.

Scan the fiction market directories and you'll increasingly see major publishers screaming in bold print: AGENTED SUBMISSIONS ONLY. For unpublished novelists, it's seemingly a miserable catch-22. Publishers won't look at their work because they have no agent. But agents won't look at their work unless they have a track record with publishers.

Happily, the situation isn't nearly so frustrating for nonfiction authors. Although they may look at the agent-submitted proposals first, most major publishers still look at professionally presented nonfiction book proposals from unrepresented authors.

But, you say, despite publishers' willingness to give me a look, should I try to get an agent anyway?

The answer is, unequivocally, yes, no, and maybe.

We'll consider each of these answers in turn after briefly considering what it is that an agent does.

What an agent does

Because it is impossible to keep properly abreast of what is happening market-wise and content-wise in every fiction and nonfiction genre, most agents find it necessary to specialize. Some, for example, may handle romance or science fiction novels exclusively and turn down any kind of nonfiction. Others may concentrate on one aspect of nonfiction, specifically, say, science, health, how-tos, sports, finance, or self-help.

Agents who specialize usually know their markets well and quickly recognize when something potentially salable crosses their desks.

Several hundred literary agents operate in the United States and Canada. Most work in and around Manhattan, where the largest publishers are located. A growing number of agents, however, can be found scattered about in small offices or home offices from North Overshoe, Maine to Fork-in-the-Road, Alaska.

Although having the ability to regularly network with the New York publishers is an obvious plus, lunching and schmoozing with them there is hardly necessary to make book sales. Agents have made million-dollar sales without ever once laying eyes on the editors who doled out the cash. E-mail and faxes allow agents to operate efficiently from just about anywhere on the globe.

Indeed, hobnobbing with the people in power, while valuable, ranks a distant second to an agent's most crucial task: selection of manuscripts.

Agents read query letters, proposals, outlines, sample chapters and various hen scratchings from thousands of authors every year. Job one for an agent is to winnow out the weak or ill-directed submissions and find the ones with potential. Since the overwhelming majority of material is, in a polite word, unpublishable, an agent's reading is more often than not unfruitful.

After clearing her desk of a mountain of submissions by mailing ninety-nine rejection letters, an agent may, if she's lucky, have one remaining proposal worthy of representation.

The agent then contacts the author and, if an agreement can be reached, a contract is signed. If the proposal needs fine-tuning, it goes back to the author. When the rewrites are over, the agent begins submitting the proposal to editors.

Agents use e-mail, faxes, telephone calls, overnight messenger service, and the United States mail to present an author's book to editors. This can go on for weeks, months, even years. An agent with stamina may submit the material to as many as thirty different publishers. On the other hand, depending on how passionate she is about the work and how broad the market is, she may try as few as three. Most sales are made with less than a dozen submissions in a span of less than twelve months. Although it may come as a surprise to some authors, many agents routinely give up the chase after eight or ten submissions.

Once a publisher makes a commitment for a book, the agent handles the duties of negotiating the highest possible advance and royalties and routing out contractual land mines. Following a domestic book rights sale, the agent may then pursue other subrights sales and may contract with coagents to sell the book overseas or perhaps to movies and television.

Agents act as liaisons between author and publisher long after the sale is made. They make sure the author's money is paid in a timely fashion and monitor royalty payments and other contractual matters—until, in fact, the book goes out of print and cannot be resold to another publisher.

Why can't I represent my own book?

Is an agent right for you? Or should you handle your work on your own? As mentioned, not every author benefits from having an agent, some authors do just fine representing their own work. To help you in the decision process, consider all of the benefits and liabilities an agent can bring to the table. Here are some of the pros, cons, and a maybe to consider:

The pros

Pro #1: An agent will act as a whip and make you revise your work until it's in its best possible shape before submitting it to publishers.

New authors almost always submit their work prematurely, usually one revision or more short of what would be considered professional. Discouragingly, the material that arrives in an agent's mail every day can be broken down roughly as follows:

87 percent amateurish and unpublishable.
3 percent material that targets the market well but is too poorly written or researched to be fixed.

4 percent pretty good material with virtually no market.

4 percent pretty good material with a saturated market.

1 percent material with good potential if the work is re-vised and polished.

1 percent material with excellent potential that is ready for submission.

Because almost every good proposal's sales potential can be improved, the agent's job is to crack the whip at the author. Anything in the proposal that suggests laziness or negligence on an author's part must be eliminated before it is submitted to an editor. Slipshod grammar and spelling? *Crack!* goes the agent's whip across the author's back. Questionable research? *Crack!* Inconsistent style? *Crack!* Sloppy mechanics? *Crack!* The goal is to remove all impediments to an editor saying "Yes."

First-time authors may be shocked to learn how many times an agent is willing to send material back for improvements. With this unexpected slave-master development, unprofessional writers may bolt. These authors may take their chances submitting incomplete or unfinished material on their own or perhaps try to find an agent with a more relaxed approach.

Smart authors endure the abuse. Editors don't say yes easily. Finding out what it takes to get editors to say yes is a part of scaling and mounting the professional plateau. Many authors simply cannot reach that plateau without an agent who lashes them regularly.

But, you may ask, are agents really qualified to critique your work like this?

Take a poll of top agents and you'll find that most are former editors from major publishing houses. Some racked up twenty years or more experience at publishing houses before starting their own literary agencies. It follows, then, that these agents not only know what publishers want, they also know how to write and how to make the writing of others better. These agents are great troubleshooters. When something in a manuscript doesn't work, they can usually spot it and figure out a way to fix it.

Having such an objective and knowledgeable critic-mentor in your corner may alone be worth the 15 percent commission.

Pro #2: Agents have more credibility with publishers.

Because agents can usually be counted on to screen out the dreck and to submit only quality material, agented submissions are read more eagerly.

Editors expect to see, as is the norm, unprofessional work from unrepresented authors. Because of this stigma, an unrepresented manuscript may sit unnoticed on an editor's desk for weeks or months, only to be finally sent back after a superficial scanning.

An editor or a first reader has only so much time in a day, and more is spent on agented manuscripts than unagented ones.

Pro #3: An agent knows how and has the courage to squeeze more money out of editors.

Experienced agents know how much to ask for as an advance. They also know how high most publishers are willing to pay in royalties.

A seasoned agent won't make an embarrassing demand for $100,000 when your book is only worth $10,000. On the other hand, if the book *is* worth $100,000, she'll know. She may be able to put it up for auction, with several publishers bidding. Most authors wouldn't have the nerve to do this and wouldn't know how anyway.

The goal in all negotiating is simple: to give up your shirt but to keep your pants. Negotiating to your advantage without making the opposite party feel like he has lost his pants as well as his Skivvies is something like walking with oversized shoes through a minefield. The skill involved is not natural. It comes with practice and from the confidence of knowing what your editor knows. Most authors don't have that kind of knowledge, and they're likely to make some terrible blunders. This ignorance will show in any number of ways, and even the nicest editor may take advantage.

Pro #4: An agent knows the pitfalls of author/publisher contracts.

Publishing contracts are loaded with pitfalls for authors. For example, does your publisher figure your royalties by *net receipts* or by a book's *list price*? Not knowing the difference can cost you thousands, even tens of thousands of dollars.

Or consider the problem of cross-accounting. Should the royalties from a hot-selling book of yours go to the publisher to repay an advance on a previous book of yours that failed to earn out the advance? That may be exactly what happens to you if you don't read and understand certain clauses in your contract.

Publishing contracts bristle with potential author bombs. A good agent can and will disarm them all.

Pro #5: An agent knows subsidiary sales.

An agent will know which, if any, rights the publisher should handle and which should be retained for the agent to market.

An author without agent representation may blindly choose to let a publisher's subrights department make sales to foreign publishing houses, to electronic book publishers, to movie or TV producers, and to other potential rights buyers.

An author could try to make these sales on his own, and he may even do an adequate job of it. But selling books overseas or to movie or TV producers can be a daunting, mind-numbing, and time-consuming process. Because of the knowledge and patience required, selling subrights is something few authors should choose to tackle on their own.

Pro #6: An agent acts as a buffer between publisher and author.

Negotiating a book's contract is only the beginning of the tense process of book publishing. Publishers often find themselves annoyed with authors for any number of reasons. Authors may refuse to deliver much-needed revisions. Or they may deliver those revisions late. Sometimes they refuse to go along with a copy editor's suggestions for changes, much to the detriment of the book. They may fail to double-check crucial facts or to attain legal permissions to reprint work. Authors may also neglect to send required promotional information to the publicity department in a timely fashion. They may refuse requests to appear on TV or to grant interviews to newspapers. The list of author annoyances goes on and on.

In some of these cases, the impatience of a bristling editor will be buffered by the author's agent. The editor may bluntly tell the agent to tell the author to get his head out of his ascot. A wise agent will, of course, couch the message in softer terms.

Conversely, the author may vent his annoyance with a publisher's gaffes and shortcomings via the same port: the agent. Again, the agent dampens the ire and sends the message on in more diplomatic terms, often saving a professional relationship for this and future projects.

This diplomatic service comes in particularly handy if you're an author with either a prima donna or Type A personality.

Pro #7: An agent can help steer you away from bad book projects and show you how to increase sales and expand your career.

Authors sometimes follow the market as closely as agents. Or they may be well versed in their own peculiar little niche, but be unschooled in others. Agents have a pretty good nose for distinguishing between book ideas that stink and book ideas that promise a rosy financial future. Even if you're well informed, the agent brings to the table an outside, educated, objective opinion.

An agent is often the most qualified person on the planet to ricochet ideas off. An agent will help you hone your market sense and will almost certainly help prevent you from jumping into a dog of a project. She may also generate great ideas of her own, which she will freely pass along to you.

Lastly, if she's well connected or networked with editors in New York, she may have just heard of two books on camcorder stunts sold in the last three months. If you were planning your own camcorder stunt book, you'll definitely want to know when the market door is closing or has been slammed shut, so you can go on to a different project.

The cons

Con #1: An agent may not be nearly as aggressive in the sales department as you would be.

Over the years, I've experimented with employing various agents. Although all of these reps had their own peculiar personalities, techniques, and levels of success, they shared one thing in common that made me crazy: None of them pitched my work anywhere near as aggressively as I would have—and ultimately did—myself.

While these agents sent out one or two queries or proposals at a time and tended to other clients, I would sit at the edge of my seat in my office, watching the phases of the moon wax and wane and then wax and wane again. The leaves of the oaks in my backyard turned from green to cherry red then fell and were raked and composted. Page after yellowing page of my desk calendar swirled into the trash can, then into the trash truck, then into oblivion.

Time passed. Rivers flowed into the ocean. The Milky Way reeled in its arc across the universe. And all the while I quietly steamed with the thought that my manuscripts were probably receiving less attention from editors than were mold spores.

Not that I thought I could do better. I *knew* I could do better. Far better. *Two* queries at a time? Why not ten? Why not twenty? How hard could it be to make ten identical copies of queries or proposals and pop them into the mail?

Sometimes I would get on the phone and ask these agents point-blank, "Why don't we submit to publishers B, C, and D instead of waiting for the next ice age for publisher A to respond? Also, wouldn't it be prudent after so much time has passed to drop publisher A a polite note inquiring as to the proposal's progress?"

I was told to be patient, that the publishing world operated in its own time zone—where two weeks means a month and two months equals twelve weeks—and it was best not to be in such a hurry or I'd get all stressed out over something nobody could control, and it would be much better if I just started another project and stopped bugging him.

After one agent held on to one of my books for eight months without any status report (I thought he must have died), the aura of agent as minor god began to shatter.

These agents had made only a handful of submissions when, exasperated, I pulled the plug on them. It was clear their slothful ways would never satisfy me. The old cliche began to haunt me: If you want something done right, do it yourself.

In the process, I learned something important about myself: I was not cut out to be a client.

With an aggressive sales campaign of my own, I ultimately sold all of my books myself. I also ended up learning another great lesson: With one client—yourself—it's easy to make masses of multiple submissions and to follow through with notes and phone calls to editors. You not only have the time, you have the clear motivation: If you don't make a sale soon, your family will be taking up residence in a cave with nice, natural air conditioning but with no central heating or cable.

An agent with ten, twenty, or thirty clients, on the other hand, does not have an abundance of time. During my own stint as an agent for other authors, I was receiving more than 300 pieces of mail per week. Among these were manuscripts of every size and degree, demanding to be read or at least skimmed. I realized I would have to answer the mail *and* make multiple submissions for clients *and* send follow-up notes to tardy editors *and* read manuscripts *and* go over contracts *and* amend the pitfalls in each *and* take out the office trash? And, in the words of my seven-year-old: Holy mackerel.

Nor can an agent be expected to dredge up nearly as much enthusiasm for your work as you can yourself. It's not the agent's name that will appear on the book's jacket. It's not the agent who will get the great reviews. It's not the agent who will get his picture in the local paper or be asked to give interviews for talk shows. It's not the agent who will collect the prince's share of the royalties. It's not the agent who will get the adoring looks from his mother and his children.

And, unless you've got the earning power of a Stephen King or a Richard Carlson, the agent doesn't really need you. Literally thousands of other authors clamor for the agent's attention each year. Among these thousands will, in all likelihood, be somebody whose writing will sell just as well as yours.

The bottom line is this: unless your book gives off the aroma of a potential best-seller or auction candidate, an agent *can't* and *won't* do for you what you could do for yourself, assuming you had all of the agent's knowledge and skills.

So if you sign with an agent, be prepared to witness a sales assault that very well may be far less ambitious than you might launch yourself.

Con #2: Most agents will not submit your book to small publishers.

This is a no-brainer. Many independent publishers pay advances of $2,000 or less. The agent's commission in this case—$300—wouldn't even cover the cost of his effort. The average book sale costs agents roughly $350 in expenses. Consequently, agents often refuse to submit books to independents.

The odds, however, are often better with a smaller publisher. A small publisher may keep your book in print longer, and you may have a closer relationship with the editor. Acceptance with a small publisher will get your writing career underway and your foot in the door. The money may not be great, but the sale will boost your confidence, provide you with the right to brag—I'm a published author!—and help open doors to bigger publishers down the road.

Some authors will want to skip the years of heartache that can be involved in trying to woo a big, Manhattan publisher and take the short-cut to publication at one of these smaller publishers. These authors should completely forget about getting an agent.

Finally, the maybe

The maybe: Agents charge 15 percent or more, but some earn it.

This, of course, is the major problem authors have with agents. That 15 percent is charged on *all* proceeds, which includes the advance and all royalties thereafter—even on royalties paid decades after the book was originally sold. That's 15 percent of paperback sales, 15 percent of book club rights, 15 percent of serial rights, 20 percent (half of which is split with a coagent) of overseas rights, 15 percent of electronic rights, 15 percent of merchandising rights, and so on.

Just when you think you've been thoroughly milked, you'll discover that agents take 15 percent of income generated not by the agent's efforts, but by the efforts of a publisher's own in-house subrights sales department! (A book sold to an overseas publisher by a publisher's in-house subrights department is a good example.)

Is it worth it?

What rubs many authors is that the 15 percent is earned whether an agent puts in an hour of work or a year. Agents have been known to labor intensely for as long as two years to make one modest sale. But sometimes they do nothing more than send out a single mailing; read over a standard, ten-page contract; have you sign on the dotted line; and then cash the checks.

In the past, the agent's typical commission was 10 percent. Today some agents charge 20 percent. These days, many charge the author for the agent's out-of-pocket expenses for photocopies, postage, messenger services, and so on, in addition to their commissions.

Fifteen percent of $10,000 is $1,500.

Fifteen percent of $100,000 is $15,000.

Fifteen percent of $1,000,000 is $150,000.

Is it worth it?

Let's take a typical scenario and add it all up.

Most authors will gladly take whatever advance and royalty publishers offer. Editors always initially offer less than what they've actually budgeted. So, if you're offered $7,500 right off the bat, you can be fairly confident that in most cases an agent would have countered with $12,000 and gotten $10,000. Already, you'd be $2,500 ahead and the agent's commission would be covered, with a little gravy for you!

The same dynamic is at work with royalties. Authors are usually offered a smaller rate than the editor has actually budgeted. An agent recognizes when a royalty being offered is too low and will campaign for more. He is likely to get at least 1 percent and possibly as much as 5 percent more. For our purposes, we'll call it 2 percent.

A 10 percent royalty on a $25 book selling 10,000 copies would add up to $25,000. You might, as many authors would, be pleased with that. But let's assume an agent can get you 12 percent on that same $25 book. Now the royalties add up to $30,000. Subtract the agent's commission of 15 percent and you're left with $25,500. That's $500 better than what you would have gotten on your own, and your effort in making the sale, negotiating the contract, *and* earning this extra cash would have been zero.

Is it worth it?

If you're too shy to ask publishers for a large advance and a fair royalty, if you're ignorant about contractual pitfalls (there are many), if you haven't a clue as to how to sell your book overseas or to TV producers (but then again, only one in fifty books sells overseas anyway, and even fewer nonfiction books end up as TV shows or movies), if you prefer to spend your time writing rather than marketing, if you hate negotiating, if you need someone to tell you honestly when your work reeks and when you're headed for disaster, then, yes, unambiguously, the 15 percent is worth it.

That is, assuming your agent is competent.

How to choose a competent agent

Although many agents are, as I mentioned, former book editors, others come from all walks of life and clearly have less than encyclopedic knowledge of contracts and the market. There is no licensing requirement for agents. *Anyone* can be one. Housewives. Pig farmers. Mob members. Some agents are rip-off artists. Others are lazy or, to put it in kinder terms, unmotivated. Some are just plain stiffs. It's not much of a stretch to imagine that some poorly schooled agents lose money for their clients.

All things considered, then, having an agent can be terrifically beneficial for you. But if you get a bad one, he may not only get you into trouble contractually, but obtain for you far less money than you might get on your own. He may even sabotage your entire career for you.

You should choose an agent as carefully as you'd choose a cardiac specialist because either one can break your heart.

Before signing any agency contract, be brave enough to ask your potential agent some critical, qualifying questions. If the agent is offended by the questions or is evasive in any way, go on to another agent. Legitimate representatives have nothing to fear from a businesslike probing and will answer your questions with confidence.

> "You should choose an agent as carefully as you'd choose a cardiac specialist because either one can break your heart."

Is your potential agent a member of AAR, the Association of Authors' Representatives? Agents must have sold a formidable number of books in the last two years in order to join this highly regarded organization and they must swear to conduct business in an ethical manner, specifically by following AAR's strict code of conduct. An AAR member thus has great credibility.

AAR members are, by definition, successful agents. They usually have a strong client list already in place. Therefore, if you're a new author, you may have trouble attracting any interest from them. Although I recommend trying a number of these association member agents first, don't be surprised if their responses are nothing more than preprinted rejection notes.

If an AAR agent refuses to give you a whirl, consider a non-AAR agent. A non-AAR agent isn't necessarily incompetent or shady. He may be new to the game. Building a client list strong enough to make the multiple sales AAR requires can take anywhere from two to four years. Some agents may never meet the minimum sale requirement because they only work part-time with a small client list. If you go with a non-AAR agent, look for affiliations in other writers' groups, such as the Author's Guild, which offer a number of great services for both agents and authors.

Keep in mind that new agents are hungry agents. They're likely to hustle for their bacon. They have bills to pay and probably a family to support. They need clients and sales badly. But don't sign with just any new agent. Interview all prospective agents first. Are they former editors? Former authors with book sales of their own? Are they lawyers? What qualifies them to be agents anyway? Have they made any book sales in the past year? If so, what? Would they be willing to share a couple of names of clients with you so that you may get a reference from them? Do they offer a contract that binds you to them for a year or more, or do they work from book-to-book? (Don't lock in with any agent for more than a few months until you've gotten to know how he operates.) An agent who only works from book-to-book will have to work hard to keep you happy and on his client list. An agent having a contractual three-year lock on you, on the other hand, could afford to be far less motivated.

Keep in mind that new agents have less clout and less credibility than established agents. Editors will review their submissions with greater skepticism. Still, even beginning agents will be granted greater credibility than unrepresented authors. Here are questions to ask an agent *after* she has expressed an interest in representing you—not before; agents do not have the time to be interrogated by every unknown writer who approaches them.

• How many people work in your agency?

Bigger is not necessarily better, as new writers can be lost in the shuffle. On the other hand, size of staff is obviously an indication of long-term success. A large sales staff may employ a number of specialists—some handling domestic sales, some handling foreign sales, some handling motion picture sales, and so on, and that's a good thing, for the most part. Just don't expect a lot of touchy-feely, personal attention from any one person here, as you might get with a one-man or one-woman operation.

• Are there specialists in your agency who handle foreign rights and other subrights?

A Note About Fee-Charging Agents

Some agents charge fees ranging from $50 to $500 to evaluate manuscripts. These agents maintain that their fees are fair and justified since new writers are far less likely to have anything worthy to sell, and agents end up being uncompensated for their time. Although these agents have a good point, many fee-chargers clearly are less than ethical. Some will try to get you to pay for an evaluation and/or editing services by telling you how much promise your work has. They may allude, with all the integrity of a cockroach in a candy store, that if you'll contract with them for reading, evaluation, and editing services, they'll represent your book to publishers.

Maybe they will. Maybe they won't. Some of these agents may have had class-action suits filed against them on behalf of scores of abused writers. Such lawsuits, unfortunately, have tarnished the entire fee-charging industry. The Association of Authors' Representatives, in fact, forbids its members to charge reading, evaluation, and editing fees because such commerce is simply too easy to abuse.

Not all fee-chargers are weasels, of course. The legitimate ones will give you a complete reading and provide a solid, helpful critique. But ask an agent for her qualifications before sending her any money. What qualifies her to provide the services she is proposing? Is she a former editor or book author? Has she sold books to legitimate publishers? If so, which ones and when?

My advice is to approach agents who charge fees only after exhausting the field of agents who don't charge fees or when you want an objective reading and critique of your manuscript and nothing more. If you expect little in the way of actual sales from fee-charging agents, you won't be disappointed. Their sales records often leave much to be desired.

These are more likely to be found at large agencies. Smaller agencies depend more on coagents to help them makes subsales.

• How many clients do you handle?

The number divided by the size of the staff will give you an indication of how much TLC you can expect. You won't feel very special if you're one of a small army of clients clamoring for attention.

• Will you send me a specimen contract, with explanations of any complicated clauses?

An agent who won't do this may already have too many responsibilities on her plate. Take her refusal as an indication of how little time she may have for your manuscript.

• How often will you communicate with me about the status of my work, especially concerning rejections and plans for future submissions?

In my opinion, you should hear some kind of status report from your agent at least once every four to six weeks.

• Will you provide career guidance and editorial input with my work?

The answer should be "Yes."

• What are your commission rates?

The standard is 15 percent for domestic sales, 20 percent for foreign.

• Do you charge for such office costs as photocopying, messenger service, postage, etc.?

Charges of this sort are standard now, but ask that a ceiling be placed on them.

• How easy will it be to terminate relations with you should I become dissatisfied?

With sufficient written notice (thirty to ninety days), you should be able to end—subject to sales made due to the agent's efforts previous to the termination date—an agent's representation of you and your work.

No matter what her answers are to your questions, make sure your agent has loads of enthusiasm for your book. If she says she absolutely *loves* it and raves about its potential, you've landed the right agent. She has the passion necessary to see your book through the gauntlet of discouraging rejections it may generate. Don't go with an agent who seems to be only lukewarm or tentative about your book's prospects or who admits to reading only the first chapter; this agent may be history after only a couple of rejections.

> "Make sure your agent has loads of enthusiasm for your book. If she says she absolutely loves it and raves about its potential, you've landed the right agent."

Here's a copy of a fair agency contract to help guide you.

SMITH AGENCY AGREEMENT

I hereby appoint Joy Smith of the Smith Agency to, at the best of her ability, advise me in my writing career, and to sell my book, *Hunting Flying Weasels for Fun and Profit*, to an acceptable publisher.

I agree to allow Joy Smith to deduct as a commission 15 percent of all income due to the author from advances, royalties, and subsidiary payments from domestic sales and 20 percent on all income from foreign sales. Joy Smith will collect all income due, deduct her percentage, and mail the remainder to the author within ten days of receipt.

Joy Smith will consult with me before accepting all offers on my book. I must approve of an offer before acceptance is given.

The above commissions shall be in effect throughout the life of the book, as long as it is in print, and throughout new updating, revisions, new editions, etc.

All commissions received by Joy Smith shall not be returned should I (the author) fail to uphold my agreement with a publisher to satisfactorily carry out any assigned and agreed-upon tasks, resulting in the forfeiture of my advance.

If I am approached by a publisher to buy my work, I will refer the buyer to Joy Smith.

Joy Smith will not be responsible for the author's legal fees, should the need for legal counsel arise.

If Joy Smith is unable to make a sale and ceases making submissions, I will be free to pursue a sale on my own, owing no obligation to Joy Smith.

Any sales that come through *after* termination due to Joy Smith's efforts previous to termination shall be negotiated and collected by Joy Smith, who will receive the commissions as stated above, unless otherwise agreed upon by Joy Smith and myself.

If Joy Smith refuses to handle my next book for any reason, I am free to seek representation elsewhere without obligation.

Joy Smith may cease representation of my work at any time for any reason. I may end my professional relationship with Joy Smith with a 30-day written notice.

Author X_____

Agent X_____

Where to find agents

Numerous directories of agents, updated yearly, can be found in your local public library, in any large bookstore, or through Amazon.com. The following are examples of available directories:

- *The Guide to Literary Agents*, Writer's Digest Books.

- *Literary Market Place*, R.R. Bowker.

- *International Literary Market Place*, R.R. Bowker. (Lists overseas agents.)

- *Jeff Herman's Guide to Publishers, Editors and Literary Agents*, Prima Publishing.

The website for the Association of Authors Representatives, among other helpful material, includes a database of over 350 AAR agents with their mailing or e-mail addresses, brief notes on what type of material each handles, and whether each is currently accepting new clients. Go to AAR-online.org for more details.

Scores of nonfiction authors have successfully represented themselves over the years. Numerous guidebooks on negotiations and fair book contracts are available to teach you the ropes. Many nonfiction book contracts are routine. Figuring them out is not rocket science. Yes, you *can* act as your own agent. Yes, you *can* ask for and get every penny that an agent would have gotten for you. But doing that requires time and knowledge.

If you're the intrepid, entrepreneurial sort, and you haven't gotten discouraged yet, jump to the next chapter—the real adventure is yet to begin.

Chapter Seven

Toughen Yourself to Rejection

Don't feel like the Lone Ranger…

My first book, *The Compass in Your Nose & Other Astonishing Facts About Humans*, was rejected seventeen times before finally selling to Jeremy Tarcher. Along the way one of the most prestigious agents in the country told me point blank that "it would never sell because it was comprised of too much rehash." The book not only became a featured Book-of-the-Month Club selection, ultimately reaching number five on its summer 1990 best-seller list, it went on to sell somewhere around 300,000 copies worldwide. Not bad for rehash.

My second book, *Descriptionary*, was rejected twenty-one times. I finally caught the interest of two publishers simultaneously and conducted an auction between them. That book, too, became a BOMC selection and now, with a string of new editions, has the potential to stay in print for the rest of my life.

One of my best-selling books, *Roget's Super Thesaurus*, was rejected ten times. "Too much competition," the rejecting editors said in chorus. Writer's Digest Books ended up paying me the biggest advance in their history for it. It is one of its perennial best-sellers.

If you're uninspired by my own experiences, consider once again those of Jack Canfield and Mark Victor Hansen. Their *Chicken Soup for the Soul* book was rejected more than 140 times before landing a deal with a small publisher in Florida. Agents and editors were certain the book wouldn't fly. Yet today, along with its endless spin-offs, it stands among the biggest best-sellers of the 1990s.

Don't be put off by rejections. They are a standard part of the publishing business. In my eighteen years of writing, I've collected well over a thousand of them. At one time, I even used them as wallpaper to decorate my office.

"Rejection is the norm," says Jerry McTigue, who has racked up big sales with his *Life's Little Frustration Book, How Not to Make Love to a*

Woman, and *You Know You're Over 40 When*....Some of his books have been rejected fifteen to twenty times before selling. Many proposals, he admits, have bombed altogether, illustrating the hit-or-miss reality of selling, well, virtually anything in publishing.

"When my rejection slip file threatened to get thicker than my manuscript, I pulled up an old lesson I learned during my modeling and television commercial career," says Dianne Schwartz, author of *Whose Face Is in the Mirror?*

"If I auditioned for a commercial and didn't get the job, it wasn't because I wasn't talented or pretty enough—I simply didn't have a certain look the producer for a particular product was looking for. The same is true with publishing. Rejection slips don't mean you're untalented, even though the evil troll sitting on your shoulder may try to tell you so. Your book just isn't right for them. So, you keep going, don't give up, and don't take it personally. Never let your ego interfere."

It never ceases to amaze me how easily new writers give up on their books. I once met an extremely intelligent psychotherapist, with excellent credentials, who had written a truly lovely and exceptional self-help guide. She threw in the towel after a single rejection. Yikes! If a psychotherapist can't hang in there through rejection, how can the rest of us?

When you're unpublished, it's difficult to get agents or editors to take you seriously ("Every man with a new idea is a crank," Mark Twain said), but it's eminently harder to take yourself seriously. Most of us are filled with self-doubts. The other guy, we think, is always smarter, better, more qualified. Published authors are special people with just a higher IQ and superior formal schooling. Right?

What the unpublished writer fails to recognize is that one factor stands above all the degrees, credentials, and high IQ in the world, and that is—sorry for the hokey cliche, but it happens to be true—*belief in yourself.*

It's simple, really. If you don't believe in yourself or your work, you'll quit too soon. And your failure will become, not proof of your incompetence or low IQ, but your own self-fulfilling prophecy.

The successful author, somebody once said, is the onetime amateur who never quit. *Bingo!*

Reasons for rejections

Your book was rejected with a form letter. Does that mean your book stinks? Maybe. But just as often, it may mean any one or more of the following:

• The first reader was so swamped with manuscripts that he never really took the time to read your proposal, but simply placed it in its return envelope and mailed it back.

• The publisher already has a similar book in the works.

• The first reader or the editor was completely unfamiliar with the potential market for your book and sent it back to you out of sheer ignorance. Editors are not omniscient gods. They don't know what has the potential to succeed in all genres or categories. Most editors know only a half a dozen or fewer categories well.

• The publisher may never have published a book quite like yours before. Publishers are notoriously afraid of the unknown. Untested waters may suck them under. Nothing neurotic about good old, healthy fear. Publishers may spend at least $30,000 to bring a book to the public. If that were your money, you'd be afraid to try something new, too. Publishers love to see variations of what has succeeded in the marketplace before, not original ideas.

• Your book may be good, but it may have offended the editor. A book which bashes men sent to a male editor may get the boot out of pure irritation. (On the other hand, the fellow may have a sense of humor and love it.) How about a book advocating gun control sent to an editor who strongly supports the NRA?

If you can, try to learn of an editor's leanings before submitting. A good way to do this is to check the books that she has worked on in the past. Another, if she is well known, is to read about her opinions in *Publishers Weekly* and elsewhere. As a practical matter, however, you usually don't have an easy way to ascertain an editor's personal likes and dislikes and are forced to take your chances.

• Your manuscript may have too many red flags. Agents and editors look for obvious signs of amateurism in the opening pages of your proposal. If they see too many, they may send you a form rejection, without ever really delving into your proposal. Red flags include misspelling, grammatical errors, sloppiness, and factual errors. The existence of a number of red flags is almost always a reliable indicator of unpublishable work. Of course, this isn't always the case, but most editors and agents go with the odds and risk overlooking a hidden gem due to sheer time constraints.

• The publisher is overstocked; a moratorium is placed on buying anything new or anything new in the genre in which your book resides.

• Your directory is out of date, and the publisher is no longer publishing the type of book you sent.

• The editor thought your manuscript had potential, but he didn't have the time to tell you what needed fixing to make it more marketable.

While viewing my rejection-papered walls, someone (who assumed I was out of earshot) once said that I reminded them of the *Peanuts* comic strip character, Charlie Brown, because I couldn't do anything right.

Those words seared across my brain. Charlie Brown? Can't do anything right? *Ouch!* Fortunately, little, more-potent, motivational rocket fuel exists than words that cut into your self-image. Such words can make you mad as hell to prove otherwise. They did for me.

So, if someone puts you down or rejects you with a form letter, get mad. And use that rage to prove them wrong. Getting that quiet little last laugh, I promise you, is one of life's deepest pleasures!

Chapter Eight

The Query Letter

Be professional…Sample letters…
What to include…What to omit…Anticipate rejections

Your idea is a lock. A large portion of your research material has been gathered and organized. You've cracked your knuckles, and your fingertips hover over your word processor's keyboard like a concert pianist preparing to reel off *The Flight of the Bumblebee*. You are psyched. You are ready.

At this point, you may be expecting me to offer some tips on writing to help you get your book underway in earnest. What, after all, would a book about writing a book be without tips on actually writing a book?

It may seem odd, but the writing tips in this book are actually coming in the *last* chapter.

There's a good reason for that. If you're lucky, you may not have to write as much as a single paragraph of your book in order to attract a publisher's interest.

It doesn't take reams of paper and months of research to hook a publisher. You can do it with a simple letter called a query.

What's a query?

The initial presentation in a sales campaign to a publisher is a pitch called a *query letter*. A query letter is a one- to two-page, thumbnail description of your book project, including a sentence or two illuminating the potential market and any existing competition, plus a brief bio (one paragraph, not a resume) of yourself containing any pertinent qualifications, credentials, or publishing credits.

Many publishers wish to see a query letter before a formal proposal. The reasoning is simple: Queries take up less space on a desk and can be read quickly. Most book projects—for any number of reasons which may or may not pertain to the quality of the project—are turned down at the git-go. Many submissions simply don't fit a company's publishing program. Editors can skim and process these inappropriate queries far more efficiently than they can slog through masses of proposals. The query letter saves both the author and the editor time.

It is not only completely ethical but wise to mail out simultaneous queries to multiple publishers. This cuts down on your waiting time and expands your possibilities, not to mention raising the odds of a possible auction situation. Most publishers accept simultaneous queries, albeit somewhat grudgingly.

Unless only one publisher exists for the kind of book I'm writing, I always send out queries *en masse*. I have, in fact, sent out as many as twenty queries at one time.

No need to tell editors that you're sending the exact same letters to twenty other publishers. You may, if you wish, but don't assume that the threat of competition will necessarily expedite a reply. While it might if they think you have something unusually valuable to offer, it probably won't.

The query you send to an editor is the same query you would send to an agent, if you're thinking of working with one. Of course you could query agents and editors simultaneously.

Neatness counts

In publishing, as in any business, appearance counts. Never settle for a hastily scrawled note on cheap paper. As an agent, I was stunned to see writers dash off handwritten or hastily typed and error-filled queries on dirt cheap, see-through paper. The message it conveyed was loud and clear: *I don't have the time or the inclination to do things right.*

Invest in professional-looking letterhead and envelopes on high-grade paper. A letterhead conveys a quiet little message: *I'm a professional, and I'm willing to expend the extra effort and cash to prove it.* Even though you may have never had anything published at this point, the letterhead will give the impression that you have and that you're in business for the long haul. As a literary agent, I always approached these slick-looking queries with more optimism and respect.

While manuscripts and proposals should be double-spaced, single-space your query.

Rejections Are Our Friends (Sometimes)

Please, please, please! Don't be surprised when you receive rejections. As I can vouch from my stint as a literary agent, the book ideas of most beginning authors do not appeal to publishers.

If you're turned down or ignored by a couple of dozen agents and editors, you can be pretty sure—but never completely sure—that the project you're proposing isn't viable. If that's the case, be glad you found out before spending six months writing the book. Just come up with another idea or another variation of your original idea, and start the query process over. You aren't beaten until you quit.

As an extra touch of professionalism, type or print out the publisher's address on the envelope with your word processor, instead of handwriting it.

It's important to address your query to an agent or editor by name, not "To Whom It May Concern" or "Dear Editor" or "Sir." Make sure you spell the name correctly. Again, if you don't bother to take this extra step, it will convey a very loud message: *I'm lazy and clueless.*

If you don't know who to address your query to, consult a current publishing directory, including *Literary Market Place, Writer's Market,* or any of the others. Don't use last year's directory. Editors move around a lot. Heads of departments and imprints change as frequently. It's best, even when you have a new directory, to pick up the phone and double-check.

Samples of actual query letters

Following the writer's golden rule to show, not tell, here are a few sample queries. Some are actual letters I've used successfully, some composites of letters I've received as an agent.

This first query is for a children's book. Note how concise and punchy it is, with a focus on "just the facts." Remember a rule fiction writers hold dear: "No tears for the writer, no tears for the reader." That holds true for queries as well. If what you've written doesn't stir something in you emotionally—whether it's awe, fascination, outrage, sadness, alarm, repugnance, or excitement—it won't stir anything in an editor, either. This is the query that sold my book, *The Beast in You: Activities & Questions to Explore Evolution.*

Jack Williamson
Williamson Publishing
Church Hill Road
Charlotte, VT 05445

Dear Mr. Williamson:

Did you ever look in the mirror and notice evolution staring back at you?

Some kids don't believe we evolved from animals. But all they may need to be convinced is a close examination of their own bodies.

Fingernails from claws.

Goosebumps (erector pili muscles) that try in vain to erect a coat of hair that has nearly vanished.

Hackles that stand up on our necks when we're petrified.

And surely you've noticed those nasty-looking canine teeth?

My book, *The Beast in You, Activities and Questions to Explore Evolution,* introduces kids to evolution by first having them examine their own bodies. As Charles Darwin knew, the human body bristles with vestiges and clues to the past. With the evidence so close at hand—so *personal*—the concept of evolution becomes a living entity, something kids can instantly relate to.

The book proceeds with a discussion of evolution that highlights Charles Darwin, the laws of natural selection, mutations, and the creationism controversy.

Fascinating sidebars examine everything from the re-mains of a 70,000-year-old Neanderthal toddler who had the braincase of a modern six-year-old to the massive teeth of a mysterious ape creature that stood ten feet tall (*Gigan-topithecus*).

The final section includes a thorough description of all the hominids (*afarensis, africanus, Homo erectus,* etc.) that pre-ceded modern human beings.

In the 80s, I wrote regularly for *Science Digest* and *Omni* magazines, popularizing dozens of science developments on everything from "singing planets" to "hominid dreams." In 1990, my first book, *The Compass in Your Nose & Other As-tonishing Facts About Humans* (Putnam/Tarcher), sold 300,000 copies and reached #5 on Book-of-the-Month Club's summer best-seller list. I've written several books since, including *Roget's Super Thesaurus* (Writer's Digest Books) and *Grandfather's Christmas Camp* (Clarion), which earned starred reviews from *Publishers Weekly* and *School Library Journal.* My work has also appeared in *Reader's Digest, Cosmopolitan* and *USA Today.*

The Beast in You is written for readers eight years old and up.

A thorough inspection through *Books in Print* reveals an astonishing lack of youth books on human evolution. There is definitely a void waiting to be filled.

Thanks for all your time and thoughtful consideration. I'll be looking forward to hearing from you soon.

Sincerely,

Marc McCutcheon

Below is the query I used to sell the book you now hold in your hands. Note the "leave them astonished" postscript. It really helps to nail the "anyone can do this" slant.

Stephen Blake Mettee
Quill Driver Books
8386 N. Madsen Avenue
Clovis, CA 93611

Dear Mr. Mettee:

The *high school dropout's* tour of the human body...

The *gay man's* guide to pleasuring *women*...

The *farmer's* cookbook...

The *housewife's* battle with obesity...

The *gym teacher's* belly flattener...

The *elderly woman's* adventure in solitude...

The *teenager's* solution to a puzzling national obsession...

The *alcoholic's* chronicle of addiction...

The *home baker's* directions for giant cookies...

The elementary *school teacher's* encyclopedia of all things disgusting...

Best-sellers all...

Ordinary people all.

Working from kitchen tables and home offices across America.

The ordinary Jill or Joe from next door will be next. And if they're savvy, they'll figure out the secrets to doing this *full time.*

Damn, Why Didn't I Write That!: How Ordinary People Are Raking in $100,000 or More Writing Nonfiction Books & How You Can Too! tells how.

I *am* that high school dropout mentioned above , and I've authored ten such niche nonfiction books and I *have* made $100,000 and far more. With no formal training of any kind. One international best-seller. Three Book-of-the-Month Club titles. Starred reviews in *Publishers Weekly*.

Plus, reference books that will remain in print and collect royalties for not five or seven or ten years, but as long as *fifty years or more!*

There are *hundreds* more like me out there. Ordinary people (neither brainiacs nor workaholics) who have figured out a way to make a nice living from what I think is—hands down—the greatest home business anywhere on the planet: *niche nonfiction book writing.*

Would you like to see the complete proposal and sample chapters? Please e-mail, write, or call, and I'll send you the whole package pronto.

One secret prevails above all, and I learned it early in my career: *Treat your writing as a business, not as a hobby, and you will be amply rewarded.*

I appreciate all your time and consideration. I look forward to hearing from you soon.

Sincerely,

Marc McCutcheon

P.S. People always worry that they don't have the proper "credentials" to write a book. When I tell them that one of the greatest-selling guides to sexually fulfilling women was written by two *gay* men, jaws drop with delicious incredulity.

If they continue to have doubts, I fall back on my "convincer": a how-to book that sold over six million copies in one year alone, and still stands as one of the fastest-selling nonfiction books of all time.

It was written by a *teenager.*

Here's a great example of an ordinary writer without degrees or credentials of any kind collaborating with a doctor in order to give her book the "authority" the market requires.

Christine Belleris
Health Communications
3201 SW 15th Street
Deerfield, FL 33442

Dear Ms. Belleris:

Increasingly, Americans are medicating their stress, blue moods, boredom, and poor self-esteem with Dunkin' Donuts, Lay's Potato Chips, and Dairy Queen ice cream.

So what? you say.

On any given day, 48 million Americans, more than ever before, are trying to lose weight. Many are on yo-yo diets that will ultimately leave them fatter and *even more stressed* than before. In fact, Americans are now the fattest they've ever been.

"Mood eating" is eating to soothe what's eating *us*, and it has become a national pastime. Munch, chomp, nibble, nosh. Turn up the stress, break open the Oreos. Sound familiar? Some of us are literally wearing our emotional baggage on our hips and bellies.

Enter Mary Martin, M.D., director of the Weight Management Center of California. She addresses such mood eating in our book-in-progress, *Mood Control, Food Control.*

In this "back to sanity" weight-loss guide, Dr. Martin discusses eating disorders; dieting failures and their long-term health consequences; the roles anxiety, boredom and depression play in overeating; the critical importance of exercise in beating not only flab but the bad moods that compel us to overeat; the long-term solutions to low self-esteem in the obese, and much more. This is no fad diet book. This is the advice endorsed by the medical mainstream.

For overweight people, Dr. Martin offers a one-two punch, offering help for weight problems as well as the emotional burdens tethered to them.

Dr. Martin oversees the treatment of thousands of overweight patients at her eight weight-loss clinics across California. She knows firsthand the anguish that yo-yo dieters face, as one of her specialties is treating depressed, obese patients. Martin teaches them how to get off the dieting treadmill and on to a permanent lifestyle change that will bring their weight down and keep it down for good.

I am a freelance journalist working in collaboration with Dr. Martin and am eager, as is she, to promote this most sensible of weight-control plans to the nation.

This is, I think, the book dieters will turn to when their fad diets fail them yet again.

Dr. Martin and I would love to have the opportunity to send you a complete proposal with sample chapters. Please give us a call, e-mail, or drop us a line in the enclosed SASE.

I appreciate all your time and thoughtful consideration, and I look forward to hearing from you very soon.

Sincerely,

Jane Smith

Here's an example of a writer, again without credentials, using national experts to give his book that crucial ring of authority that editors demand.

Jamie Miller
Prima Publishing
3875 Atherton Road
Rocklin, CA 95765-3716

Dear Jamie:

Arthritis. Bursitis. Dislocation. Hamstring strain. Jumper's knee. Ligament sprain. Meniscus tear. Runner's knee. Tendinitis. "Trick" knees.

Orthopedic specialists cry that we're woefully ignorant of how serious knee injuries and diseases are and that we don't give this delicate joint the tender-loving care and respect it deserves.

The result? Millions of Americans, particularly athletes, middle-agers, and the elderly, are suffering from a broad spectrum of nagging and sometimes excruciatingly painful knee problems.

Enter my proposed book, *The Knee Care and Recovery Book*. From around the nation, I've gathered firsthand research and interview material from twenty of the nation's leading orthopedic specialists, along with all of the latest studies and statistics, and put it all together into a body-wise owner's manual—a guide to parts, maintenance, injury prevention, and repair of our most abused joint.

According to the American Academy of Orthopedic Surgeons, 11.2 million Americans visit their physicians for knee injuries each year (that figure does not count arthritis and other knee diseases); 700,000 undergo arthroscopies, and 312,000 have total knee replacements. Many of these, the experts say, undergo expensive procedures unnecessarily.

My book would have surprisingly little in the way of competition. The only recent knee book published by a large house is *Dr. Scott's Knee Book* from Fireside which, despite being in print for several years, is ranked in sales at a healthy 7,031 out of the 2 million titles *Amazon.com* sells.

All of the experts contributing to the book are board-certified orthopedic surgeons. Some have worked on a personal level with world class Olympians. One has even agreed to write an introduction.

I have a proposal and three-chapter sample ready to go. Would you like to see it? Let me know, and I'll overnight a copy to you.

Thank you for taking time out. I'll be looking forward to hearing your reaction.

Sincerely,

Marc McCutcheon

P.S. Did you know that in addition to being highly prone to injury and arthritis, the knee is the body's most common location for tumors, including cancerous ones?

Dos and Don'ts of query letters

Here's a checklist of things to do and things not to do when writing your query letter.

Do:

✔ *Open by firmly pulling the trigger.*

Your first paragraph should go BOOM. Use a fascinating fact, a stunning statistic, a staggering anecdote, an intriguing teaser, or clear evidence that the book you're about to describe will make a publisher lots of money. Your opening must compel an editor to read the entire letter. Remember, editors are in a big hurry to clear their desks of submissions. You may not be given the luxury of making a big impression on page two.

✔ *Keep it short and sweet.*

A one-page query is ideal. Although it can be longer, it should never ramble on for more than two pages. Editors don't need any more information than what you can cover in one or two pages to make a decision, and it is very possible to kill interest by saying too much.

✔ *Revise and polish your query until it scintillates.*

When it comes to writing queries, most writers take the lazy way out. Odds are you won't get it right the first time, nor the second, nor the third time. The query must contain your best writing. It is your calling card, your invitation to an editor to sample your wares. If you saw a picture of a dirty plate filled with sloppily presented, half-baked food, would you order it from a menu?

Not a single imperfection must be allowed in your query letter—not a minor grammatical or spelling error, not a redundancy, not a smudge, not a crumple, nor a cross-out. A brochure I once received from a "professional" editing service contained at least *four* grammatical errors. Needless to say, I didn't recommend their work to any of my clients.

Use a nice letterhead-quality paper, not the cheap stuff, and make sure your print ribbon or cartridge is flowing smoothly and printing characters sharply.

✔ *Identify the potential market clearly.*

Hard numbers are great when you can get them. (25 million men and women play softball at least once a week. 85 percent of all homes in America will have a home computer by the year 2012. The number of people contracting Lyme disease is increasing 4 percent each year.) Statistics are everywhere and are almost always easy to find on virtually every topic. Any kind of evidence of a large body of potential book buyers will get your editor's attention. Don't, however, try to convince an editor by simply saying you "think" the market for a woman's book would be big because half the population is female. That kind of lameness won't cut it.

✔ *Make a brief note of the weaknesses of the competition.*

Note how many books on your subject exist, according to *Books in Print* and *Amazon.com*. Highlight the Achilles heels of those competitors, such as bad reviews or lack of thoroughness or outdatedness. Ironically, telling an editor that there are no competing books on the market can backfire. If there truly are no competitors, the editor will instantly wonder why. It may well be that there is no market for a book on the topic you've chosen.

✔ *Give a brief capsule of your pertinent credentials.*

List your publishing credits, if you have them, and outline your educational or vocational background only if it pertains to the subject you're writing about. Don't go overboard. No editor or agent wants to see resumes. Avoid at all costs trying to sell yourself to an editor by telling her you've had a perfect attendance record at your place of business for the past ten years, or that you sold the most widgets in a single year (unless your book is on selling widgets), or that you frequently donate your time and money to charity, or that you belong to the VFW. She doesn't care. Worse, she'll be irritated by having to read unnecessary fluff. Worse still, you'll sound like an amateur.

✔ *If you have little or no publishing history, enclose a three or four-page sample of your best writing from the proposed book.*

A sharp writing sample will speak volumes. If you have several nationally published articles or previous books to your credit, this initial writing sample is unnecessary. The editor will check out your writing in the proposal stage.

Don't:

✔ *Claim to have written the next best-seller.*

Only amateur writers make such bold, unsupported statements. Editors will only roll their eyes and immediately place you in the "neophyte" category.

✔ *Claim to be a great or gifted writer.*

Let the writing in your query speak for itself. Having to tell someone you're great makes you sound pompous and insecure. The impression you leave is just the opposite of what you want. If a famous author or well-known editor, on the other hand, has called you "great," include his quote in your letter. Coming from someone in authority, it sounds much more credible.

✔ *Mention that you're an unpublished author.*

Never supply a negative about yourself unless an editor asks you directly. Just say nothing.

✔ *Mention that your mother or neighbor thinks you or your book have great potential.*

These references are completely meaningless and editors will mark you as an amateur if you use them.

✔ *Present more than one book idea at a time.*

Many writers make the mistake of thinking that a presentation of many ideas in one letter will increase their odds of a sale. Just the opposite is true. The buckshot approach dilutes the presentation of each idea and makes each seem not quite important enough to present on its own.

When a writer claims to have a number of books available for purchase, editors immediately assume he's accumulated a lot of rejection slips over a long period of time. Present your book ideas *individually* and as freshly written, not as an old horse that's been trotted around every barn for the past decade. Don't make the mistake of leaving an old copyright date on the manuscript or proposal. If you're still trying to sell something you wrote five years ago, the thought an editor will have is: If nobody else liked it, why would I?

✔ *Make demands of what you expect for advance and royalties.*

This is presumptuous, but I've seen writers do it in query letters, and it's always instant death. No mention of contractual matters should be made at the query stage. Those items should only be brought up after an offer is made on your book.

✔ *Demand that an editor respond to you within two weeks or lose the opportunity to see your book.*

This doesn't frighten editors in the least. Unless you have an extraordinary book (one in ten thousand, if that), editors will simply ignore you.

✔ *Tell the editor how many times your book has already been rejected.*

This is just plain dumb. Would a young baseball prospect tell a baseball scout how many times he's struck out in the last year unless asked?

✔ *Claim to have spent twenty years writing your book.*

This only impresses people outside of publishing. To people inside publishing, it only means you're an incredibly slow writer, a procrastinator, possibly an alcoholic, or that you had the manuscript in a drawer, forgotten for nineteen of those twenty years. The length of time spent writing a book is no indication of quality. Some of the biggest best-sellers of all time have been written in as little as three months.

✔ *Be vague.*

This is, in my experience, the most common problem among people new to writing queries. Too many authors assume that editors are mind-readers or that they'll simply ask to see sample chapters if they need more specific information. Many writers *never* get to the proposal stage because they don't tell editors exactly what the book will contain in the query letter. Vague references such as "the story of my tough life" or "a guide to helping people have better relationships" or "my book about being successful at one's work" are not specific enough. Editors will reject these as reflexively as swatting mosquitos. By being vague, you give the impression that you haven't really thought out the contents of the book. Include specific details. Include the nitty gritty.

✔ *Make a reference to having a copyright.*

This is another indication of an amateur, and a paranoid one at that. Publishers don't steal authors' books and then print them under someone else's name in order to keep all the profits. Nor can mere ideas be copyrighted. You don't need to put the copyright symbol on your work and you don't have to register your manuscript with the copyright office; your work is protected by law from the moment you put it on paper or on your hard drive.

Usually a publisher will register a copyright in your name after the book comes off the press.

✔ *Forget to enclose a self-addressed, stamped envelope for the editor's response.* Odds are, you won't get a response without it. Don't just send loose stamps or a check for one dollar to cover postage or an unaddressed envelope. Not including an SASE makes you look unprofessional and makes an editor's job more difficult. Requiring that an editor get an envelope and address it can reduce your odds of a positive response.

✔ *Beg or vent your frustrations.* No matter how frustrated you are that nobody will give you a break, resist the urge to beg or whine in your query. Writers who sound desperate don't sound like winners. Resist the urge to purge.

Below is a good example of a bad query. Note the incorrect grammar, the misspellings, the glowing endorsements from family members, the paranoia about copyright, and the allusions to having the next best-seller—all classic signs of an inexperienced author.

Dear Sirs,

I have a book idea about which I know would be a best-seller because everyone in my family, and my neighbor which reads a lot, says its great and that I should get a publisher right away. My book idea is about aliens and how I prove they live around us and we don't even know about it.

I'm going to get a copyright on my idea soon, so it cannot be stolen. But until I get the copyright, I can't tell you just yet about everything in the book. But trust me when I describe my talents as God-given, you won't be disappointed.

Can I send you the book when I get the copyright and you won't regret it. You will have another best-seller on your hands and will earn millions, I promise.

Sincerely,

Roger Insecure

In the next query, the author makes multiple mistakes. As you read it, see if you can identify them.

Dear Sir,

I have written nine books but I am an unpublished author who needs a break. I am asking if you will please give me a chance. If you would just read any of these books, you would see big potential. I know my books are good, and you have nine of them below to choose from! If you're looking for the next best-seller, I will send any one or all to you upon your request.

Sincerely,

Joe Loser

How many did you spot? This poor fellow commits the sin of announcing he remains unpublished after writing nine books—all of which he's pitching in this query. After making himself sound pathetic by begging for a chance, he claims his books will become best-sellers.

Publishers typically require anywhere from one week to three months to respond to queries, so be patient. A couple of publishing houses are known for responding only when interested. Never assume agents or editors are simply "arrogant bastards" or the "devil's disciples"—I've been called both—should they fail to reply within a reasonable time or if they fail to respond at all. Often, there are good reasons for late or no responses, including the lack of the aforementioned SASE, inadequate postage, lost mail, or an impossible-to-get-out-from-under mountain of mail that accumulates during an illness.

If you fail to receive a reply after three months, it's likely the editors at that particular publisher just aren't thrilled with your idea. Although you can scratch off a polite letter of inquiry, asking if an editor is planning to respond soon, resist the urge to write a nasty complaint letter. The same rules apply when sending queries to agents. If they don't respond, don't sweat it. It happens all the time. Move on.

Queries should give the impression to the editor that you have a full proposal with sample chapters already available, even if you don't. Editors will have less confidence in you if you approach them without having actually written anything, but there is no law saying that you have to have written anything. Is this dishonest? A little. Is it unethical? Probably on a par with tearing that warning tag off your pillow.

In your query, simply state, "I'd be happy to send a full proposal, if you'd like." If an editor expresses interest (*Woohoo!*), it's always easy to stall for time. Just tell her you're putting a final polish on everything and send her a professional proposal a month or so down the road. As long as you follow through and deliver what you promise, when you promise, no harm, no foul.

Editors' responses to queries are usually cool and measured; they know better than to get excited about a book at this early stage. However, every now and then an editor's excitement will come through loud and clear, and it's music to an author's ear. In response to one of my own queries several years ago, William Brohaugh of Writer's Digest Books wrote: "You have me drooling over this. Send the proposal immediately."

To a writer, no sweeter words were ever spoken. Take it from me, you'll know you've written a damn good query letter if you get a response like that.

Chapter Nine

The Proposal

The parts…Sample of a successful proposal…Proper format

A proposal is a formal, comprehensive sales package sent to an editor to convince him that your book will be profitable. Although there are no carved-in-stone laws dictating, detail by detail, what a proposal must be, it is generally comprised of:

- a cover letter with a hook

- a formal description of the proposed book

- front matter that will be included, such as a foreword by a noted celebrity

- back matter that will be included, such as an index, bibliography, or glossary

- a market survey, highlighting the population of potential buyers

- a list of possible spin-offs

- a rundown of competing books and why yours would perform better or at least as well

- an estimate of word length

- time needed to complete

- ideas or opportunities for promotion and publicity

- a brief bio of yourself, explaining why you're qualified to write such a book, including any personal experience relating to the book's topic and your educational background if pertinent. (If you have no formal qualifications, this is where you detail the sources or outside experts you will consult and interview.)

- your publishing credits, if any

- a table of contents

- a chapter by chapter outline

- two or three sample chapters

The second through the tenth items in the list above are often collectively referred to as the overview or outline.

Most of the principles for pitching queries also pertain to proposals.

Some publishers are willing to look at proposals without seeing query letters first. Sometimes that's a good thing: it eliminates a time-consuming step in the sales process; it also gives you the chance to pitch your book in more elaborate detail. You may be able to convince an editor with a complete proposal, whereas you may not in a brief query. Still, there is a paradoxical rule that occasionally rears its ugly head; that is, you can sometimes kill interest by saying too much. Knowing when to keep your mouth shut in a proposal is critical. Only that which helps sell your book should be included in your proposal.

Your proposal must clearly establish:

- An obvious population of people who will almost certainly be attracted to your book and will consider buying it

- Your ability to write and complete the manuscript at a professional level

- Your ability to conduct thorough research

- Clear promotional opportunities, such as on radio or TV or in newspapers or via lectures, conferences, etc.

- That you will best the competition by including something they overlooked or by being more thorough, more up to date, or by taking a different angle on the subject.

Simultaneous Submissions

Many larger publishers don't want to see proposals submitted simultaneously to other houses. These publishers add a notice to this effect in their directory listings. Whether you should heed such warnings would probably be best answered by a business ethicist. I've broken this rule many times; I've never been caught or regretted it. Simultaneous submissions increase your odds of a sale. Would you put a used car up for sale to only one person at a time?

And, what of the time factor if each publisher keeps your proposal for only one month? It isn't uncommon for a book to go out to thirty, forty, or fifty publishers before one buys it. You do the math.

Usually, my strategy is to hit all of the publishers who *do* accept simultaneous proposals first and leave the others to submit to when all else fails.

The goal of the proposal is to leave no doubts in the editor's mind. When the editor reaches the end of your proposal, she should be thinking: "Looks like a pro here. He hasn't cut a single corner. The writing is sharp; the research is comprehensive and authoritative; the market is proven conclusively. We can trust this writer to deliver what he promises. We'd be foolish to ignore this."

Again, as with queries, think neat. Don't allow a single typo or smudge or awkward phrasing. And, don't forget to include a SASE for the proposal's return.

The best tip I can give you about proposals is this: *Put yourself in the editor's shoes.* What does she want? What motivates her?

I can tell you exactly what motivates most editors: She wants to take a convincing book proposal to her colleagues, a book proposal in which the author will have supplied all of the market research for her, including details on the population of potential buyers, the competing books, the promotional possibilities, and so on. The author, in other words, will leave no work for the editor.

The following are parts of an actual proposal I used to sell one of my books to Writer's Digest Books.

The cover letter

This could easily work as an initial query letter or as a general description to open an outline. This letter went on to serve double duty, with slight modifications, as an introduction in the book itself.

Dear Mr. Brohaugh,

Writers working on romances, mysteries, thrillers, police procedurals, historical dramas—where do they go to find obscure information on everyday life in what is easily the most story-rich period of the century—Prohibition through World War II?

For example, when did teenagers refuse to wear jeans unless their cuffs were rolled up?

How did people make their own booze during Prohibition?

When was the word *swell* on everybody's lips? And in which decade was something so cool that it had to be called the "cat's pajamas," the "cat's whiskers," the "bee's knees" and a dozen other variations?

What night of the week did the radio program "Fibber McGee and Molly" come on? What time? How about "Inner Sanctum," "The Shadow," "The Lone Ranger?"

What soap operas did most women listen to in the 1930s?

Why did so many people break their arms trying to start a Ford Model T? How did one shift gears in a Tin Lizzy? And, why were so many people seen driving over hills in one backward?

When did American men stop wearing tee shirts, and what event provoked them to do so? When did girls go crazy over bobby sox and tight sweaters?

Unfortunately, small, period-illuminating details like these are frequently difficult and time-consuming to find. While there are enough books on political events and general history to fill a fleet of 1930 Lincolns and enough works on World War II to sink a battleship, few references to *everyday life* during Prohibition through the World War II era exist.

And, that's exactly what the writer of a coming-of-age, rags-to-riches, or timeless love story needs in order to avoid spending perhaps hundreds of hours at the library winnowing minutiae, a reference book one can have at his fingertips to find out in an instant the favorite pinup girls of the World War II GI; the cars favored by gangsters; how speakeasies served liquor illegally during Prohibition and got away with it; what kitchen product housewives scraped out of their pots and pans to aid the war effort; when the zoot suit was all the rage; what hairstyle was "in" in 1940; what year a character would most likely dance the Charleston, sit on a flagpole, or swallow a live goldfish.

I've enclosed a proposal, including two sample chapters and a detailed chapter-by-chapter outline, from just such a reference book, which I'm calling *Writer's Guide to Everyday Life from Prohibition Through World War II*.

Writers would use this reference to verify facts and dates (and to avoid anachronisms!), for ideas and, mostly, for inspiration. They'll read this book and feel the period come alive, and they'll borrow from it to make their own work come alive.

Flappers. Babe Ruth. Prohibition. Lindbergh. The Depression. The advent of radio. The golden age of movies. Aviation. Amelia Earhart. The Midwest dust bowl disaster. Jesse Owens. Gangsters. John Dillinger. Pearl Harbor. FDR. Audie Murphy. The War in Europe. The War in the Pacific. The advent of the atomic age.

A thousand stories await in what I think would be a truly rich resource for writers. See what you think.

Your time and consideration are greatly appreciated. I'll be looking forward to hearing your reaction soon.

Sincerely,

Marc McCutcheon

(With the exception of the cover letter, the actual proposal was submitted double-spaced; it is reproduced here single-spaced to save room.)

OUTLINE

The outline is where you tell the editor about the book, what it is going to cover, who'll read it and how it will be promoted. In the outline you include information about an appendix, bibliography, glossary, index, or other similar material (called back matter).

Detail any important research you plan to do that is considered above the norm. For example, if you plan to interview a broad array of experts or to travel and explore an exotic location, say so loud and clear. Here's what I wrote:

To add authenticity and authority, I'll include actual "quotes" and direct references and excerpts from the era's newspapers, magazines, radio shows, etc., plus a complete chronology of historical and "everyday" events, a bibliography, and a detailed source list. I will interview at least seven people across the country who lived through the Depression and World War II and provide lively quotes from their experiences.

Whatever you do, don't skip over a mention of promotional opportunities. Even if you're not a professional public speaker and have no interest in becoming one, you must offer publishers something that you can do to promote sales, whether it is getting blurbs or prefaces from national experts or by arranging interviews with newspapers. If you have TV and radio experiences, detail them. Publishers love authors who have interview experience and who have tapes of previous shows to send to potential interviewers.

> **PROMOTIONAL OPPORTUNITIES: I maintain a comprehensive list of newspaper columnists and book reviewers who have a strong interest in history, particularly in this period, and would be great candidates for review copies and press releases. I will also make myself available for book signings and lectures throughout the year. John Doe, president of the Historical Writers Association, has agreed to supply a cover blurb.**

Identify, as specifically as you can, your potential market. Don't stretch this, though; be realistic. If you've written a plumber's guide, mention how many plumbers currently work in the United States. If you've written a book on amateur astronomy, mention how many people bought telescopes and binoculars last year. Editors love hard numbers. If you can find them, give them.

In addition to traditional outlets, would your book sell in museum gift shops? Hardware stores? Drugstores? Gourmet shops? Could it be adopted as course material for schools? Would a large corporation be interested in buying mass quantities for its employees? Could it possibly be sold as bonus freebie when packaged with another consumer item? (For example, a book on lawn care could be sold to grass seed companies to sell with their seed.) Could a television show be produced from your book? A video? A CD-Rom? If there is a credible (don't stretch the truth) possibility for any of these, be sure to mention it.

> **POTENTIAL MARKET: The largest market will be writers and authors, particularly those working on historical romances, mysteries, mainstream novels, or short stories. This book would be a natural as a featured or alternate selection in Writer's Digest Book Club. It would also be a strong candidate as a selection at the History Book Club.**

> **The library market would also be very strong, as the book will be a solid historical reference tool. A secondary market may exist in the mainstream population of readers who lived through this period. Reviews in retirement magazines may spawn additional sales among those seeking a "stroll down memory lane."**

Here comes another ethical dilemma. Editors want to see a complete rundown of competing titles in your proposal. But if you do that, you may shoot yourself in the foot. A long list of existing competitors will scare off many editors unless your book will clearly stand head and shoulders above all the rest. On the other hand, if you say there are no competing titles, the editor will strongly suspect that you're either lying or you haven't done your homework. Almost every book—including your own life story which must compete with other people's life stories—has at least one competitor.

I'll detail a complete list of competitors only when it will help my odds of getting a sale. Otherwise, I pick and choose, being sure to point to the obvious titles that the editor is likely to know about, but being selective on the rest of the field.

Look for things to bring to the editor's attention, like the fact that your book's top competitor is currently in its 16th printing and is now seven years old. This points out to an editor a potentially profitable opening, particularly if the competition's information is outdated. Saying that another book is written in academic prose, while yours will be written in a reader-friendly style, might be just the ticket.

While it is OK to mention glaring weaknesses in competing titles, don't be insulting about other authors' books; you'll just come off sounding petty. And, besides, your editor may have edited one or more of them.

> **COMPETING TITLES: A search through *Books in Print* reveals two existing books on "everyday life" from this period, but none specifically designed to aid writers in their research.**

WORD COUNT: 70,000 (Negotiable)

Be concrete about your estimated word count and time to complete. A hard number gives editors the impression that you've thought things out carefully rather than merely guessed. Giving a word count spread of no more than 10,000 words—"70-80,000" words—is acceptable, but not quite as impressive. Giving a ballpark figure—"between approximately 60,000 and 100,000 words, give or take"—suggests poor planning. Don't go overboard with length. Unless you can see potential for a return on your investment by making your book the most comprehensive on the market, try to stay just over accepted minimums, usually around 70,000-80,000 words. The goal is to write the best book on the market with the shortest acceptable length.

TIME TO COMPLETE: 6 months

When estimating the time needed to complete the book, it's wise to give yourself a shorter deadline rather than a longer one. A long deadline breeds inefficiency and low production. In other words, it'll make you lazy! A short one forces you to be disciplined and that, in the long run, will increase your income dramatically if your plans are to write for a living.

AUTHOR BIO: My health and science news reporting have appeared in *Omni, Science Digest, USA Today, Cosmopolitan*, and many other national publications. I currently have twelve books in print, including *The Writer's Guide to Everyday Life in the 1800s* and *Descriptionary*, a Book-of-the-Month Club featured selection.

Be sure to mention any previous book club sales, berths on bestseller lists, movie or TV sales, or rave reviews you've received with previous projects.

Avoid negatives in your bio. If you're unpublished, say nothing. If you dropped out of college or, worse, high school, say nothing. Don't mention that you once sold a poem to your local *Podunk Times*. Editors will not only be unimpressed, they may stamp you as a hopeless newbie. While you may not have spectacular credits—maybe no writing related credits at all—in your bio, a sharply written proposal that is thoroughly researched may be all the convincing an editor needs.

If your book lends itself to a series or to spin-off titles, explain ideas you have for these spin-offs and your interest in developing them. By detailing a second book with a paragraph or two and a table of contents, it is sometimes possible to land a two-book contract, so don't overlook this great potential. (This is very different from pitching several unrelated books at once, previously discussed as a bad idea.)

TABLE OF CONTENTS

Introduction
1. Slang, Colloquialisms, and Everyday Speech
2. Prohibition
3. The Great Depression
4. World War II
      On the Home front
      Slang and Colloquialisms of Soldiers
      Selected Weapons and Vehicles
5. Crime
      Sidebar: New York City Police Slang of the 1940s
6. Transportation
      Cars
      Air Travel
7. Clothing and Fashions
      Sidebar: Military Uniforms of World War II
8. Radio and Radio Shows
9. Music and Dance
Chronologies
      History, Events, Innovations and Fads

Hit Songs
Books
Movies
Bibliography

CHAPTER BY CHAPTER SUMMARY

Chapter One
SLANG, COLLOQUIALISMS, AND EVERYDAY SPEECH

Bushwa? Jiggery-pokery? They're jake. Hipper-dipper! They've got the goods, see? Sure are swell! The words and phrases your grandmother grew up with. With excerpts from publications of the day.

Sample entry:

swell: good; great; fine; excellent; nice. An exceedingly popular word, used by virtually everyone, from hoboes to presidents. The excerpts below only hint at the word's pervasiveness throughout society in the 1930s and 1940s.

1938: "I worked on a Broadway paper where the managing editor used to say, "Broun, Mr. Eddie X has just given us a big ad for Sunday. See that he gets a swell notice when you write your vaudeville review." *(New Republic,* Aug. 17)

1941: "It's a shame about Sarah…She's such a swell girl otherwise!" (Ad for Listerine toothpaste, December)

1945: "George and Gracie will be right back…I want to remind you that Swan is swell for everything: for baby, for you, for dishes…." (Ad, Burns and Allen radio program)

Chapter Two
PROHIBITION

Millions of drinkers scoffed at Prohibition. With its legitimate manufacture eliminated, liquor in the form of "moonshine" and "bathtub gin" were simply produced in thousands of homemade stills across the country. Between 1921 and 1925 alone, the government seized some 696,933 such stills.

Blind pigs....bootleggers....How citizens made their own hooch....Al Capone...Slang terms for liquor.... poisonings....prohibition agents....police raids...rum running...speakeasies....stills....St. Valentine's Day Massacre....the Untouchables....

Sample entry:

whisper sister: a woman proprietor of a speakeasy.

1927: "The ladylegger who runs a speakeasy is known in the trade as a 'whisper sister' in a tea shop or a restaurant or a hotel. It may be, and not infrequently is, the woman's own house. The apartment speakeasy is spreading throughout the big cities...."(*Literary Digest,* February 5)

Chapter Three
THE GREAT DEPRESSION

In 1932, 56 percent of blacks and 40 percent of whites were without jobs. Many of the jobless remained that way throughout the Depression. But even those who were lucky enough to keep their jobs saw their incomes plummet by as much as 50 percent or more...how and why it happened.

Bank runs...cellar clubs...drought and dust bowls...evictions...Herbert Hoover....Hoover blankets... Roosevelt's New Deal...relief....rent parties...morale-booster Will Rogers...unemployment and making ends meet....

Sample entry:

Hoover blankets: newspapers. So-called because many slept in the streets after being unemployed for months; a derogatory reference to President Hoover.

Chapter Four
WORLD WAR II

On the home front, Americans came together in a mass effort of camaraderie. Civilians helped the military watch the skies for approaching enemy airplanes. Civilians watched the shores for submarines. They conducted air raid drills, blackouts and dimouts. They rationed. They salvaged. They conserved. They worked overtime. They planted Victory gardens. They bought war bonds. They did everything their government asked them to do and then some.

Air raid wardens...blackouts...C-rations...Dear John letters...gas shortages...rationing...Jerries, Krauts and Nips...relocation of Japanese citizens...salvaging... spotters....Rosie the Riveter...V-homes...Victory gardens...war bonds...the dreaded notice of death....

Sample entry:

V-Homes: American households that carried out a number of duties to aid the war effort were thus honored with V-home certificates, placed in windows, from the office of Civilian Defense. The V stood for *Victory*. (I will reprint an actual V-home certificate from the Office of Civilian Defense.)

Chapter Five
CRIME

According to a committee appointed by the American Bar Association, "the criminal situation in the United States so far as crimes of violence are concerned is worse than any other civilized country." The committee was speaking not of the 20th century, but of the 1920s.

Bonnie and Clyde...chiselers...John Dillinger...flimflams...drugs...Ma Barker gang...street hustles... racketeering...street slang...assorted swindles, cons, and ripoffs...the fuzz....

Sample entry:

creep joint: a brothel with rooms equipped with closets having secret openings that slide open, so that clothing could be ransacked for money and other valuables while the patron was sexually distracted.

Chapter Six
TRANSPORTATION

Thanks largely to Henry Ford and mass production, by 1920 one in every thirteen Americans owned an automobile. In 1924, one could buy a Ford for the astonishingly low price of $290. In 1919, the average nationwide speed limit was twenty miles per hour, fifteen in residential areas and ten in cities.

Cars that no longer exist...Cord...DeSoto...Doble... Dusenberg..."fill it with ethyl"...flivvers and other slang terms...the Model A...the Model T...Hupmobile... Nash...Packard...rumble seats...Pierce Arrow...Studebaker...Stutz....In the air...the Graf Zeppelin....

Sample entry:

Studebaker: in the 1920s, a carmaker nearly as popular as Ford, building over 100,000 cars in 1922 alone. Its popularity didn't last, however. In 1932–33, its claim to fame was the six-cylinder Rockne, named after Notre Dame football coach Knute Rockne. It sold for just $600 but failed to catch the fancy of the buying public. Some suspected the name might be a problem. So the Rockne was promptly followed up with another car with a terrible name, the "Dictator," built through 1937.

Chapter Seven
CLOTHING AND FASHIONS

If there was anything that shocked 1920s America as much as gang shootings and poisoned hooch, it was the startling trend in women's clothing to show more skin. Hemlines were going up, up, up. Necklines were coming down, down, down.

Bobbed hair...bobby sox...the advent of cigarettes... fashion...flappers...men's hats...women's hats...jeans... Lindbergh jackets...the "moral" gown...raccoon coats...when women's slacks became all the rage...sloppy Joe sweaters...why men stopped wearing undershirts...zoot suits....

Sample entry:

undershirt: Men stopped wearing undershirts almost overnight after Clark Gable appeared without one in the movie, *It Happened One Night,* in 1934.

Chapter Eight
RADIO AND RADIO SHOWS

The first home "radio music boxes," as they were called, came off the assembly lines in 1922, at a cost of between fifty and one hundred dollars. Eleven million dollars worth of sets sold that first year. Sales doubled the next year and doubled again the year after that. All across the country, stores sold out of these wonderful appliances almost as quickly as they got them in. (The sets were a great improvement over the homemade crystal sets built by radio enthusiasts out of Quaker Oats boxes, wire, and copper the year before.) Soon the most common news story of the day was that of a new radio owner falling off his roof as he installed his first antenna.

The advent of radio..."The Adventures of Ozzie and Harriet"...The Aldrich Family...Amos and Andy...Arthur Godfrey Time...Blondie...Bob Hope...Buck Rogers in the 25th Century...Burns and Allen..."The Cuckoo Hour"...Dick Tracy..."The Edgar Bergen and Charlie McCarthy Show"... Fibber McGee and Molly....Flash Gordon...Gangbusters... "The Guiding Light"..."Inner Sanctum"..."The Lone Ranger"

Successful Books Get Reprinted

You can learn how many printings the books that will compete with yours have had by checking the code on the copyright page. You'll see a series of numbers that look something like this:

10 9 8 7 6 5 4

The last number designates the printing; in this case, the fourth. Sometimes publishers won't use the code but will simply say outright, "3rd printing."

Any book getting beyond a first printing can be deemed successful, and any book getting into double digit printings can be deemed hugely successful. Pointing out the success of a similar—but different or weaker in some measure than yours—title can whet an editor's appetite.

...airing of the Scopes Monkey trial...War of the Worlds broadcast...Will Rogers..."Your Hit Parade"...and much more.

Sample entry:

Walter Winchell: Winchell, "your New York correspondent," delivered news and commentary in a breathless, rapid-fire style while a code signal (which he worked himself) beeped in the background. One of the highest-rated reporters on the air. His famous opening: "Good evening, Mr. and Mrs. North and South America and all the ships at sea...let's go to press!" He could be heard over NBC at various times, including Sunday nights at 9:30.

Chapter Nine
MUSIC AND DANCE

The music was hot. Jazz. Swing. Crooners. Big bands. Swing bands. The morale-building war songs, the miss-you-when-you're-gone songs, the ballads. In the 1920s, Rudy Vallee and Paul Whiteman and his orchestra dominated the music scene. In the 1930s, it was Benny Goodman, Glenn Miller, Tommy Dorsey, Duke Ellington, Ella Fitzgerald and Bing Crosby. In the 1940s, it was all about Frank—Sinatra, that is.

The Charleston...dance halls...the fox-trot...the Lambeth walk...the Lindy hop...the hit songs from 1919 to 1945. (I will provide a list of top ten songs year by year.)

Chapter Ten
CHRONOLOGIES

The big news from year to year, from the flu epidemic in 1918 and 1919 to the end of meat and butter rationing on November 23, 1945.

If you're sending three sample chapters, you only need a rough outline of the remaining chapters, as I've done above. If you supply fewer chapters with your proposal—especially if you have no writing credits—you'll need to be more thorough in your outline than I've been here.

If you propose to do anything unusual, such as saying "I will interview twenty-five of the nation's top experts," include some sample material—in this case a representative interview—to prove that you will be able to pull it off.

Be accurate and don't exaggerate. One factual error in your proposal is enough to turn off an editor. If you can't be bothered to double-check facts in a proposal, why would an editor trust you to do so in a book? Take the time to get everything right, and don't trust your memory on *anything*. Check spellings, check dates, check grammar, check statistics, and so on. When you're done, show the proposal to your most educated friend or family member, or even better, an editor or writer, if you know one, and have this person check for misspellings and errors. You'll be amazed by how many gaffes a fresh pair of eyes can pick out.

Although editors deal every day in hype, don't exaggerate anything in your proposal. Editors are highly educated and sharp; they'll see through it and mistrust you from that point on.

Some tips on the mechanics

Preparing your proposal with a standard format helps to show the editor that you are a person who can be counted on to act professionally throughout the publishing process.

Use 8½" x 11" 20-pound white paper. Do not use erasable bond paper. Double-space all lines. Use a standard type style and size.

Be sure your printer has a fresh toner or ink cartridge.

Include your name, address, telephone, e-mail and fax number on your title page and your last name, a keyword from the book's title and the page number in the upper right corner of all subsequent pages. You can set your word processor program to do this automatically. It'll look something like this:

McCutcheon/Prohibition/pg 2

Number the pages of your proposal in consecutive order, not by sections. If the proposal is accidentally shuffled or dropped by an editor, it will be easy to put back together.

Don't justify the right margin, because the odd-spacing of words in the line makes it more difficult to read. (See page 232 for an example of how to properly format your book proposal.)

Use your word processor to spell check every page. Watch for errors that the spell checker may not catch, such as the use of "to" for "too."

Don't staple your proposal together. Place it neatly in a double-pocket construction paper portfolio. The cover letter and proposal can go in the left pocket, the sample chapters in the right, although you can do whatever seems most sensible with the material you have. Use your word processor to print your book's title and your name on a self-adhesive label to stick on the front cover.

Be sure to include in your portfolio a large SASE with adequate postage for the return of your proposal.

Once the sale is made, the editor wants to put in as little work on your book as possible. Don't entertain the misguided notion that an editor will "fix" your book's flaws. That's your job.

If she calls or writes and asks you if you can do something, your automatic answer should be "Yes, of course."

Deliver more than what is expected. In time, you will be an author publishers seek out.

Negotiating Your Book Contract

Figuring advances & royalties...Negotiating the advance
Handling subrights...Sample contract

I've always handled my own contracts, sometimes to my detriment, sometimes to my benefit. I've been surprised by some publishers who offered fair advances and contracts up front, without haggling. I've not been surprised with others who did quite the opposite. I once asked for and got the biggest advance (for a book on writing) in my publisher's history. But I have also been caught hideously off guard (early in my career) by not knowing the difference between net receipts accounting and list price accounting. In twenty-two years, I've learned about negotiating and contracts in the same way a young puppy learns about skunks and porcupines—through painful experiences.

Hopefully, you'll heed the caveats of a bruised and wary veteran before venturing too far into the woods on your own.

If you've decided to handle your own negotiations, you must form a clear idea of what your book is worth in the marketplace. The tendency is to overinflate the value of one's own work, but then, ironically, to cave in and accept whatever an editor offers, even if it is well below normal. Your goal should be to avoid either of these scenarios.

Most advances—the money a publisher pays an author up front against future royalty earnings—fall in the $7,500-$20,000 range. Basically, the advance is an estimate of what the publisher thinks a book will earn for the author if the publisher's first print run sells out completely. (First print runs, historically, have been for the quantity of books a publisher expects to sell the first twelve months the book is out, but this is changing downward as new print technology comes on line.)

This is the formula the Author's Guild embraces, and while it is a good starting point in your negotiations, in practice, it is deviated from widely.

To work this formula, you must find out two things: the royalty rate and the projected first printing. The second one is simple: Just ask the editor the number of books they've projected to print the first year.

The royalty rate, however, may require a bit of negotiation. Although there are many variations from book to book and publisher to publisher, the general consensus of fair royalties from larger publishers looks something like this:

- Hardcover: 10 percent of retail cover price on the first 5,000 copies, 12½ percent on the next 5,000, and 15 percent thereafter. (Some houses will start the upward progression at 10,000 copies.)

- Trade paperback: 7½ to 8 percent of retail cover price. (This can go as high as 10 percent with a particularly valuable book and a sharp negotiator.)

- Mass-market paperback: 6 percent of cover price on first 150,000 copies, 8 percent thereafter.

Here's an example on how to figure an advance on a hardcover book that retails for $25.00 and earns a 10 percent royalty, with a first print run of 5,000 copies:

10% x $25.00 = $2.50,
$2.50 x 5,000 = $12,500 advance

For a mass-market paperback book earning 6 percent of the cover price of $7.99 and an initial print run of 25,000:

6% x $7.99 = $0.48,
$0.48 x 25,000 = $12,000 advance

Some small publishers don't offer royalties as high as these examples. These publishers have carved out a niche for themselves by profiting from books on which others would lose money. Their profit margins, of course, are helped by their authors' lower royalty rates. If you sign with such a publisher, ask for an escalation clause that pays you royalties at a higher percentage if the book happens to take off. Perhaps on sales in excess of 25,000 copies, a higher rate would be reasonable.

When an editor calls with an offer, it's going to be difficult to relax, yet things will go better if you've prepared beforehand.

Be prepared with responses and counteroffers. I always keep a printout right next to my phone of what I want for advances and royalties from my books. I also have arguments already drawn out for any contingency an editor may throw at me.

℘ **Note:** You don't need to prepare ahead of time for every contractual point. With the first contact, you will only be negotiating advance, royalties, and rights territories. The other details will be outlined in the contract they send you. You can then take time studying this contract and suggest changes or amendments.

Try to build some kind of rapport before tackling a negotiation. If you recognize the editor from reading about her in *Publishers Weekly* or elsewhere, say so and, if you're conversant with the books she has put out in the last year or two, by all means voice your familiarity—"Oh, yes, didn't you edit the Samantha Brown book on so and so…" A little friendly small talk can go a long way in reducing tensions.

I once had an editor call with an offer while my kids were screaming and fighting in the background. Utterly mortified, I apologized for the fracas, but the editor just laughed and related her own child war stories, which got us both chuckling and in a great mood for negotiating. Getting someone to laugh is always a great icebreaker.

Once the initial small talk phase is over, the editor will tell you how much she likes your book. Thank her for her kind words and tell her how happy you are to hear that because you feel the same way. She may try to feel you out about possible revision work, whether you'd accept that chore, and your only response should be, "Of course. I'm all for making my book better." Once she is assured that you're going to comport yourself like a professional through the book publishing process, she'll likely get down to business, saying something along the lines of, "What do you need for an advance?"

The question might completely throw you. You may have been expecting her to make a concrete offer. Some editors do. But some don't. A general rule in all negotiations is: "The first person to mention a number loses." However, that's not always true.

Don't become flustered.

Your response at this point should be, "Well, what did *you* have in mind for an advance?" This is a wise response because there is the chance she will offer you more than what you would have initially asked for yourself.

If she comes back with, "Well, we were thinking X dollars," you should respond with: "Oh." Then silence.

If the editor doesn't jump back in immediately (everyone hates uncomfortable silences and will sometimes trip themselves up in order to fill them quickly), wait three or four seconds and counter, "Actually, I was thinking twice that."

If she counters with her own silence, hoping that you'll read hostility in it and cave in (hostile silences or faux-hostile silences are the deadliest weapons negotiators use; it's a little game of chicken), don't let it shake you. Remain quiet and wait for her response.

Once you've suggested doubling the offer, you now have a negotiating point to zero in on. Often that will be the number halfway between the editor's offer and your counteroffer.

The editor may well offer only a small increase. Your move is to come down exactly as much as she has come up. Keep this incremental joust going until you find some common ground. She may make some good arguments why she can't pay you the amount you want. Listen carefully to those arguments. She may be telling it straight. On the other hand, she may be taking advantage of your naiveté. Editors can and sometimes do resort to the negotiating tactic known as *ad ignorantium* (statements that are true only to the degree of the listener's ignorance) to get what they want.

As I've mentioned, some editors will simply tell you what they're going to give you for an advance and royalties, and that's that. They may approach you with a no-haggle policy, and if that's the case, you'll find out quickly enough when she refuses to budge on virtually everything. Most editors, however, will play ball with you.

No matter how tense things get, try to remain calm, confident, and completely nonhostile. My rule here is: Make no enemies, make no friends. This is a business transaction, not a criminal trial or a bid for pals. That means you're not fawning or servile, but you're not snide or rude, and you're certainly not chomping a cigar and pounding your fist down on your desk. Think "politely assertive."

If you're brave enough to refuse the first offer an editor makes, you're already doing well compared to other authors. If you can hang on for a second refusal, you'll be entering the league of literary agents, and whatever you obtain for yourself after that point should be considered gravy.

Of course, if you're particularly brassy and you're confident about the value of your book, you may insist on the advance you ask for and nothing less.

Rights

Before you discuss advances and royalties, you should know exactly what "rights" you're allowing the publisher to purchase. (For a more complete outline of the rights an author has in her work, see "The Author's Bundle of Rights" on page 230.)

You could give your publisher the exclusive right to publish in the United States, its territories, and Canada only—although this agreement is becoming increasingly rare. In this scenario, you would retain the right to sell your book to one or more publishers in other countries. According to what you agree to, these foreign publishers might then publish your book in English or in that country's native language.

Granting worldwide English rights along with foreign rights, on the other hand, is becoming more and more common.

"When negotiating with the American publisher," says New York foreign rights agent Dan Bial, "you should have some concept of what worldwide English and foreign rights are worth. And, one way of figuring this is to ask the prospective publisher how many copies he envisions selling and at what price. In many cases, a book will be so American-specific—many books simply don't 'travel' well—these rights will be worth nothing and you won't be able to get an extra dime out of the publisher. Even if the book has foreign sales potential, you might still want the publisher to keep the rights. You'd only want to take on foreign rights if you think you'll do a better job than a publisher," Bial says.

Although it is possible to make these foreign rights sales yourself, most agents would discourage you from the task. Selling foreign rights is expensive and time consuming, and most often results in very limited returns. The general recommendation for an unrepresented author is to let the American publisher have world rights and to have a clause in the contract that secures for you a fair piece of the proceeds.

Of course, just because a publisher retains world rights doesn't necessarily mean an attempt will be made to actually try to sell the book in other countries. Publishers often wait to see what kind of sales develop in the United States before making any concrete plans. Only one in fifty books is ultimately sold in foreign markets.

After the negotiations are complete and the contract signed, don't compare your deal with another author's deal. That kind of exercise will give you no end of grief. Book contracts are all different, and that's especially true in nonfiction.

If you don't get what you dreamed of for an advance, remind yourself that most authors don't. Those six-figure advances make headlines for a reason: They're rare. If you negotiate a fair royalty, console yourself with this reality: There are some actual advantages to that modest advance. To begin with, you'll "earn out" the advance and start collecting royalties much sooner than you would otherwise. This income, paid twice a year, will feel like free money, almost like some sort of investment dividend. To me, it's like forced savings, and it almost invariably arrives in the mailbox just when I really need it. By contrast, a large advance has a tendency to be spent and squandered quickly.

When advances are earned out, publishers are happy. It means they're making a good profit on your book. It means they'll be that much more inclined to give you a whirl with a second book, and you won't be placed on their list of taboo or high-risk authors.

Sample contract

Here's a sample contract I've drawn up to help familiarize you with the basics. The contract is actually a composite of clauses from five different publishing houses.

For space limitations, not everything is covered here. You can receive a sample copy of a fair publishing contract, one of the many benefits of joining the Author's Guild.

AGREEMENT

AGREEMENT made by and between Joe Author who is a citizen of the United States of America (hereinafter referred to as "Author"), his heirs, executors, administrators, successors, and assigns;

And Fabulous Publishing, Inc. (hereinafter referred to as "Publisher"), its successors, and assigns.

The Work
The Author contracts with the Publisher to deliver the following described and tentatively titled work,
Wildest Dreams (hereinafter called the Work):

The completed manuscript for the Work shall be approximately 80,000 words in length and shall be submitted to the Publisher on disk (in a program mutually agreed to by the Author and Publisher) and in hard copy. The text of the manuscript in hard copy shall be an *exact* duplicate of the text on the disk. The hard copy shall be typed correctly, neatly, and doubly-spaced, or in such other form as the Publisher may specify. If the disk submitted is not in the agreed-upon program or otherwise in a format usable by the Publisher, the

Publisher may make arrangements to convert or manipulate the electronic files to make them acceptable and deduct the cost from any sums due or which may become due to the Author. If the hard copy is not in legible condition, the Publisher may make arrangements for the manuscript to be retyped and/or reprinted and shall deduct the cost from any sums due or which may become due to the Author.

This is perfectly reasonable and fair. The author is contracting to deliver a "professional" product, not something the publisher will have to rekeyboard. If you are still pecking away at an old-fashioned typewriter, you'll have to have your hard copy converted to a word-processing file, which can be expensive. In the long run, you may end up spending more on hard copy conversions to disks than you would by investing in a computer.

Delivery and Acceptance

The Author is aware of the publication commitments of the Publisher and that time is of the essence in performing the Author's obligations specified in this Agreement. The Author shall prepare and deliver the Work to the Publisher satisfactory in both form and content, according to the following schedule:

January 1, 2012: the first half of the manuscript;
May 1, 2012: the second half of the manuscript.

Within a reasonable amount of time after receipt of each portion of the manuscript, the Publisher shall either deem it acceptable in form and content or send it back to the Author for revision and correction.

In the event the Author fails to deliver the manuscript on schedule, or the Author fails or refuses to perform any correction or revision of the manuscript within the time specified by the Publisher, the Publisher shall have the right to

terminate this Agreement on 30 days written notice to the Author, in which case the Author shall return all advances paid to date within 30 days of such termination.

This is fair. The publisher goes to work setting up and promoting a book long before the author has finished it. The publisher must schedule advertisements, placement in catalogs, mailings of review copies, and much more and has every right to demand the return of an author's advance if the author fails to deliver a professional product on time.

Sometimes publishers will add a provision allowing them to go to an outside contractor to repair shoddy work that an author cannot repair on his own and to deduct the cost from the advance. That's also going to be fair in most cases. Keep in mind that manuscripts are almost always returned to the author for revision work or additions after the contract is signed. At the very least, authors should expect to be copyedited to ensure that the work is grammatically correct and factually accurate.

Make sure the publisher includes a clause giving you the right to terminate the contract, should the house fail to publish your book by the date agreed upon. If you terminate because a publisher's failure to live up to contractual agreements, the Author's Guild advises that you should retain all rights and all of the advance money.

Permissions

The Author agrees to inform the Publisher of any material created or controlled by others which he or she has incorporated into the Work. The Author will obtain at the Author's expense and deliver to the Publisher, within one month of delivery of the completed manuscript, written permission for any and all such material.

This covers the use in the book of excerpts from the works of others, in addition to photographs, illustrations, maps, charts, etc. Getting permission to use this material should be the author's job.

Grant of Rights

The Author grants and transfers to the Publisher, for the duration of the copyright in each territory granted, the following:

(1) the exclusive right to publish the Work in hardcover and/or softcover book form in the English language and all other languages throughout the United States, its dependencies and territories, the Republic of the Philippines and Canada;

(2) the nonexclusive right to publish, in English in other countries except the British Commonwealth (except Canada) or adapt the Work or any part of the Work for sale, distribution, or other exploitation, in print or in any other form as herein provided;

(3) the right to license third parties to publish, use, or adapt the Work or any part of the Work for sale, distribution, or other exploitation, in print or in any other form as herein provided.

What you retain for rights depends on how likely you are to pursue the outside sale of these rights.

Be sure to include a clause that states that all rights not specifically granted to the publisher are reserved by the author. This may help cover you in case a new technology develops down the road that nobody foresees. You may be able to sell or license your work in a way not yet dreamed of, especially if your book stays in print for a long time. This is especially relevant when considering all the new electronic possibilities that exist today.

Advance and Royalties

In consideration of the rights granted herein and as full payment to the Author, the Publisher shall pay to the Author the following:

(a) $15,000 as an advance against all amounts payable to the Author under this Agreement, payable as follows:

$5,000 on signing this Agreement;
$5,000 on acceptance of first half of manuscript;
$5,000 on acceptance of completed manuscript.

Authors shouldn't expect an advance to be paid in one lump sum. Publishers routinely pay advances in installments to insure that the author delivers his work in a satisfactory manner.

(b) Ten percent (10%) of the Publisher's retail price of each hardcover copy of the Work sold by the Publisher for use or distribution within the United States, or its dependencies, and Canada on the first 5,000 copies sold, twelve and a half percent (12.5%) of the retail price of the next 5,000 copies sold, and fifteen percent (15%) of all copies sold thereafter.

(c) Eight percent (8%) of the Publisher's retail price of each trade paperback copy of the Work sold by the Publisher for use or distribution in the United States, or its dependencies, and Canada on the first 20,000 copies sold, ten percent (10%) of all copies sold thereafter.

(d) Six percent (6%) of the Publisher's retail price on the first 150,000 copies and eight percent (8%) thereafter of any mass-market, rack-size paperback.

These are fair royalty rates, but depending on factors, such as the size of the publisher, the type of book, and the author's track record, these rates may be adjusted up or down. Clauses may also be added that spell out a reduced royalty rate when the publisher makes large volume sales that carry a higher than normal discount, such as sales to businesses which in turn use the book as a premium or an incentive.

Publisher Overstock
Should the Publisher find itself with an overstock of the Work on hand when, in its sole judgment, the demand for the Work would not use up the stock within 2 years, it

shall have the right to sell (remainder) such copies at the best price it can secure. If the Publisher finds it necessary to remainder its entire stock or the remaining copies of an edition which has become obsolete and is being replaced by a revised edition, and if the remainder selling price is less than the manufacturing expense, no royalty will be paid the Author. However, if the remainder selling price exceeds manufacturing expense, the Publisher will pay the Author ten percent (10%) of the actual cash received over manufacturing expense for such a sale. No remainder sale may take place before one year from the date of first publication of the Work in book form, and the Author shall have first option to purchase remainder copies in a minimum quantity of 25 of the Work, at the best price obtainable from any third party or at the cost of manufacture, if there is no such offer.

No author should expect to be paid royalties on books sold below cost of manufacture.

Royalties on Subsidiary Rights
On a license of the right to another to publish a paperback or hardcover edition of the Work, 50 percent (50%) of Publisher's receipts.

This is the traditional split between publisher and author.

On a license to book clubs to produce the Work, either in whole or in condensation, and distribute it to their members: fifty percent (50%) of Publisher's receipts.

This is the right for a book club to produce its own cheaper version of your book. This is the traditional split.

On copies of the Work sold to other book clubs, fifty percent (50%) of the royalty received by the Publisher.

The publisher's own copies sold to a book club for resale. This is the typical split between publisher and author.

On a sale of the right to publish the Work in English outside of the United States, or the right to translate the Work and publish it in other languages, fifty percent (50%) of the Publisher's receipts.

An agent would sometimes retain these rights and then pay a coagent 10 percent to sell the book to a British Commonwealth publisher and then separately to foreign publishers. The author's cost per sale is 20 percent. That is, he'd keep 80 percent of the money instead of—through the American publisher's efforts—50 percent. If you don't have an agent, you can ask for a better percentage from the publisher or you can try to keep these rights and try to make these sales on your own. Be aware, however, that more and more publishers are asking for world rights. And don't forget, as mentioned above, most books published in the United States fail to find overseas markets, for a variety of reasons.

On a sale of First Serial rights to the Work, the Author shall receive fifty percent (50%) of Publisher's receipts.

These are excerpts from your book purchased by magazines, newspapers, newsletters, etc., before the book's publication. Some agents insist that 90 percent of these proceeds go to the author. That may or may not be in an author's best interest. Will a publisher's subrights department even bother to make an excerpt sale if they're only going to earn 10 percent? This one will hinge on how hot a book's excerpts sales will be to periodical publishers and how much the sales might bring.

On a sale of Second Serialization, the Author shall receive fifty percent (50%) of Publisher's receipts.

These are book excerpts sold to a magazine or newspaper after the book's publication. This is the traditional split.

On a license, with the Author's approval, for products or novelties based on the Work, or taking their name from the Work, the monies received shall be divided as follows: eighty percent (80%) to Author and twenty percent (20%) to Publisher.

This would cover anything from bookmarks to coffee mugs to posters to tee shirts. For an author, 80-20 is a very good split.

Audiovisual or audio recording rights to the Work: If such rights are exercised by the Publisher, the Author shall receive seventy-five percent (75%) of the Publisher's receipts.

This is a good deal for the author; a more likely split would be 50-50.

For electronic rights, such as databases, CD-ROMS, on-line Web sites, information storage and retrieval, computer programs, interactive, optical disk and Videotext rights, the Author shall receive fifty percent (50%) of Publisher's receipts.

Electronic rights are currently an unsettled issue because of the uncertainty of the future impact of the electronic—also called "digital"—technology, such as E-books and other devices. Alan Kaufman, a literary agent and publishing attorney, recommends that authors demand the same royalty rate on an E-book that they get from a standard book. At this writing, however, some agents are demanding that E-book rights be licensed as a subsidiary right, from which authors should receive 50 percent of all proceeds. Regular print books sold via Web sites such as Amazon.com should receive full royalties.

For Motion Picture and Television Rights, the Author shall receive fifty percent (50%) of all proceeds.

An author should get much more than this. An attempt should be made to get 90 percent.

Joint Accounting

Any sums owing from the Author to the Publisher arising out of this Agreement may be charged against any sums accruing to the Author under any other agreement.

Tilt! This clause means that the publisher may take royalties owed to you from one book to pay off losses on a previous book or on a future book. This is not fair and is hotly rejected by all agents and writers' organizations. Each book should be accounted separately.

Royalty-free Provisions

(A) No royalty shall be paid on free copies of the Work furnished to the Author or to others for purposes of review, sample, or similar purposes, or on damaged copies sold at or below manufacturing cost, or on copies which are destroyed by the Publisher.

This is fair.

(B) The Publisher is authorized to permit publication of the Work in Braille, or other reproduction of the Work for the physically handicapped without payment or fees and without compensation to the Author, provided no compensation is received by the Publisher.

Nobody argues with this one. It's for a good cause.

(C) The Publisher may grant permission to publish extracts of the Work containing not more than 1,000 words, without compensation to Author or Publisher.

Such excerpts could help sales, or they may be used in a charitable fashion. Some small publications cannot afford to pay to publish excerpts, but even these small venues can help publicize your book.

Copyright

Registration and Notice. Upon first publication of the Work in the United States, the Publisher will insert in every copy of the Work, in the name of the Author, the copyright notice required for protection under the Universal Copyright Convention and will require the same of its licensees and will register copyright for the Work in the United States within 90 days of its publication. The Publisher shall have the right to secure copyright protection for the Work in individual countries other than the United States, whether or not such countries are parties to said Convention.

Authors rarely need worry about copyright. It's all handled by the publisher. Just make sure the copyright is registered in your name.

Revisions, New Editions

When the work is deemed outdated or in need of new, revised, or additional information and when sales warrant such action, the Author shall prepare matter for a new edition and carry out the necessary changes, at the Publisher's request. If the Author is unwilling or unable to prepare such new matter, the Publisher will render the necessary revisions at the Publisher's expense, such expense to be charged against the Author's earnings.

This always seems fair to publishers, but not to authors. This is nearly the equivalent of selling a new book to a publisher without being paid an advance. A request for a new edition means demand for your book is ongoing; that's a good thing. But compiling it without an advance will feel something akin to slavery and your motivation may be lacking. Try to amend this to include the line, "for a negotiable advance against future royalties." I can't give you a hard figure on what's fair because a new edition may include only a 10 or 15 percent change in content. Thus the advance must be figured on a case-by-case basis.

Having an outside party do a new edition for you is fine, but don't expect to earn full royalties for work you didn't do.

Option
The Author agrees to give the Publisher the exclusive first opportunity to consider the Author's next full-length work for publication.

It's usually in your best interest to let your publisher get a first crack at your next book, but do put a time limit on how long it gets to mull over the decision. Insert a clause that says, in effect, that if after thirty to sixty days, a decision hasn't been rendered and negotiations for purchase aren't entered into, you have the full right to pursue a sale with other publishers. If you don't, the publisher can hold on to your second manuscript for a year or even longer. Such stalling gives it time to see how well your first book performs in the marketplace, which is great for them, but awful for you, especially if you're prolific. Do you really want to constantly endure these long waiting periods between the publication of each of your books?

Statements to Author
A. After publication, the Publisher will render semiannual statements of account in the months of March and September covering receipts from sales and licenses of the Work through the last day of December and the last day of June preceding and shall pay with the statement the net amounts due the Author hereunder, subject to the following exception:

(1) Reserves for Returns. To avoid overpayment to the Author and to provide for return of stock by booksellers, the Publisher may withhold a reasonable reserve against the royalties accrued to the Author on all sales of the Work in any of the Publisher's editions. Such reserve shall be withheld for not more than the first semiannual statement following publication of any edition, and any amounts withheld under such

reserve shall be due and payable when they are no longer needed to cover actual or reasonably foreseeable returns and in any event not later than the next semiannual statement.

This is reasonable. Booksellers return books. Sometimes they return a lot of books. You will, therefore, have accrued unearned royalties on such books, which the publisher wisely must account for ahead of time.

Competing Works

While this agreement is in effect, the Author shall not, without the prior written consent of the Publisher, write, edit, or publish, or cause to be written, edited, or published, any other directly competing work or any other edition of the Work, whether revised, enlarged, abridged, or otherwise, nor shall the Author permit the use of his name or likeness in connection with any such work.

Reasonable in most cases. However, think this one over carefully. The words "directly competing" are open to broad interpretation. Does that mean if you've published a cookbook with publisher A, you can't publish a different cookbook with Publisher B? If you can foresee the need for exceptions, by all means try to amend this clause to keep your options open. For example, if your contract is for a book on low-fat chicken recipes, specify in the clause that the prohibition only covers another "low-fat chicken" cookbook.

Publication

A. The Publisher will publish the Work at its expense, except as otherwise provided herein, within three years after acceptance of the completed, acceptable manuscript.

This is awful. Who wants to wait three years to see his book published? At the very least, try to amend the clause to eighteen months. Your publisher may meet you part way and accept two years. The ideal, of course, is one year or less. Still, be cognizant of the different demands posed by certain kinds of books. Some may require a heavy load of illustrations, which may be contracted for separately. Others may be put on hold in order to be released during an optimum period for publicity, say, a year before an historical anniversary. Some publishers simply maintain big backlogs of books, and they can't get to them all in a timely fashion. Publishers' directories often note how long a house typically requires to bring out a book. I always place publishers who routinely need more than eighteen months at the back of my submissions list.

B. The Publisher shall have the right to publish the Work in such form as it deems best suited to the sale of the Work; to fix or alter the prices at which the Work shall be sold; and to determine the methods and means of advertising, publicizing, and selling the Work, the number and destination of free copies, and all other publishing details. All of the Publisher's decisions about format, title, design, editorial style, and production specifications shall be final.

Many authors experience abject disgust over their publisher's choice of cover design. But only name-brand authors with track records and proven big-time profits get to add to a contract: cover art to be approved by author. Of course, if you're bent on getting a great, eye-catching cover, you can always offer to apply a chunk of your advance toward cover art, on approval by you, and see if your editor will bite. What has she got to lose?

First-time authors are particularly sensitive about cover art because they know that many friends and distant relatives who may never actually read the book will, however, judge its quality by its outward appearance.

Use of Author's Name
The Publisher may use the Author's name and likeness or photograph in connection with the advertising and pro-

motion of the Work, and the Author will make himself available, upon the Publisher's request, to publicize and promote the Work at the Publisher's expense.

Promotion is vital, but if you think you'd faint if you were forced to appear and speak articulately on television, you'd better amend this clause to protect yourself. You should never turn down any promotional opportunity, but if you have phobia issues or health issues or child care issues that prevent you from taking part in the book's promotion—and that may include a whirlwind, coast-to-coast book tour with endless radio and TV interviews—be sure to discuss these with your editor. Your reticence to perform publicity won't be met warmly unless you can provide some other means to increase sales, via print media, reviews, or otherwise.

Author's Warranties

A. The Author represents and warrants that the Work is and will be in accordance with the following:

(1) Disclosure Affecting Rights Granted. Unless otherwise disclosed to the Publisher in writing, the Author warrants that:

(a) the Work has not been published in whole or in part;

(b) the Work is not and, prior to the normal expiration of copyright, will not be in the public domain in whole or in part;

(c) the Work is and will be original and the Author is its sole author and creator;

(d) no third party has or will have any claim to or interest in the Work as a coauthor or otherwise; and

(e) the Author has not entered and will not enter into any agreement conflicting with the Publisher's rights with any third party relating to the creation, subject matter, or publication of the Work.

(2) Risk of Liability. The Work will not infringe any copyright, contain any matter that libels or violates the privacy or

publicity or any rights of any person or entity, or otherwise be in contravention of law; and the Author has used and will use all reasonable care in the creation, research, and preparation of the Work to ensure that all facts and statements in the Work are true and correct in all material respects.

(3) Risk of Injury. The Work will not contain any statement, formula, direction, recipe, prescription or other matter that involves a foreseeable risk of injury or damage to the Work's readers or others.

> ●
> "Many authors experience abject disgust over their publisher's choice of cover design. But only name-brand authors with track records and proven big-time profits get to add to a contract: cover art to be approved by author."

(4) Third Party Claims. The Author is not aware of any claim or proceeding by any third party inconsistent with any of the Author's Warranties, and the Author will inform the Publisher if any such claim is made or threatened in the future.

(5) Other Publication. The Author has not published or authorized publication of any work that would compete directly with the Work or materially diminish the value of the rights granted to the Publisher in this Agreement and will not do so during the term of this Agreement.

(6) Cooperation. The Author agrees to cooperate with the Publisher and its insurance carrier in the defense of any claim or proceeding arising out of the Work.

(7) Legal Changes. The Publisher may request the Author to make changes to the Work in consideration of the legal rights of others. If the Author is unwilling to make such changes, the Publisher or the Author may terminate this agreement and the Author will reimburse the Publisher for advances paid to the Author.

The author's manuscript must be original and written by the author, with no parts written by others or considered to be in the public domain or published previously, unless disclosed to the publisher. In short, an author must not infringe on the copyright of another. These clauses also spell out clearly that the book's contents are the responsibility of the author. Anything potentially libelous or inaccurate or that causes a reader harm in any way should be edited out before publication, not after.

Reversion of Rights

The Work shall be deemed "out of print" and discontinued if it is taken off the Publisher's publication lists, and those publication lists of licensees or parties to which the Publisher assigned any of its rights hereunder, for more than a year and is not restored within 90 days after written notice is received from the Author requesting that either the Work be restored to the Publisher's publication lists or that the rights revert to the Author, provided, however, that if the Publisher (or such licensees or assignees) shall have been prevented from restoring the Work to the Publisher's publication lists by fires, strikes, shortages of labor or materials, mechanical difficulties, governmental restrictions, the breakdown of market distribution facilities or other circumstances beyond the Publisher's control, such notice from the Author shall be effective only after the Publisher continues its failure for a period of six months after termination of the circumstances which prevented restoration to the Publisher's publication lists. In the event of such discontinuance, all rights shall revert to the Author, subject to any license, contract or option granted to third parties by the Publisher before the discontinuance and the Publisher's right to its share of the proceeds from such grants after the discontinuance and the Publisher's continuing right to sell all remaining bound copies and sheets of the Work, and all its derivative works, which are on hand at the time of the discontinuance.

> **After the Publisher has discontinued publication of the Work, the Author shall have the right, upon written request, to buy copies of the Work at a price equal to the Publisher's manufacturing unit cost or the best remainder bid, whichever is greater.**

New technology is now allowing publishers to print books "on demand," on a one-at-a-time basis, with virtually no in-print inventory. Consequently "out of print" clauses in most contracts are outdated. With the new technology, publishers can, in effect, keep books "in print" forever. Try to include a clause stating that a certain number of your books (100? 1,000? the number will depend on what is satisfactory between you and the publisher) must be sold each year or it will be officially deemed out of print and the rights reverted back to you.

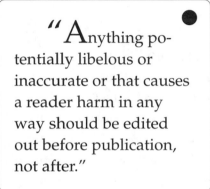

> "Anything potentially libelous or inaccurate or that causes a reader harm in any way should be edited out before publication, not after."

Author's Copies

> **The Publisher shall furnish to the Author free of charge ten copies of any print edition of the Work published by the Publisher. The Author shall be entitled to receive additional copies at a discount of forty percent (40%) off the retail price.**

Unless the book is unusually expensive to produce, I often ask for fifteen hardcover copies. Asking for fifteen to twenty trade paperback copies is also perfectly reasonable. Being able to buy books at a 40 percent discount allows you to sell them in various ways, including back-of-the-room-sales at talks or seminars you present. Profits from sales of this type can be a welcome supplement to an author's income.

Finally, make sure your contract contains a clause allowing you or your accountant to conduct an audit of the publisher's books, relating to the sale and revenue of your book at any time. A recent survey by a publishing accounting firm revealed that publishers commonly make mistakes in royalty statements.

Many writers' organizations, such as the Author's Guild, offer detailed information on book contracts and may even offer model contracts to be used as negotiating guides, one of the many benefits of becoming a member of one of these groups. If you're anywhere close to selling a book, membership in one of these organizations is strongly recommended.

Chapter Eleven

Promotion

Working with your publisher's publicist...Obtaining prepublication blurbs...Promotion to-do checklist...Resources

J ack Canfield's and Mark Victor Hansen's *Chicken Soup for the Soul* books didn't become among the greatest selling books of the century by accident. Nor were they so massively successful because they offered such exceptional reads. They were, in fact, the most heavily promoted titles of the 1990s.

That the original *Chicken Soup* book was peddled unsuccessfully to over thirty-three publishers in New York and 111 more at the American Book Publishers Association convention in Anaheim, California, before being picked up by a publisher only begins to hint at the authors' sharklike marketing aggression. If these rejecting publishers had only known just how much of a push these authors would have given to their own sales departments!

Once Canfield and Hansen had their book in print, they didn't sit back and wait for somebody else to do all the publicity for them. The authors asked hundreds of famous people for blurbs and endorsements. They called all of the large metropolitan newspapers and asked their editors if they would like to do stories on their book. They wrangled spots on every television show that would give them the time of day. They gave away thousands of review copies, wrote articles for newspapers, magazines, and newsletters; they did book signings, radio talk shows at all hours of the day and night (they averaged three to five interviews per day their first year), and even sold their books in gas stations and beauty salons!

Today the *Chicken Soup* series is as popular and recognizable as any franchise. But it didn't happen through luck. It happened through promotion.

Promotion pays. Big time.

Just when you think the work on your book is finally over, when you've researched, written, and revised it ad nauseam and you're chafing at the bit to go on to something entirely new, the promotional and publicity campaign will kick in, and now instead of researching and writing your book's subject to death, you can talk it to death, too.

Although the prospect of becoming pitchmen for their own products is about as appealing to many authors as lancing a boil, it is a necessary evil. Every book published this year competes with 50,000 others published this year, plus all the others still in print. Unless you write a reference book, which buyers will seek out on their own without much of a promotional boost, you must be prepared to launch some kind of publicity scheme to help your publisher move copies.

Depending on the book, the publisher, the personality of the author, and numerous other factors, such publicity may include book signings and readings at bookstores, lectures given at schools and colleges, interviews with newspaper and magazine reporters, appearances on radio and TV programs, plus the writing of media releases and newsworthy articles, the gathering of endorsements and blurbs, the mailing out of review copies, and much more.

Authors are rarely satisfied with the amount of publicity generated by a publisher's in-house publicity department. And, it's no wonder when you consider that some publicists may be publicizing as many as fifty different titles in the course of an average week! Consequently, more and more authors are either hiring their own private publicists (see *Literary Market Place* or the ads in the back of *Publishers Weekly* for leads) or are supplementing their publisher's efforts with their own.

"Your baby in the maternity ward is not going to get all-day care," humorist Jerry McTigue says of the average time a publisher's publicist can spend on any individual title, pointing out the dire need to get in the promotion trenches yourself.

Although I can't recommend such supplementation highly enough, great care must be exercised in coordinating promotional efforts with publishers. You may not only end up duplicating their efforts, for no gain, you may end up causing mass confusion.

The first step is to find out the name of your publisher's publicist,

> ## Self-Promotion, for a Successful Author, is a Way of Life
>
> "You can't count on publishers to do any promotion. School visits sell lots and lots of books as do other personal appearances. My website, designed by my son, also sells lots of books."
>
> —Vicki Cobb, *Science Experiments You Can Eat*

get her e-mail address or phone number, and start talking. Once you have a clear idea of the media outlets she plans to contact with your book, you may launch your own publicity campaign with all those outlets she overlooks. (And there will be plenty, don't worry.)

Before your manuscript even goes to the printer, one extremely worthwhile thing you can do is to contact well-known authorities or celebrities in your book subject's field and ask if they might be interested in reviewing your work and supplying blurbs for the front and back covers. "Blurb" is publishing lingo for a testimonial. Here's one from my *Roget's Super Thesaurus*:

> **"It has one drawback. After I found the word I was looking for, I could not stop browsing. I kept finding more interesting words and phrases that kept leading me to other interesting words and phrases in which I began to fear was a never-ending cycle! This thesaurus is a pleasure to use...an extremely useful and wonderful literary tool."**
>
> **—M. L. Godshalk**
> **Professor of English, University of Cincinnati**

People who have never supplied blurbs before are often thrilled at the opportunity to have their names and recommendation plastered across the cover of someone's book. It's a fun, status-building thing to do, so getting someone to do the hours of reading involved is easier than most writers think. Roughly half the people from whom I request blurbs respond favorably.

Still, your request must be worded delicately, without the slightest hint of presumption or sense of entitlement. You must acknowledge the big investment in time you're requesting—that you will certainly understand if the authority can't help, for whatever reason, and that he may feel free to dump the manuscript in the nearest trash can if he is so inclined.

> "Promotion pays. Big time."

Small gifts are nice as inducements. (A signed copy or two of the finished book is appropriate.) You can even offer cash. But be careful. Paying for a glowing blurb crosses the ethics line. Simply ask your authority for his honest opinion of your book, and if that happens to be a glowing one, might he supply a blurb to that effect?

Getting prepublication blurbs serves many purposes. They buy your book not only credibility but an aura of worthiness, especially if you're an not an established authority on your topic. Publishers' sales people are impressed by blurbs. So are bookstore owners and acquisitions librarians, not to mention the ordinary bookstore customer.

To get the blurb above, I simply consulted a university directory and contacted those professors whom I thought might be appropriate candidates. (See chapter 5 for ideas on where to contact experts.)

After sending your blurbs on to your editor or publicist (he'll be delighted by your extra effort), your next step will be to get a firm idea of when your book's pub (publication) date will be. Once you have a firm commitment from your editor, you can plan to mount a publicity assault in earnest. Here is a checklist of just a few of the things you can do to dramatically increase your sales, starting now.

Promotion checklist

✔ *Write media releases.* The 1,500 daily and 8,500 weekly newspapers in this country are always hungry for news. The features editors at Sunday newspapers are highly receptive to stories gleaned from book authors. Magazine editors are constantly on the lookout for anything from interesting feature material, including book excerpts, to short fillers.

Think hard about the contents of your book and try to zero in on a newsworthy angle. With my evolution book, *The Beast in You: Activities and Questions to Explore Evolution,* I wrote a media release that served as a rebuttal for the Kansas School Board's decision to drop evolution from its required curriculum in 1999. The media release featured statistics on how ignorant the American mainstream was about evolution and gave a brief rundown on some of the vital science on which Kansas students would be missing out. The timing was nearly perfect and captured attention for my book that never would have happened without the accompanying controversy.

If you've written an exercise book, you might write a media release on how most people perform exercises incorrectly and risk injuries. If you've written a history book, you might be able to pinpoint a dangerous correlation between a past event and one that is happening today. If you've written a book on developing better relationships, you might write a release revealing how to make friends easier and deepen our intimacy with our spouses.

Your media release should sound more like a news story than a pitch for your book, otherwise, news organizations will toss it in the trash can, along with the hundreds of other book pitches they receive every week.

One trick to making a release sound like news is to interview yourself and "quote" yourself liberally. News outlets will either quote your release directly or call you for a more in-depth interview. Here's a portion of my release for *The Beast in You:*

For Release: Anytime

Permission is hereby granted to reprint all or part of this release with or without permission from the author or publisher. This media release is available via e-mail. Marc McCutcheon is available for interviews via e-mail at DMMcCutc642@cs.com or by phone at 555-555-5555.

SHOULD YOUR CHILD BE TAUGHT EVOLUTION? FINALLY, A GUIDE FOR PARENTS

True or false, evolution has largely been debunked, and scientists are more and more accepting the Bible's literal interpretation of how life was created?

Despite polls showing that nearly 50 percent of the American population reject evolution, the answer is a resounding "false."

Marc McCutcheon, science writer and author of *The Beast in You*, a hands-on guide to evolution for children aged 8 to 12, says if you're debunking evolution with your child, you're doing him a tremendous disservice.

"Knowledge of evolution is vital throughout the school system and particularly at the college level. You simply can't learn biology and many other disciplines without a firm grounding in evolutionary principles," he notes.

Of the school board decision to eliminate evolution from the curriculum in Kansas, McCutcheon sounds a familiar refrain: "They might as well have thrown out slavery or the Constitution from United States history classes."

McCutcheon says he wasn't surprised by the move, however. When he visited his local bookstore looking for a book on human evolution for his children two years ago, he was dismayed to find what he calls a "yawning black hole." A bookstore manager told him, "People aren't interested in children's evolution books, so we don't stock them."

"I found the same hole in every bookstore I visited," McCutcheon recalls. "Books on human evolution were conspicuous by their absence. It was like this passive censorship thing. Here in the bookstore aisle were more than 50 titles on dinosaurs and space and not one on Darwin or Neanderthal Man."

McCutcheon was shocked to find just three modest children's titles on human evolution in print, with three times as many "creationist" books actually tearing down Darwin.

The dearth of "real" science books in the market yanked the former science reporter for *Omni* and other science magazines from reference books (*Roget's Super Thesaurus*, among others) back to science writing in a hurry. "As a book author, my mantra is always, if you see a hole, fill it. But this wasn't just a hole, it was a bomb crater."

Of the century-long battle over teaching evolution versus not teaching evolution, McCutcheon observes, "Sometimes

Sex and Promotion *Both* Sell

Self-styled sex expert Laura Corn self-published *101 Nights of Grrreat Sex*, the first of her many sex guides, and sold 525,000 copies. Such healthy sales don't happen on their own. Corn has appeared on more than 1,000 radio shows pitching her books nationwide.

we tell our children what we *want* to believe, not what is. But telling your children that we descended from Adam and Eve without Darwin is the equivalent of telling them that two plus two equals five or that the Holocaust never happened. It comes down to telling the truth."

The question for parents is, should we tell the truth?

"Evolution can be an unpleasant reality," McCutcheon says, "but we can't make it go away through denial or any other form of mental contortion. The Emperor is unequivocally naked, and most kids, even though they may not say so, quietly notice in time."

And how have his own children, aged seven and ten, reacted to his book? "They didn't suddenly revert to apelike behavior and start swinging from the trees," he says, "because they were already doing that. But, really, their ethics and morals didn't disappear. They were simply deeply fascinated. They wanted to know where we came from and how we got here. That's something we all want to know more about."

McCutcheon says there is one very compelling reason evolution (and not creation science) is taught in all of the secular universities of the world and most nonsecular ones, including Brigham Young and Notre Dame. It's neither conspiracy nor dogma, McCutcheon says. "The evidence for evolution has simply passed the peer review process in literally tens of thousands of studies, while creation science has not."

Varied Promotion Works Best

"Promoting a cookbook involves making all kinds of appearances—conferences, private groups, cooking schools, benefits, relevant trade shows, and all the TV and radio you or your publicist can drum up. I also promote by writing articles on the book's subject and through my web page. I think web promotion will become even more important as more and more folks go online."

—Nancy Baggett, *The International Cookie Cookbook*

That particular release actually went on in detail for another two pages, offering media outlets all kinds of juicy fascinating facts, statistics, and so on. It's wise to limit your release to three pages or under, however, as few editors have the time to read everything you send and may be too time pressured to even consider anything that appears voluminous.

When you send out a media release, send a review copy of the book or a picture of its front cover with a card the receiver can return requesting a review copy. Also, send a page of your prepublication blurbs and quotes from reviews to show editors that people are raving about your book before it has even hit the stores. How much effort and money you want to risk up front is up to you.

A variation of the standard media release is a Q & A. This is also a newsworthy release, but it takes the format of questions and answers fielded by you.

Another variation is a Top Ten List. The subject matter of some books obviously won't lend itself to creating a newsworthy top ten list, but if you've written, say, a guide on gardening, you could draw up a list of Top Ten Perennials, or Ten Best-Loved Roses or Ten Ways to Control Bugs Without Pesticides. Of course, you'd work the title of your book into the release.

✔ *Write your own book review.* Write a two- to three-paragraph review of your book. Be descriptive, succinct, and don't tout your own writing. Just present the facts. Some of the magazines and newsletters with smaller circulations will actually use your review exactly as you wrote it. Most readers are never the wiser.

You can write media releases, book reviews, and other promotional material anytime, but the timing for mailing them out to the media is critical. Newspapers may work your material into the paper in as little as a week, while magazines may have a six-month or longer lead time. Make sure you time your material so it doesn't appear in print before your book is available in stores. There's nothing worse than wasted publicity. Remember, in most media venues, you'll only be given one shot at publicity, and you may not have another chance for a year or more, if at all.

Media releases on paper are still acceptable but some media outlets like to see releases on diskettes. Whatever you do, don't overwhelm editors with too much material on any single submission. It's much wiser to send your material in convenient units, say, a generic media release, bio, and request for a review copy card first, followed a couple of weeks later by, say, a "Top Ten List," a "Q & A," a book review, or even a second media release focusing on another aspect of your book.

Follow-ups are important, because just as people often reject sales pitches the first time around, a certain percentage will weaken the second, third, or fourth time around. Pitch as often as your energy and money allow, and newspaper and magazine editors will eventually bite.

✔ *Write an op-ed piece.* An op-ed piece is a column or essay in which you state your opinion and make important observations on the news. A typical column is between 500 and 800 words in length. In newspapers, op-ed pieces appear "opposite" the "editorial" page. However, that doesn't mean your opinion must oppose that found on the editorial page. All that's required is a sharply and intelligently written article that ties in to recent developments, the more controversial the better.

If anything in your book can be tied in with current events, you've got a shot at the op-ed pages. Although writing such a column is no walk through the park, the effort can score some fabulous free publicity. Even though you may not actually mention the name of your book in the column, the newspaper's editor almost always will do so in the short bio that is often run at the end of these pieces. Many newspapers have circulations from 20,000 to 1,000,000, so even if only 1 percent of the readership seriously considered buying your book, your investment would pay off.

Timing, again, is everything. As soon as a story you can comment on breaks in the news, call or e-mail several newspapers and ask them if they'd be interested in seeing an op-ed piece. Don't delay. News stories grow stale very quickly. Likewise, editors' interests change as frequently as the tides.

Find out about submission requirements before you sit down to write. Ask about prescribed lengths, manuscript mechanics, hard copy or disk, and whether you should submit by e-mail, fax, or snail mail.

When sending media releases or other stories to many newspapers at one time, you can address them to the appropriate department (food editor, city desk, etc.) instead of addressing an editor by name. Editors move around a lot. Sometimes they go on vacation or call in sick. Addressing a department instead of an editor assures that your material will be seen by the appropriate person in a timely manner. (Note that this is the opposite of what you want to do when sending a query or proposal to a book publisher, where you *must* get the editor's name and use it.)

Check your public library for a copy of *Bacon's Newspaper Directory*, which includes listings for editorial/opinion pages nationwide.

✔ *Write letters to the editor*. Lots of people read these. In newspapers with average circulations, you'll most certainly be reaching thousands or tens of thousands of readers with your words. This is a great place to sound off on your topic and quietly plug your book.

✔ *Produce your own interview on your local public access channel.* You could be a cable star! Well, at least you can get some free publicity. Get someone with good verbal skills to interview you. Because you'll be the producer, nobody will limit how many times you can plug your book! Contact your local cable company.

✔ *Post a website.* These may not generate a lot of sales directly, but they can generate requests for interviews, readings, and other public appearances. "I think a website is a necessity if you want to offer updates, as I do, or if you want to connect to your readers through newsletters and discussion groups," says Jean Armour Polly, author of the popular *Internet Kids and Family Yellow Pages,* now in its fourth edition. "My website gets many hits, and it's linked around the world. I think it has helped to drive sales and interest."

As do many authors with websites, Polly, who is the original coiner of the phrase, "surfing the Internet," has an Amazon.com associates link on her site to sell her books. "We aren't making a lot of money," she admits, "but it's enough to make the program worthwhile, a few dinners out every quarter." Contact Amazon.com for details.

✔ *Get a nice review at Amazon.com.* How's that, you say? If you've got associates who have professed to love your book, why not ask them to actually post their glowing review at Amazon.com and the other major online bookstores? "Sometimes I send a free copy of a book to influential people and ask them to please write a signed review of it on Amazon.com or another site in return," says Jean Polly. Cheating? Not if the reviews are honest!

✔ *Sponsor contests or annual polls and surveys and send the results to the media.*

To promote it's book *Hi! It's Me ,Your Dog!* by Emmy-winning journalist Lisa Mendoza, Quill Driver Books held dog photo contests at over thirty Borders superstores. Local news coverage of these events brought in scores of photos and hundreds of books were sold because of the attention the book received. The media love these events. Just make sure you're accurate and fair.

✔ *Send review copies and brief, fascinating excerpts to radio and TV talk show hosts.* Think it's unlikely a national talk star would read excerpts from your book on the air? You may be surprised. Johnny Carson not only read some of the fascinating facts from my book, *The Compass in Your Nose & Other Astonishing Facts About Humans,* on air on *The Tonight Show,* he spoofed it with some silly facts of his own!

Psychologist Joy Brown also read excerpts from the book between call-ins on her radio show. Talk hosts are always looking for something interesting to talk about to fill air time, so if you've got something provocative or funny or just plain amusing in your book, send it in.

✔ *Present seminars or workshops.* Not only is this a great way to get a following, back-of-the-room sales during a break or after the presentation are an effective way to sell books. Since authors usually are allowed to purchase their own books at the same discount a retailer gets, many authors use back-of-the-room sales to augment their income. Many actually make more money selling books this way than they do in royalties. As an added bonus, the publisher normally pays full royalties on all copies of the book the author buys on top of allowing the retailer's discount.

✔ *Do book signings at bookstores.* I placed this one last because the consensus among many authors is that signings often sell too few books to be worth the time or trouble. "The only appearances that I don't really think usually pay off are book store signings," says best-selling cookbook author Nancy Baggett. "Unless you're a celebrity, people just don't respond."

Every well-traveled author—even best-selling authors—have stories to tell about the times no one showed up for a signing except the bookstore staff. Yet, when promoted correctly, signings have benefits beyond the actual sales made during the signing. Often the signing provokes a feature article in the local paper, and, if it doesn't, most papers have event calendars that give the author's name and the book's title as well as the time and place. Even if readers don't attend the signing, reading about it in the calendar is one more time they have been exposed to the book's title. Some will look for the book the next time they are in a bookstore, others, spotting the book in a store will think to themselves, "Hey, there's that book I've heard about." Librarians may make a note to order a copy.

Another benefit to signings is that the store often promotes the book in-house by bringing in extra copies for the shelf, building a display, putting up signs, and mentioning the book in the store's newsletter. All of these help to promote the book and impact sales, but one of the most important things that happens with a signing is that the bookstore staff is introduced to both the title and the author.

Word-of-mouth is the best salesman and nearly every time a bookstore staff member suggests your book, you'll get a sale. One clerk in a store in San Francisco sold over 1,000 copies of a book she liked just by mentioning it to her customers. You can bet if a staff member you've met and befriended gets a request for a book on your book's topic, she'll recommend yours.

But signings don't have to be just signings. The most effective ones are those to which collateral dimensions have been added. Promote your signings as talks and give your talk some snappy title like "Ten Ways to Make Your Lover Smile" or "Things the IRS Doesn't Want You to Know." At the very least, announce that you'll be happy to answer questions.

Another good idea is to promote that you'll be handing out something free. This could be a list of helpful hints, samples made from the recipes in your book or instructions on how to build some item for the house or yard.

Promotional resources

Here are some great promotional resources to investigate. For even more ideas, get a copy of *1001 Ways to Market Your Books* by John Kremer. It is the *must-have* promotional guide of every nonfiction book author. Another that shouldn't be missed is *Jump Start Your Book Sales*, by Marilyn and Tom Ross.

• *Gebbie Press* (gebbie.com/). Maintains a great website providing free links to most of the radio, TV, magazine and newspaper websites and databases nationwide. Its all-in-one directory (not free) features listings of 23,000 TV and radio stations, newspapers, magazines, news syndicates, and more.

• *Radio-TV Interview Report* (rtir.com), Bradley Communications, 135 E. Plumstead Ave., Box 1206, Lansdowne, PA 19050-8206. Phone: 610-259-0707. This is an eighty-page publication that sells ad space to authors, celebrities, and experts who wish to publicize their availability for interviews on radio and TV programs. The magazine is sent to about 4,000 producers nationwide. Humor writer Jerry McTigue swears by it. "I landed 200 interviews by being in there," he says. *Chicken Soup's* Jack Canfield and Mark Victor Hansen are equally emphatic about its effectiveness. "We've done several things for marketing which worked well and advertising in *Radio-TV Interview Report* was one of the most effective tools we used."

• *C-Span2's BookTV.* Bookworms adore this programming marathon, and no wonder; it's forty-eight hours of books and authors, from 8 A.M. Saturday (EST) to 8 A.M. Monday. There are loads of author interviews, readings, book signings, book release parties, and more. If your book falls anywhere under the categories of biography, history, politics, social issues, or other "serious" nonfiction, you've got a good chance of getting on. You can e-mail the producer at booktv@c-span.org or call 202-737-3220. Visit the website at booktv.org.

• *How You Can Get On Radio Talk Shows All Across America Without Leaving Your Home Office.* A very useful guide and directory to the who and how behind phone-in radio talk shows, written by Joe Sabah, who has, as of this writing, appeared on some 629 such shows pitching his book, *How to Get the Job You Really Want and Get Employers to Call You.* He charges $99 for his book, database of 700 talk shows, and mailing labels; if you land just one radio interview from it, it's a bargain. Check out his website for more info, plus *10 Radio Talk Show Interview Tips.*

(members.aol.com/talkshows/); e-mail: JSabah@aol.com; phone: 800-945-2488.

• *Bookflash.com.* For a fee, this website will showcase your media releases, archive them indefinitely, and then forward them to thousands of reviewers, editors, newspapers, magazines, librarians, and retailers.

• *PartyLine, The Weekly Roundup of Media Placement Opportunities* (partylinepublishing.com). A newsletter with the inside dope on how to attract the attention of TV and radio programs, magazines, and newspapers and who to contact for interviews. A recent sample issue gave the names of who to call to get on Bryant Gumbel's *The Early Show*; ABC's *Good Morning America*; NBC's *Today Show*; Fox's *Queen Latifah Show* and *Martha Stewart Living*, Talk Radio's *Bob Dornan* program, and about thirty other venues. At this writing, subscriptions run $180 per year. Phone: 212-755-3487.

• *Inside Borders.* A free monthly, fifty-page magazine featuring a wide variety of books sold at Borders bookstores nationwide. Included are book reviews, author interviews and profiles, and articles on everything from reading to publishing. Customers typically pick up their free copies at the checkout. For a shot at getting your own book profiled, contact Beth Fhaner, editor, *Inside Borders,* 100 Phoenix Dr., Ann Arbor, MI 48108. Phone: 734-477-1100.

• *The Publicity Hound* (publicityhound.com), 3434 Country KK, Port Washington, WI 53074. Phone: 262-284-7451. This is a bimonthly newsletter featuring tips, tricks, and tools for obtaining free or almost-free publicity. "During twenty-two years in the newspaper business," says editor Joan Stewart, "I have seen many people literally beg the media to pay attention to them, but they fail repeatedly because they don't know what the media want or how to give it to them." The newsletter includes information on how to prepare for interviews with reporters, establishing strong media relationships, and clever marketing and promotional ideas. $49.50 for six issues.

• *National Directory of Newspaper Op-Ed Pages*, Marilyn Ross, Communication Creativity. Call 800-331-8355. A great resource by the always thorough Ross.

• *The National PR Pitch Book*, InfoCom Group. This bills itself as "the most accurate, in-depth, up-to-date directory to the nation's leading editors, reporters and producers." The directory includes complete contact information, including direct phone, fax and e-mail, plus detailed advice on how journalists want to be pitched. InfoCom Group publishes lots of directories and books to help authors score publicity. Check out the website at infocomgroup.com or call toll free at 800-959-1059.

• *Book Marketing Update*. A newsletter of book publicity opportunities edited by book marketing superstar John Kremer. Absolutely fabulous. Open Horizones, P.O. Box 205, Fairfield, IA 52556. Kremer's website, bookmarket.com, offers a host of useful free information and you can sign up for a free e-mail newsletter.

David Hornfischer, coauthor of *Mother Knew Best* and *Father Knew Best*, says the biggest mistake of his publishing experience was "relying on the publisher to do all the publicity." His feelings are shared by thousands of other publicity-poor authors.

Get yourself out there. Knock on doors. Sign books. Get some air time. Peddle media releases. Write an op-ed or two or three. Then do it all again. *It's the cumulative effort that moves books; there is no silver bullet.* The time to begin your work is long before your book's pub date. Think promotion. Plan now.

Chapter Twelve

Lean and Mean:
The Secrets to Full-Time Writing Success

It's a business…1,000 words a day…Focus…
A writer's checklist for success

I've been writing for twenty-eight years, making a solid, full-time living for sixteen. My apprenticeship was long. But it didn't have to be.

My desire from high school onward had been to become a full-time writer, yet I never believed deep down that I could actually achieve it. Looking back, it's little wonder.

My work habits were erratic, sloppy, inefficient, and capricious. I had no concrete business plan, no chart of short- and long-term goals. Failing to study the market, as everyone advised, I employed a buck-shot strategy of diversification, writing poetry, then science fiction, then health articles, then novels, then joke books, then science news, then back to poetry, and maybe a song or two, taking no real aim toward any one category or genre.

I worked only when I felt like it, waiting, stupidly, for inspiration before lifting a finger. Or, I looked for a million-dollar idea to fall into my lap.

Editors and agents sometimes told me that my writing "had no market" or that it needed work, yet I had no idea what either of these meant. So I made the same mistakes over and over again, month after month, year after year, never once asking (or *paying*) a professional to point out and help me correct my shortcomings.

I treated writing as a hobby, not as a business, and I made almost no money at it. Needless to say, I could never have supported myself on my writing income.

I was, to borrow my neighbor's favorite phrase, *young and dumb*.

Fortunately, I've grown up a bit, and what a difference a little maturity makes.

Today, I easily support my family of four, working part-time. I sit at my desk roughly four mornings per week. The rest of the time I putter in my garden or go hiking or play ball with the kids or dabble in screenplays or play a round of golf or lie on my hammock and read a good book. That is my life, as I write this, and the nice thing is, *I don't even have to work those four mornings per week. I only do it because I enjoy it.*

I boast only to illustrate where you can find yourself if you treat your writing like a business. It makes, quite literally, the difference between financial security and financial bust.

So, how does one treat writing as a business anyway? Over the years, I've made lots of mistakes. I'll tell you what those are, so you won't repeat them. I've also developed good working habits (which I don't always have to use now). I'll tell you what those are, so you can repeat them, again and again.

In fact, here's a checklist to help you succeed.

The writer's checklist for success

✔ *Set aside a set number of hours per week.*

This is your job, your business, your livelihood. Don't treat it like your stamp collection and don't expect to love every minute of it. If you write only when you "feel" like it, the odds are high that you'll never finish a single project. With no boss to peer over your shoulder and no customers or clients coming through the door every fifteen minutes to keep you on your toes, you must find a way to keep yourself honest. That's where the next item comes in.

✔ *Write 1,000 words a day.*

"One thousand words a day" is a tenet that writers have been sharing with one another for decades, perhaps for centuries. Shakespeare no doubt lived and breathed by this rule. I'm certain every successful writer today swears by it.

In a nutshell, you cannot quit work for the day until you've completed at least 1,000 words of writing—and ideally, that's finished writing, revised, polished, and put to bed. One thousand words per day is 5,000 per week, 20,000 per month. Keep to the schedule and in three and one half to four months, you'll have a complete book. Some writers push themselves to do 1,500 words a day or more. That's perfectly sensible: Some books are far easier to write than others.

The 1,000-words-a-day rule works because it not only gives you a

---

Writing is a Business

"If you want to write for publication, you have to treat it as a job. You wouldn't go up to your boss and say, 'Hey, I'm sorry, I'm just not motivated to make that sale today.' That isn't acceptable. Why, then, should we consider it acceptable to say, 'Oh, I'm blocked. I can't write anything today'? Business is business, and you work until you get a good product."

—John Gilstrap

---

concrete goal, but it provides an incentive: If you complete the 1,000 words early, you can take the rest of the day off!

It's important to make a big deal out of the 1,000-words-a-day rule. Write it up in block letters on a poster and hang it over your desk. Repeat it aloud like a mantra before you begin work in the morning.

When you start to feel sorry for yourself, think of the work ethic of the late Isaac Asimov, author of more than three hundred books. "I can write up to eighteen hours a day," he once said. "Typing ninety words a minute, I've done better than fifty pages a day. Nothing interferes with my concentration. You could put on an orgy in my office and I wouldn't look up—well, maybe once."

Unfortunately, while you slog away on completing those 1,000 words, the home environment is going to distract and endlessly tempt you. Maybe not with orgies, of course. But….

Relatives arrive at the door for a surprise visit: four hours of work time, *poof!* The children get into a scrap and you feel the need to settle it: a half hour, *zing!* You reach a difficult bit of writing and suddenly a messy house looks far more appealing and compels you to pick up a broom and a duster: two hours, *bom!* Your phone rings; you answer it and take a message for a family member. Twenty minutes later, your phone rings again; you answer. Another message. Fifteen minutes later it rings again; you answer again. By the end of the day, you've spent twenty-five minutes taking messages, *gazongk!*

A daughter needs you to fix the basketball hoop: fifteen minutes. Your wife needs you to watch the kids while she goes grocery shopping: one hour. A neighbor tempts you with nine holes of golf: two hours. The doorbell rings…the toilet overflows…the dog vomits on the new carpet….

And it goes on and on and on with virtually endless variations.

Working at home is not the insulated Shangri-la many people think it is. It is loaded with conflict. Labor versus domestic life. Domestic life versus labor. It's the kind of conflict that just doesn't happen in those swank offices in downtown Manhattan.

When I first began writing full-time, these clashes not only drew me away from my desk again and again, but they put a serious dent in the patina of that beloved slogan, *Home Sweet Home.*

Home sweet minefield was more like it.

My wife and my children and I fought. *A lot.*

The work-at-home brouhahas threatened not only my marriage but my livelihood as a writer. How could I possibly make a living if I was continuously yanked away from my desk for every little domestic contingency?

The answer is, I couldn't.

One of the most common traps that springs from working at home is the "flexible" schedule you think you're entitled to. You can work mornings five days a week, midafternoons seven days a week, overnight, graveyard shifts, three thirteen-hour day shifts, every other hour, or every other week, and so on. To make matters worse, every schedule is interchangeable with all the others, and the temptation to mix-and-match is irresistible.

If you live alone, *under a rock,* with no obligations to anyone, you can get away with working when you feel like it. Otherwise, you can't. You just *can't.*

The trouble with a flexible schedule is, *nobody knows when you're working*. Nobody knows when you're going to work and nobody knows when you plan to knock off. If your spouse can't plan on when exactly you'll be working, she can't plan her week. When can she count on you to do your share of the child care, for example? Is it fair to expect her to wait until the last minute to find out? What about friends or neighbors or outside family members who want to socialize with you? How are they supposed to know when they're being rude by calling you at this particular moment when you seem to work all the time one week and never the next? What about your son who wants to play ball? Why are you working when everybody else's dad has been home from his job for hours?

To avoid these kinds of conflicts, you must, at the very least, have a rough schedule that the people near you can count on. For me, it's mornings. My wife knows that four designated weekday mornings are *mine.* They must not be interrupted or interfered with. Yank me away from my desk for any other reason than a broken bone or a tax audit and I will grow fangs to rival a saber-toothed tiger. When I'm at my desk, with my office door closed, my wife must never approach me with the water bill, ask me to watch the kids so she can get her hair done, remind me that the trash is overflowing, or try to get me to plan our vacation destination. I am at work. During this time, I tell my wife to pretend that I'm away, employed at Microsoft, with Bill Gates, a horse-whip in one hand and a cattle prod in the other, glaring over my shoulder. Would she approach me with such domestic problems in that situation? I think not!

That's how seriously family members and friends must take your work. That's how seriously you must take the need for a set schedule.

The second horn of this dilemma is that devil, temptation. Hmmmm, should I write another page or watch *Dr. Phil?* What about that Stephen King novel that's been calling to me from the couch? Hey, doesn't the garden need weeding? Ooh, is that the ice cream truck I hear coming up the street! What a nice morning for a walk on the beach!

Heed your 1,000-words-a-day rule. And get your work done early.

✔ *Don't diversify too much.*

Remember the cliche: Jack of all trades, master of none. Success hinges on knowing deeply your niche markets: the publishers, the editors, the competing authors, the trends, the fads, the sudden opportunities, the books that have done well and the books that have bombed.

Pick one major and one minor, and, perhaps, one minor-minor subject area. Learn these niche markets as if your every breath depended on it.

Get copies of the catalogs of publishers who publish your field of books. Get to know what's been done, what's being done, and what still needs to be done.

✔ *Look hard for a series.*

Look first and foremost for a subject which you're passionate about and which offers the opportunity for a potential series. Landing a contract for a series is, aside from obtaining a berth on the best-seller lists, the crown jewel of writers' goals. Any size series is a good size. Three. Six. Ten. Kenneth Davis signed a contract to write twenty books in the *Don't Know Much About* series! Talk about striking gold.

A series relieves you of researching and writing new queries and proposals to publishers. By eliminating those time-consuming tasks, you drop perhaps a third of your workload as an author. What's more, you'll be vanquishing the unknown. For several years—or perhaps for the rest of your life—you won't have to worry about what your next book will be, how or if you'll sell it, and how much money—if any—you'll make in any given year. You'll have a very good idea of what your work schedule will be like, what your income will be, and what you can expect for difficulties.

Series' authors build their audiences book by book. A reader buying one title will often go back and buy another in a series, and another, and another. That increases your overall sales, reduces the publisher's marketing costs, creates a brand-name following, and makes everyone happy.

A superb example of a hot nonfiction series is one that people give each other as gifts at Christmas or on birthdays. *Don't Sweat the Small Stuff* and its spin-offs were quintessential gift books. So were *Life's Little Instruction Book* and its spin-offs. Both of these series gave great advice, but equally important was the easy reading perception they projected with their bite-size chunks of wisdom. It was precisely this perception that made them great gifts for people who don't ordinarily read books and helped propel them into the stellar sales brackets.

Think niche! Think series!

✔ *Write the definitive book in your field.*

Once you've landed a contract, write the unequivocal standout title in your field. Do not write the weakest book. Do not write a good book. Do not write an acceptable book. Write the best book.

Write the book that will stand head and shoulders above the competition, a book that reviewers will call the definitive guide and thus compel librarians the world over to purchase not one, but multiple copies and bookstore owners to stock entire shelves full of it. Write the book that will compel talk show hosts and newspaper editors to clamor to interview you. Write the book that will lead book clubs to an automatic decision to buy in mass quantities. The definitive title is a no-brainer for booksellers; it is a title they must have in volume.

Never mind that your competition already went an extra mile. You're going to go an extra mile and a quarter.

Yes, doing the additional research will be tiring. Yes, tracking down that hard-to-find expert will be troublesome and time-consuming. Yes, making your book just a tad more comprehensive and a tad more sharply written than the competition will test your resolve. But the reward *will* be worth it.

When you write the *best* there is, the publishing house will be behind you with its promotional and advertising dollars, the critics will be behind you with their praise, the librarians and booksellers will be behind you with their purchase orders, and your family and friends will look upon you with newfound respect and awe.

Writing a great book buys you instant credibility as an author. Thereafter, the doors of publishing will swing wide open to greet your future writing projects. People will listen to you. Editors will write you personal letters. You'll have your pick of agents, who will be scrambling to get you instead of the other way around.

In 1998, the editors at Amazon.com voted my *Roget's Super The-saurus* among the "Top Ten Reference Books," not only of 1998, but of the previous several years. I've been reaping the benefits of that praise ever since, in increased sales and in a nice inner glow of pride.

Finally, and perhaps most important, your book is not only going to sell well right out of the gate, it's going to do something most books do not—it's *going to stay in print*. Month after month. Year after year. Maybe even decade after decade!

Staying in print is money in the bank. Twice a year you'll be rewarded—and sometimes richly so—for going through that extra trouble, and you'll be *so* glad you did.

✔ *Feather your nest.*

Running out of office supplies provides too convenient of an excuse to abandon your writing for the day. *Twice per year, s*tock your office with six months of supplies. That includes stamps, envelopes, priority mailers, disk mailers, print cartridges, paper, pens, and floppy disks. The store you patronize should be one of those giant warehouse establishments, like Staples. My local, upscale office merchant sells my favorite paper for fifteen dollars per ream. My local Staples sells it for four dollars. If you're buying a six-month supply of paper at once, that's a nice savings.

Once you get the supplies home, place them all within easy grasp, not scattered all over your house. I try to keep twenty pens in my penholder. Pens, like socks in the dryer, have a tendency to migrate to some mysterious land of the lost. Time spent hunting for a pen adds up over the course of a year. Plus, little irritations like this can be amazingly stressful when you couple them with all of the other little irritations.

Line your office with back copies of magazines and newsletters in your field of interest (I've subscribed to *Writer's Digest* for twenty years and have collected enough back copies of *Publishers Weekly* to dam a river), plus up-to-date dictionaries; encyclopedias; histories; quotation compendiums; guides to writing, publishing, and publishing contracts; publishers' catalogs; etc. The goal is to find facts fast, with a minimum of interruption or hassle and to avoid making trips to the library. A good reference library of your own will eventually save you hundreds of hours worth of drive time and dozens of hours on the Net.

You'll need a filing cabinet. As your business grows, you'll need a second and a third. *File*—don't leave stuff spread out on the floor or under your desk or shoved in a drawer. Pawing through drawers and cabinets and shoe boxes for an important document can burn up minutes of precious time and, if you have to go on the hunt several times a year—which you will— you'll burn up hours.

When I was starting out, I had virtually no filing system; there were times I spent as long as three hours turning my house upside down in search of some important newspaper clipping or manuscript. It takes less time and trouble to file and label properly than to launch search and rescue missions every time you need something, believe me.

> "Yes, doing the additional research will be tiring. Yes, tracking down that hard-to-find expert will be troublesome and time-consuming. Yes, making your book just a tad more comprehensive and a tad more sharply written than the competition will test your resolve. But the reward *will* be worth it."

A wonderful piece of equipment I use in addition to filing cabinets is a compartmentalized shelf. Mine has twenty-four spaces exactly the right size for holding manuscripts. Over the years, I've generated stacks of book drafts, plus bits and pieces of manuscripts that never quite got off the ground but may in the future—Voila!—into the slots they go. These pigeon holes are also great for holding newspaper clippings, photos, and various research materials.

A desktop wire rack or shelf is great for holding letters or any kind of document that you may need to consult frequently. "In" and "Out" holders keep things nicely organized.

Cheap office equipment is amazingly easy to find, and a sharp entrepreneur should insist on nothing less than bargains. My first desk was an old wooden door laid out on milk cartons. Talk about having plenty of elbow room! Later I found a horizontal bookshelf system, which was clean and in perfect condition, at the local dump. I set the unit up at the back of my door-desk and filled it with reference books and manuscripts. The two looked custom-built for each other! At a yard sale, I found a filing cabinet and paid five dollars cash for it. At a secondhand shop, my wife bought me an office chair for a quarter of its original price. Eventually, I picked up my huge metal desk—a 1960s relic—for nothing. Someone put it in his front yard and placed a sign that said, FREE FOR THE TAKING. I put it on the roof of my car, with no help, and drove it home.

Need I go on?

Because I don't entertain the public in my place of business, my equipment only needs to be practical, not pretty.

Stay away from office furniture stores. You'll be sorely tempted to spend princely sums on an integrated desk unit with all of the nooks, crannies, and pigeon holes. If you truly want a fancy-looking office, use that desire as an incentive to finish and sell your first book. Then give yourself permission, after that first book sale, to go out and splurge. With each new sale, feel perfectly justified to buy a shiny new piece of equipment if it makes you happy. But don't buy it all *before* you get started. Right now, your goal is maximum efficiency and cost control.

If you're in the market for a computer, resist the urge to buy something with more features than you need. Your most important computer needs are a fast modem for quick Internet surfing, a good word-processing program and lots and lots of memory. Don't agonize over your choice of word-processing programs. Most handle the job admirably, and due to nifty file conversion programs, most publishers can accept files created on nearly any word-processing software.

The experts tell me that secondhand computers are often perfectly reliable, especially considering that many people are trading up every two years. You can buy one of these two-year-old computers at a quarter of the cost of a new unit. On the other hand, new computers are so cheap now, that secondhand doesn't always make good economic sense.

Similar rules apply to printers. Prices have plunged in recent years, but even so, don't be tempted to buy more machine—with more features—than you need. The most important features to look for in a printer are print speed (you don't need the fastest on the market, by any means, but you don't want the slowest, either), reliability, jam prevention, and envelope printing. Check out the prices for a printer's print cartridges before buying—you may be in for a horrifying shock. The price of print cartridges alone may determine which unit you'll want.

✔ *Plan tomorrow today.*

At the end of your writing shift, draw up a list of things to do the next working day. Pretend that this is a directive written by your boss, and consider it your mandatory assignment. With a to-do list, you can schedule your time and plan ahead.

✔ *Avoid the "nothing to do" illusion.*

You should never have *nothing* to do just because you're waiting for a publisher to reply to a query. That may be the biggest sin that all new writers commit. There is *always* something more to do, something that will either make you more efficient later, increase your odds of a sale, or propel you forward in your career. These are just a few of the things to do when you think you're out of writing assignments:

- Send out additional queries and proposals.

- Brainstorm new book ideas and make a list of possibilities.

- Immediately start another book project. (You should know what your next book project will be long before you've finished your current one.)

- Research avenues for publicity.

- Contact people for additional endorsements.

- Draw up a master list of book reviewers who would be interested in your book.

- Write press releases for book reviewers.

- Print out a supply of self-addressed return envelopes and stamp them for use as future queries.

• Clip articles in magazines, newspapers, and newsletters for use as research for your next book.

• Order publishers' catalogs and study them.

• Read *Publishers Weekly*.

• Read the latest issue of *Writer's Digest*.

• Visit your local bookstore for ideas and to see what's selling well.

• Visit the websites of writers' organizations that interest you and that may contain leads for new work or book ideas. (Avoid "chatting" online, as it often burns up tremendous amounts of time, with nothing to show for it.)

• Add new names of editors, agents, publishers, reviewers, etc. and their addresses to your contact management software.

• Write an article to send to a magazine.

If you were attracted to writing for the downtime, think again. If you want your business to thrive, there is no such thing as downtime until you've put in an eight-hour day or written 1,000 words and attended to the things listed above.

✔ *Use a home office.*

Don't even think about renting a place to write. But, you say, you don't have room for a home office? Many successful authors don't. For years, I used a corner of my bedroom. A few years ago I graduated to a walk-in closet with a window. What luxury! Others build a little cubby hole in a garage or up in an attic. Some keep it really simple and use a kitchen table.

A rental office may cost anywhere from $300 to $1,500 per month. A home office will cost you nothing and, if you use it exclusively for work, you can usually write off its cost on your taxes. (Consult the IRS or your accountant for the latest rules.) This is a no-brainer.

Now, having said that, although cheap is good, know when to draw the line. I've found that having sunlight come into my office is extremely important for my mood. I simply can't work in a window-less cellar. Many people feel the same. A gloomy work space is depressing. Sunlight is as important as air to breathe; psychological studies on clinical depression and SAD (seasonal affective disorder) prove it.

Musty isn't good, either. Neither is dirty. Make your office a pleasant refuge—light-colored walls, pictures of attractive scenes, quiet background music—and you'll be much more apt to spend more time working there.

They say patients in a hospital room with a nice view recover faster than those in a room with no view. I can't help but believe the same factors come into play concerning a writer's productivity.

✔ *Learn how to use all of the features of your computer.*

You may be content just to learn the basics of your word-processor program, but you'll reap greater benefits and end up saving lots of time by becoming familiar with all the other neat office functions—graphic design, spreadsheet, contact management—your computer can do. Commit one day each month to learning one new feature. It will be well worth the effort.

✔ *Get connected to the Internet.*

No author should be without this vital connection. Today, the Internet is as critical to an author as a word processor. If you're writing nonfiction books and you're not on the Internet, you're pedaling a bicycle at the Indy 500.

In what is an ever-growing marvel to me, I find I now conduct more than half of all of my book research over the information super-highway and only rarely visit my local library. With free search engines, such as Alta-Vista, you need only key in your subject, say, "space," and you'll find yourself connected within seconds to websites for NASA, the Hubble Space Telescope, the Jet Propulsion Laboratory, Lick Observatory, the Planetary Society, literally hundreds of sites—all providing juicy and, often, up-to-the-minute information. You also have access to hundreds of magazines and virtually tens of thousands of magazine articles on virtually every subject. I promise you that, no matter how obscure your subject may be, you'll find websites for it and at least a magazine article or two.

I once had to find out when the pencil was invented and mass-produced. I simply typed "history of the pencil" into a search engine and was immediately directed to a website that not only had all of the answers I needed, but directed me to a book which I could order written entirely about the pencil. I found what I needed in *less than two minutes*. I would have spent more time just driving to the library.

> "Get connected to the Net. No author should be without this vital connection."

Internet browsers allow you to "bookmark" a website so you can get to it easily the next time you need it. This is tremendously helpful. With every book project I tackle, I compile an online reference library of websites to access with a touch of a button.

E-mail has shaved my correspondence time with editors by weeks or even months. We routinely e-mail contractual matters, editorial questions, copies of manuscripts, and so on. Once you've developed a relationship with an editor, e-mail can even be used to send casual queries. "Hey, have you guys ever thought about doing a book on…?" Having an e-mail address makes you easy to contact. When an editor comes up with an idea for a possible new book, it may be you whom she approaches rather than a rival without e-mail.

I routinely e-mail experts in the field I'm writing about. These experts may be located anywhere in the world. Using e-mail, I can quickly approach university professors, doctors, scientists, heads of organizations, and even other authors. These experts verify information, provide quotes, check my manuscripts for accuracy, and sometimes even supply blurbs.

I once e-mailed a paleoanthropologist who had just found a pre-human skeleton halfway around the world, and I asked him if I could get a photograph of the find for a book I was writing. Within hours, I had the photograph. In the past, such a task would have taken weeks of airmail correspondence.

✔ *Take all of the tax write-offs due you.*

During the year, keep sales slips for every writing-related purchase, whether it's for paper, reference books, print cartridges, or a new modem. Many sales slips contain a printout of what was purchased and on what date. These are great for record keeping. For those slips with only a cash amount, write on the back what was purchased and the date. Keep all sales slips, receipts, and check stubs in safe storage until tax time. Detail all transactions in a ledger, either paper or on your computer.

Here's a list of things you may be able to deduct from your income, provided they were purchased and used for business.

• Trade magazines

• Magazines and newsletters used for research or source information (If you're a science writer, a subscription to *Science News* would be fully deductible.)

• Books

• Software used for business purposes only

• All office supplies

• Fees for interview subjects, fact checkers, etc.

• Home office (It must be used exclusively for business and not double as a rec room or clothes closet. Consult the latest IRS rules on this one; it can be tricky. The IRS website is irs.ustreas.gov/. Request the publications, "Your Federal Income Tax," "Tax Guide for Small Business," "Business Use of Your Home," and "Self-Employment Tax.")

✔ *Be prepared for droughts.*

The nonfiction book business, like any other entrepreneurial endeavor, is prone to occasional droughts. I once survived a twenty-six month period when I made no new book sales. Fortunately, I had prepared for such a shortfall by socking away plenty of money. Plus I had a solid income of royalties from past books to provide a safety net.

If you expect and plan on dry spells, you'll be less likely to panic when they hit. Believe it or not, these down times are actually *good* for you, because the lack of money is a tremendous motivator. If you let yourself get lazy or slack, a drought will put you back on track in a hurry.

To prove it, consider that my own drought ended with the arrival of five book contracts in a span of less than six months! Those contracts didn't materialize out of thin air. They were the result of some serious scrambling on my part.

Writing full time is constantly challenging, make no mistake. But I've never found any other line of work nearly as rewarding. I feel like a businessman, yet I have no storefront or factory. I feel like a scholar, yet I have no degree. I schmooze (well, at least online) with illustrious editors at world-class publishers, yet I'm home and instantly available when my family needs me in a crisis.

All this while sitting in my power jammies! Could any job be as delicious as this?

Chapter Thirteen

A Grab Bag of Tips

Beating the block...Entitling titles...
Writing tips...Finding more time to write

Block out writer's block

 W hat if you can't get as far as the rejection process because you're too mired in writer's block to even produce anything?

Writer's block is almost always caused by one of just five things:

- A lack of belief in your ability to write and ultimately sell the work

- Lack of adequate research material with a struggle to invent "filler" out of thin air

- An unrealistic demand for perfection on your initial drafts

- Exhaustion

- Lack of passion for what you're writing

Let's look at each of these problems in detail.

A lack of belief in your abilities can stymie not only the effort necessary for finishing a book, but that even needed to begin. Before you jump in, you must believe that you can pull off your project or it will be doomed from the start.

Contrary to what some "feel good" psychologists might advise, it's impossible to gain confidence simply by telling yourself over and over again that you're a competent writer and that you deserve to be published. That's as realistic as waving a magic wand over your head and expecting Stephen King to emerge through your fingertips.

Self-Doubt is Self-Defeating

"The greatest block to any writer is self-doubt. This inner demon nags, criticizes, calls us names, and undermines our faith by focusing on our weaknesses instead of building our strengths. Self-doubt drains our creative energy, sends us into self-perpetuating negative spirals that can plunge us into depression. The best defense against it is recognition and deflection. At the first sign of this pest, do something constructive. Say a prayer, invoke the muse, repeat an affirmation, seek support from other writers…. The best way to grow as a writer is to write."

—Diane Dreher, *The Tao of Womanhood*

In the real world, we gain self-esteem and confidence through a cycle of effort, failure, practice to overcome that failure, and, ultimately, competence. In the case of a beginner, small, incremental steps in the direction of competence is all that's needed to get and keep that confidence ball rolling.

Unfortunately, if you're a beginner, it is hard to know when you're achieving competence without some form of outside affirmation, which is precisely why you should *never* write an entire book without first getting feedback on your idea and, perhaps, your first chapter or two. Once you've heard from a professional, an editor, agent, or nationally published author—not your neighbor, work buddies, or Mom—that your project appears viable, your confidence level will immediately soar. That reassurance that you're onto something can be terribly exciting and will help propel you through the challenging work ahead.

Even with this affirmation, you won't exactly lose all those awful voices of doubt in your head, whispering incessantly to you that *you're wasting your time…you're never going to finish this…this will never sell…your writing stinks…you're too stupid to be a writer.*

So here's something practical to tell youself when you find you are stuck on the first page: You're not writing an entire book right now.

You're writing a query letter or a proposal and first chapter or two to test the waters *first*. Now, is that so intimidating?

Still lacking confidence?

A good way to gain confidence *and* win some credibility with editors is to write a few articles for magazines. Feature articles are often a hard sell, but newsbreaks—short 200-300-word pieces on health, science, or other subjects—are really quite easy and pay well, often one dollar per word or more. Check the magazine listings in *The American Directory of Writer's Guidelines* or *Writer's Market* to see who is buying what. I started my writing career writing such newsbreaks for *Omni* and other science magazines. Magazine publication can do wonders for your resume. In your book proposal, you can say something like, "I have written pieces on everything from singing planets to flying robots for *Omni* and several other national magazines."

Article writing forces you to learn how to research, how to contact and interview national experts, and how to write concisely. A single page of a book is no more complicated than a 500-word article. So if you can master a short piece and get it published, you can write a book and get it published. And, the great thing is, you'll *know* it.

Lack of adequate research material. Major symptom: You don't know what to write and you feel as if you're ad-libbing on paper. If you've got plenty of material—statistics, medical studies, anecdotes, quotes from experts, descriptions, directions, and so forth, you'll never have this problem. You only need to organize it all into a sensible sequence and start reporting it all.

An unrealistic demand for perfection on first drafts keeps many writers in unnecessary shackles. Because they don't achieve an acceptable level of brilliance in the initial draft, they manage to convince themselves that they never will. A word from Ernest Hemingway should clear matters up:

"The first draft of anything," he said, "is shit."

Did you hear that, fellow suffering authors?

If Hemingway produced such first drafts, please give yourself permission to do the same. Just call your first draft the crap draft. Tell yourself "it is going to stink—it is *supposed* to stink."

Exhaustion. You can't write when you're exhausted. You simply won't have the ability to concentrate. Stop when you are fatigued. Get some rest and start again when you're fresh and wide-eyed.

A lack of passion for what your writing will stop you cold every time. That's why it's critical to write what intensely interests you. Passion is fuel. If you try to write something strictly for the market and have no interest in the topic, you're going to have a tough time of it. You'll very likely run out of motivation before you're halfway through.

Finally, remember that writer's block is almost always kept at bay by momentum. Because beginnings and first pages lack momentum, they can be notoriously difficult to launch. Yet once started, the work almost invariably gets easier, usually within just a few minutes. Try to begin your first half hour each day with something easy—a simple passage or a light revision of what you wrote the day before. Never stop writing for the day at a dull or difficult passage. That's an invitation to writer's block tomorrow. Always leave in the middle of an exciting or easy piece of writing. You'll approach your next writing session with joyful anticipation, not dread.

Equally important: Don't allow a research question to stop your writing cold. When you're going full speed and suddenly encounter something that must be looked up, simply write in "to be added later" and continue. Research should be done before or after a writing session, *never during!*

Blocks or any other kind of procrastination should never keep you from writing for more than one hour. If you're truly stuck, you can do something that works almost every time for me: I abandon my 1,000-word-a-day rule and tell myself to simply write *one page for an entire day's work*. One page is remarkably unintimidating. It never ceases to amaze me how quickly it cuts through the worst of my procrastination ploys. Tell yourself that even if one page is all you can handle on a daily basis, you'll still manage to write an entire book by year's end! One page is not frightening. It can sometimes mean as little as thirty minutes' work.

Look at the Trail, Not the Summit

Starting a 300-page book project can be like standing at the foothills of Mt. Everest. Don't keep looking up to see how far away the peak is. Think only of the hummock in front of you. Work one chapter at a time. A chapter is usually no more than twenty to thirty pages. If that's still too intimidating, divide the chapters into segments and focus on one segment at a time. Don't worry about the next segment until you've scaled the one facing you now.

Once you've stacked a few pages of finished work next to your word processor, you'll gain confidence, and you can gradually bring yourself back to the 1,000-words-a-day rule. Believe me, it's much better to drastically reduce your workload and intimidation factor than to get bogged down in a writer's block that perpetuates itself for months at a time and keeps you from producing *anything*.

Use your thesaurus liberally

If you think your mind is as good for discovering synonyms as a thesaurus, try this test. In two minutes (it actually takes less than that to consult a thesaurus entry), write down all the synonyms you can for *walk*. Now, check to see how your list compares to that found in a comprehensive thesaurus:

> stroll, hike, tramp, amble, pad, march, promenade, hoof it, traipse, step, stride, wend one's way, go on foot, perambulate, shuffle, mosey, waddle, toddle, saunter, strut, swagger, tiptoe, edge along, inch along, creep, lurk, slink, prowl about, troop, parade, stagger, falter, totter, lumber, hobble, limp, plod, shamble, trudge, slog, sidle (through a crowd), bull one's way through, take mincing steps, pick one's way along, negotiate around, bushwack, blaze, stalk out, storm out, stomp out, backpedal, retrace one's steps

Be aware of your moods

Never revise or reread a manuscript when you're in a bad mood. When you're depressed, everything looks awful, including your writing.

Join a critique group

Much can be learned from comments of writers and would-be writers. Join a writer's group. Read and critique and be critiqued. Don't go to a group to be told how wonderful your work is. Go to be told how *bad* it is and why.

Make a loud noise softly

When writing, be assertive, be passionate, be provocative, but present your case with facts, statistics, and anecdotes. Don't be obnoxious or insulting or you'll just come off as an angry, loudmouthed fool.

Don't be blind to political correctness

Your editor may ask you to cut or change "delicate" passages in your book that may be deemed politically incorrect, racist, misogynic, bigoted, ethnically offensive, or libelous. Even if you disagree with these changes, often you'll be wise to give in. Such material may jeopardize sales or tempt lawsuits.

However, political correctness is not always best. In my *Everyday Life in the 1800s* book, an editor pressed me to delete all references to the word "nigger" because, he said, it was highly offensive. The word, I argued, was also part of our history, and you can't or shouldn't expunge history; so it stayed. Not a single person wrote or called me to complain after the book was published.

When my *Roget's Super Thesaurus* began gaining a reputation as the "thesaurus with the most eye-popping swear words and terms," my editors asked me to tone down the second edition and remove some of the most offensive words and slang. I balked at first because, in my opinion, language should never be censored. But when I learned that many school libraries (perhaps hundreds or thousands) might not buy a copy because parents might object, I saw the light and acquiesced.

Even though I was proud of having the thesaurus with the most "honest" language on the planet, I wasn't willing to lighten my wallet because of it.

Don't react reflexively to an editor's request to make cuts or to tone down volatile language. Think it over carefully and discuss the pros and cons.

Use cooling off periods

Let your manuscript "cool off" in a drawer for at least two weeks before reading it for weaknesses. Every day you wait, you'll gain critical objectivity to help you revise more acutely.

Carry a notepad at all times

Ideas can strike anytime but will often be forgotten unless written down promptly. Always carry a pocket notebook and keep one by your bed at night.

Consider employing a book doctor

If your proposal or manuscript is faulty and you're unsure how to go about correcting it, you may want to seek out a book doctor or freelance editor. These professionals charge anywhere from $1-$5 per page, or up to $100 an hour, depending on the length and difficulty of the project. Most book doctors are competent. I've seen a few perform miracles. Of course, as in any group, a few are nincompoops. As I mentioned previously, I once received a sales brochure from an editing service that contained no less than four grammatical errors! No thanks!

You can find a book doctor or editing service in the ads at the back of *Writer's Digest Magazine*. The magazine has a reputation for fielding complaints about its advertisers, so anyone who is grossly incompetent or shady is unlikely to have a continuing ad.

Revise and rewrite

There are no great writers—only great rewriters.

Rewrite. Revise. Edit. Cut. Rearrange. And don't be shocked or consider yourself untalented when you have to toss out entire chapters and start all over again. It happens to the best authors.

Read *The Elements of Style* by William Strunk, Jr. and E. B. White and *Getting the Words Right*: *How to Rewrite, Edit and Revise* by Theodore Cheney. Study them. No need to take night courses or to get your degree in English composition. These books are all you need.

Hone your titles

As any agent or editor can tell you, beginning authors almost uniformly have zero talent for inventing book titles.

My hunch is that authors spend the least amount of their creative time trying to come up with something catchy, thinking incorrectly that the content of their manuscript is far more important. Quite the contrary, the title is, far and away, the most critical piece of writing you'll do in your entire book. Without a sharp title, neither agent nor editor may give your manuscript a second thought before scratching off a rejection slip.

Titles sell books. A book with a great title will far outsell a book of equal caliber with a poor title. That's why agents are always trying to get their clients to think harder about titles. That's why editors sometimes meet with the entire publishing and marketing teams to vote on them.

"I take pride in my titles," says Vicki Cobb, author of the bestselling *Science Experiments You Can Eat* and several other highly successful kids' books. "Coming up with a good title, one that intrigues or captivates the reader, is much like writing poetry. The essence of the adventure that is in the book has to be summed up in as few words as possible. It can sometimes take me months to come up with the right title, but when it's right, it grows on me."

This is a woman who knows; she had no fewer than eight books slated for publication when I last spoke to her, including *Squirts and Spurts*, a book about—guess what—shooting and spraying water!

"A title should just grab you and concisely summarize what's inside," says Jerry McTigue, who saw a fabulous opportunity to turn the string of rejections for his book, *Don't You Just Hate It When…*into a sale by cleverly changing the title to *Life's Little Frustration Book*, thereby riding the coattails of the massive best-seller, *Life's Little Instruction Book*. Brilliant!

The single greatest shortcoming of amateur titles is that they almost always sound academic. In my agency, I saw piles of manuscripts with titles similar to *Preventing Unhealthy Stress Levels* or *How to Control Negative Emotions*. In a crowded field, no editor or book buyer would likely look twice at these books. However, if you renamed them, *Don't Sweat the Small Stuff* (*And It's All Small Stuff*) or *Anger Kills*, you'd get his undivided attention. These titles have bite; they say it all without resorting to worn-out words which produce all the flavor of unsalted cardboard.

Some titling tricks are always in vogue: The words "Top Secret," "World's Best," "The 100 Top," and "The Complete Guide to..." are perennial attention getters, as are clever turns of phrase such as *Woe is I*, and shockers such as *How to Shit in the Woods* (*yes*, that's a real title, and it sold like crazy). Drama sells, of course. Exaggeration and hype also help.

How would you improve the following title to make it leap off the cover at a casual glance?

Changing Christian Modalities to Improve Church Attendance in the 21st Century

If you were author John Shelby Spong, a bishop and a master at eye-opening titles, you hit potential book buyers over the head and call it *Why Christianity Must Change or Die*, and you would give it not one, but two illustrative subtitles: *A Bishop Speaks to Believers in Exile: A New Reformation of the Church's Faith and Practice*.

If *that* doesn't pique most Christians' curiosity, nothing will. The book, of course, turned out to be a best-seller, and you can bet that the title gets part of the credit.

Spend time on your title. Don't settle for the first one to pop into your mind. I always think about my titles for weeks, sometimes drawing up lists of dozens of possible candidates. I do the same for subtitles.

How effective can a title change be to your marketing luck? My second book, *A Dictionary of Descriptive Terms,* was rejected twenty-two times but caught the attention and bids from two editors the month after I changed the title to *Descriptionary.* I had the same experience with my first book, *Human Being,* which was rejected seventeen times before it was finally accepted as *The Compass In Your Nose and Other Astonishing Facts About Humans.*

A Rose by Any Other Name...

An interesting book entitled *The Birds and the Bees* was originally rejected by editors. However, it went on to become one of the most popular sex books of all time when it was retitled *Everything You Wanted to Know About Sex But Were Afraid to Ask.*

Let's do a little exercise. Which titles sound more tantalizing? Which, if you were an editor, do you believe would sell more copies?

Excellent Restaurant Recipes or
   Top Secret Restaurant Recipes
Guide to Good Grammar or
   Woe Is I: The Grammarphobe's Guide to Better English
A History of Bad Judgment in Criminals or
   America's Dumbest Criminals
How to Make Extra Large Cookies or
   Monster Cookies
Guide to College or
   Been There, Should've Done That: 505 Tips for Making the Most of College
Golf Fundamentals or
   40 Common Errors in Golf and How to Correct Them
A Fisherman's Tragedy or
   The Perfect Storm
How Men Can Improve Sexually or

How to Satisfy a Woman Every Time
Religious History of the Irish **or**
      How the Irish Saved Civilization
Guide to Enhancing Your Appearance **or**
      1001 Beauty Solutions
The Healthy Personality Profile **or**
      Are You Normal?
Contracts for Writers **or**
      The Writer Got Screwed (But Didn't Have To)
How to Entertain Your Children **or**
      365 TV-Free Activities You Can Do With Your Child
Are You Dumb and Southern? **or**
      You Might Be a Redneck if...

If your book idea isn't getting the attention with editors and agents you think it deserves, try tweaking the title. Sometimes a simple sharpening of the title is all it takes to land a sale.

Now, as I promised at the beginning of chapter 7, here are some amazingly simple but effective writing tips.

Be specific

Specific verbs paint vivid pictures; general verbs paint vague ones. Avoid writing, *The man went through the mud*. Instead try, *The man squelched through the mud* or *The man slogged through the mud*. Take a look at the lines below. Which verbs are more vivid?

The woman went up the mountain.
The woman inched her way up the mountain.
A dog was by the door.
A dog sniffed at the door.
The car came to a quick stop.
The car squealed to a stop.
The child had difficulty breathing.
The child wheezed.

Use the same rule of specifics for nouns.

> **The dog ran after me.**
> *The Doberman ran after me.*
> **She parked the car with utmost care.**
> *She parked the Rolls Royce with utmost care.*

Be imaginative

Beautiful brown eyes are nice, but they barely register on a reader's imagination scale. Go deeper; think specific; think fresh. Great descriptive terms take effort. How about eyes the color of *autumn leaves?* Or eyes as *deep and brown as the Mississippi River?* Can't think of anymore? How about these: *acorn; biscuit; bronze; burnt almond; camel; dirt road after a summer rain; dusky; dusty; earth; ebony; elk; fawn; fox; Grand Canyon; grizzly bear; hawk brown; hazel; burnt honey; leather; mahogany; mill pond; moccasin; molasses; Nubian; nut brown; olive; raven; Rio Grande; russet; sandy; sorrel; sparrow brown; tarnished penny; tawny; umber?*

Cut away ugly fat

Place these words above your writing desk:

"Cutting Sharpens"

Try for a high ratio of ideas to words:

> **In the blinking of an eye, Mary then jumped out of her seat.**
> *Suddenly, Mary jumped from her seat.*
> **She didn't pay the slightest attention to him.**
> *She ignored him.*

Needless words dilute prose and dull comprehension. Lose non-essential words.

The adjective is the enemy of the noun. Dump every one you can. The adverb is the enemy of the verb. Dump them, too. Regard anything you think as clever with suspicion; it's probably purple prose.

How much can you cut the following sentence and retain all of its meaning?

Personally, I have always wondered how in the world long-distance marathon runners could hold out for as long as they do without collapsing.

How about:

Where do marathoners get their stamina?

Hook first, explain later

Start the first chapter of a narrative by opening in the *middle* of a crisis or conflict. Once the reader is intrigued, you can use chapter two to clarify and set down explanatory details.

The opening is no place for endless blocks of exposition. Pull a trigger and let the reader hear the boom. For example, if you're writing a book about hiking in the wilderness, you might start with a chilling anecdote about a bear attack or of a hiker getting himself hopelessly lost. A "you are there" description of a hike through exceptionally dramatic scenery might work. Avoid beginning with the banal and the boring.

Vary sentence lengths

Uniform sentences bore. See how they bore? There is no change in rhythm. They are the same. They are predictable. Surprise the reader. Keep the reader guessing. Sprinkle your prose liberally with medium sentences like this one. But be sure to add a long sentence and an even longer one every now and then to keep the reader wondering when it is going to end, because it is quite monotonous to read "See Spot run" sentences one after another.

Write vividly, not pompously

Use common words unless an uncommon word is either more precise or more colorful. Your goal as a writer is to communicate, not to show off.

Rarely acceptable:
  The farmer warned that the stalls were mephitic.
Occassionally acceptable:
  The farmer warned that the stalls were odoriferous.
Always acceptable:
  The farmer warned that the stalls stunk.

Words are especially objectionable when they're obscure, like "mephitic."

Rule of thumb: Key your word choices to your audience.

If you are writing for the average reader, avoid sounding academic. If you're using terms that sound pompous, technical, or dry, replace them with more casual words.

Uncommon words may be used when the reader can discern their meaning from the context in which they are used. Here's an example:

Most mountains are simply too steep for straight up-and-down trails, thus most hikers are grateful for *switchbacks*.

Research the proper terminology of a thing before you describe it. A mountain lake is called a *tarn*. High altitude air is *rarefied*. A mountain pass is a *col* or a *defile*. A zigzagging trail up a mountain is a *switchback*. If you always use the most precise word, your writing will resonate with authority.

Kill cliches

If you've heard it three times or more, discard it. Cliches are like wet firecrackers: Every one is a dud. Surprise readers with the unexpected.

Weak: **They were slower than molasses.**
Better: **They were slower than a tax refund.**

Spare the qualifiers

Avoid qualifiers. A loud noise is plenty loud to the reader; making it a *very* loud noise only adds an unnecessary word. If the noise truly is profound, use a *bone-jarring* noise or an *ear-piercing* noise.

Weak: It was a pretty warm day.
Better: It was a warm day.
Weak: The food was rather tasteless.
Better: The food was bland.

Use not, not

Avoid writing what is "not." Put statements in the positive form.

Wrong: He was not often funny.
Right: He was rarely funny.
Wrong: It was not a good day.
Right: It was a lousy day.

Combine setting with action

Stand-alone settings slow the pace of a narrative. To keep things moving, weave glimpses of setting around a character's actions.

Weak: The road was a bad one. It was loaded with chuckholes and loose rocks and wound narrowly up a steep hill. The Public Works Department should have been advised of this road. With the rain, it is was even worse. Still, Jonathan made it safely to the highway.

Better: The Ford's headlights cut shallowly into the storm. Jonathan thrust his head forward, squinting. *Thunk.* His left tire hit a chuckhole. *Thunk,* another, even bigger one. *Thunk. Thunk.* The Ford bounced crazily. An exposed stone scraped off a piece of muffler. The old motor roared. He yanked the column shift into first gear and braced himself as the car reached an uphill grade. The tires whined as they spun and slopped through the mud. Finally, he topped the rise, the headlights falling to illuminate the safety of a four-lane highway.

Use exclamation points sparingly!

Exclamation points make writers sound like amateurs! Often, their effect is comic, not dramatic! Don't forget this!!!

Use dialogue qualifiers with care

Resist the urge to write, "'You did a wonderful job,' she *praised*." "'I love you so much,' she said *lovingly*." "'I hate your guts,' he stated *hatefully*." State the obvious with your sentence, not with the qualifier.

Avoid needless sentence openers

Avoid starting sentences with "There is," "There are," or "It is." They're almost always superfluous.

> Weak: There is a mountain called Bald Peak just west of here.
>
> Better: Bald Peak Mountain is just west of here.
>
> Weak: There is no point in getting angry about things you can't change.
>
> Better: Getting angry about things you can't change is pointless.
>
> Weak: It is always a good idea to take an umbrella with you on an overcast day.
>
> Better: Taking an umbrella on an overcast day is wise.

Don't needlessly preface sentences with lines like, "It is interesting to note...." or "It is in my humble opinion that...."

> Weak: It is interesting to note that roses require large amounts of water.
>
> Better: Roses require lots of water.

Weak: It is in my humble opinion that our football team would be better served with a bigger center.

Better: Our football team needs a bigger center.

Rearrange words for maximum impact

The most powerful word in a sentence is the last one. Which of the following two sentences do you find most effective?

When she died, she was lamentably young.
She was lamentably young when she died.

Eliminate, cut, slice, or trim redundancies

Avoid redundancies. No need to write *small in size. Small* says it all. A *record* is no greater if it is an *all-time record.* To *merge together* is to *merge.* That *unexpected surprise* is no more unexpected than a *surprise.* The *reason why* is either the *reason* or *why* but not both.

Mind your who's and whose

Don't make the common mistake of confusing *who's* with *whose. Who's* is a contraction for *who is* or *who has. Whose* is the possessive form of who and which.

Who's (who has) got the flashlight?
Whose flashlight is this?
A man *whose* time has come.

Steer clear of "personally"

The word *personally* is almost always unnecessary.

Weak: Personally, I couldn't care less.

Better: I couldn't care less.

Weak: Speaking personally, I wouldn't have done it that way.

Better: I wouldn't have done it that way.

Finding More Time to Write

Writers who hold down a 40-hour job and raise kids complain that "there isn't any time to write." But you can always find at least some time, if you really try. Here's how:

• Eliminate TV-watching. Or at least eliminate an hour per day. Think about how many non-crucial, inane, noneducational programs you watch in a week. If you're like most of us, you can make some big cuts here.

• Take a half an hour for lunch instead of an hour.

• Get up thirty minutes earlier in the morning, preferably before everyone else is up.

• Plan your time more carefully and consolidate your errands into a single trip.

• Cut thirty minutes from the time you talk on the telephone each week.

• Take a pad and research material in the car. When you're stuck in traffic, jot notes or sneak in a few paragraphs of reading.

• Do your research reading on your exercise machine. Some machines even come with book holders.

Show, don't tell

"Show, don't tell" should be the mantra of every professional writer.

> Tell: **It was very cold.**
> Show: **They hunched their shoulders against the wind and shivered.**
> Tell: **She was embarrassed.**
> Show: **Her toes curled in her shoes and she blushed.**
> Tell: **He was mad.**
> Show: **His face reddened and he clenched his teeth.**

Use examples

Ben Franklin said it most succinctly: "The best sermon is an example." If you would persuade with words, use example first, opinion second. Examples can include anecdotes, case studies, clinical studies, statistics, test results, etc. These carry far more weight than personal opinion.

Evoke all five senses

Smell, taste, and touch can be remarkably powerful but are often underused. "Good writing," said E. L. Doctorow, "is supposed to evoke sensation in the reader—not the fact that it's raining, but the feel of being rained upon."

Her smooth, white throat smelled of Ivory Soap.

The perfume behind her earlobe stung the tip of my tongue.

Take care with "then" and "than"

One little letter makes all the differnce.

Incorrect:	**Jan is better *then* her opponent.**
Correct:	**Jan is better *than* her opponent.**
Incorrect:	**It is better, *than*, to stir the noodles quickly.**
Correct:	**It is better, *then*, to stir the noodles quickly.**

Be aware, the word *then* is often superfluous.

He then took the lasso and roped a calf.
He took the lasso and roped the calf.
It was then that she noticed the full moon.
She noticed the full moon.

Use abbreviations sparingly

Don't use abbreviations unless they're commonly known by your readers.

> First, my CPU unit crashed along with the SCSI, then my CRT exploded. If only I had loaded that DDT earlier!

The object of writing is to be clear, not to show off how hip you are.

Don't write gobbledygook

Avoid official-sounding gobbledygook. It is not only unclear but frequently pompous.

> **Officialese: As soon as the defrayal is in receivement, the package will be delivered.**
> **Plain English: We'll ship the package as soon as we receive your check.**
> **Officialese: There should be an interface for decisioning to prevent destabilization.**
> **Plain English: We should have a meeting and come to a decision before there is an uproar.**

Write metaphorically

The exact use of metaphors adds dimension to your descriptions.

> **Plain: The desert is a sandy wasteland.**
> **Metaphoric: The desert, that *neglected plot in God's garden*.**
> **Plain: The desert was dry but beautiful.**
> **Metaphoric: A *parched Eden* lay before us.**
> **Plain: The landscape was weird and threatening.**
> **Metaphoric: We felt as if we were entering the *Devil's backyard*.**

Using the tips provided, let's see how we can improve the following sentence.

> **It was at that moment that the bullets went into the wall behind us, and then we saw the car drive off very quickly.**

Use the "cutting sharpens" principle. "It was at that moment that" is superfluous, as are the words "very" and "and then we saw." We'll trim them.

The bullets in the first sentence are strangely silent. Let's replace "went into" with "pinged into." The bullets can now be clearly heard, which adds a sensual dimension in the mind of the reader.

"Car" is vague. It paints no clear picture. Let's be vivid and substitute "Maserati."

Now, while we've already discarded the word "very" and changed "car" to "Maserati," "The Maserati drove off quickly" is still pretty banal. Let's spice it up by writing "The Maserati smoked its Goodyears and roared off."

Now we've got:

As the bullets pinged into the wall behind us, the Maserati smoked its Goodyears and roared off.

What do you think? Which would you prefer to read?

Why you're working so hard

You may at times forget why you're working so hard. When an editor or agent calls that first time with the good news, it will all become suddenly clear to you.

"It was the greatest high I've ever experienced," says Dianne Schwartz on learning her first book, *Whose Face Is in the Mirror,* was going to be published. "I told my agent I had to hang up because I couldn't talk—I was too overwhelmed. I told my children the news and we hugged each other and broke down and sobbed."

That's what you're working for.

Dianne has these words of advice to her fellow struggling authors, and they are the words I'll leave you with:

"It's a long and sometimes painful process, but don't ever give up. You never know when success is just around the corner."

Now get out there and get started and make us proud.

The Author's Bundle of Rights

According to United States copyright law, the writer's work is considered copyrighted from the moment it is written. This automatically gives the author ownership of a bundle of rights to his or her work. (Copyright laws differ from country to country so be sure to review and understand your country's copyright laws. In most instances, many of the terms and concepts listed here will still be applicable.)

This bundle of rights may be divided and sold in any number of pieces and with any limitations the author can conceive of and get a publisher to agree to. The writer assigns the right to use the work to publishers, according to the contract between the writer and the publisher.

This is just a brief summary of some of the components of the bundle of rights. For specific questions, it is always best to consult an attorney who specializes in communications, copyright, or publication law.

All rights—Just what it sounds like. When a writer sells "all rights" to a work to a publisher, the writer no longer has any say in future publication of the work. It's always a good idea to avoid selling "all rights," unless the amount offered is very good or the writer decides that the sale—for prestige or another reason—is worth abdicating all rights to the piece.

Electronic or digital rights—This is a term used to define a bundle of rights related to computer technology. It may include the right to reproduce the material on CD-ROMs, in online databases, in multimedia or interactive media, for distribution in a format to be used with E-books, or with publishing-on-demand systems. Just like all other rights, an author may wish to assign certain electronic rights and retain others.

North American rights—Yep, you guessed it. This is the right to publish the work in North America. This could be limited to just the English language or in any other way an author and a publisher agree upon.

First serial rights—The right to be the first periodical to publish the material. May be limited geographically. Used when an excerpt from a book is published in a periodical, usually previous to or simultaneously with the publication of the book.

Foreign language rights—The right to reproduce the material in one or more foreign language. This also may involve geographic limitations, for instance, the right to publish in Spanish in Mexico, but not in South America.

Foreign rights—These include the right to publish the material outside of the originating country. These may be broken down by country or by some other geographical division such as European rights and may involve foreign language rights.

Simultaneous rights—The right to publish the material at the same time, purchased by two or more publishers. This may be the case with books published in the United States and another country.

Subsidiary rights—This is a term that refers to any secondary rights including, but not limited to,

Audio rights
Book club rights
Character rights
Condensation rights
Dramatic rights
   TV rights
   Film rights
Mass-market paperback rights
Merchandising rights
Trade paperback rights
Translation rights

Arrangements with the publisher should always be made for the author to receive a fair share of any revenue generated by the sale or use of subrights, or the subrights should be retained by the author.

World English-language rights—This gives the publisher exclusive rights to publish the book in the English language anywhere in the world.

Standard Format for
Book Proposals and Manuscripts

There is no single, correct physical format for a book proposal, but following common manuscript format conventions, as shown here, is a good way to say to an editor: "I am a professional." Always use letterhead-sized, white paper. Always be sure the print is dark and legible. Paper clip sheets together or use a two-pocket folder; never staple.

Author's Name
Street Address
City, State Zip
Phone Number
E-mail address

Copyright © Year
Approx.: XX,XXX words

Some say a copyright notice is the mark of a novice. Most editors won't care either way.

For a manuscript, round estimated word count to nearest 1,000. Don't list a book proposal's word count.

TITLE OF BOOK

by Author's Name

Come down about one-third and type the title in all caps. Double-space and type "by" and the author's name.

Lorem ipsum dolor sit amet, consectetuer adipiscing elit, sed diam nonummy nibh euismod tincidunt ut laoreet dolore magna aliquam erat volutpat. Ut wisi enim ad minim veniam, quis nostrud exerci tation ullamcorper suscipit lobortis nisl ut aliquip ex ea commodo consequat.

Duis autem vel eum iriure dolor in hendrerit in vulputate velit esse molestie consequat, vel illum dolore eu feugiat nulla facilisis at vero eros et accumsan et iusto odio dignissim qui blandit praesent luptatum zzril delenit augue duis dolore te feugait nulla facilisi.

Lorem ipsum dolor sit amet, consectetuer adipiscing elit, sed diam nonummy nibh euismod tincidunt ut laoreet

Leave four blank lines, then start the text.

Indent paragraphs.

Double-space text. Do not justify the right margin.

Left, right, and bottom margins should be 1"-1½" wide.

Lastname/Title/4

Leave 1½" blank at top of sheet.

dolore magna aliquam erat volutpat. Ut wisi enim ad minim veniam, quis nostrud exerci tation ullamcorper suscipit lobortis nisl ut aliquip ex ea commodo consequat. Duis autem vel eum iriure dolor in hendrerit in vulputate velit esse

molestie consequat, vel illum dolore eu feugiat nulla facilisis at.

END

Place a slug line: last name/a key word from the title/page number, one-quarter of an inch down, right justified, on all but first page.

Drop four lines below end of text on the last page and type "END."

Resources

Books…Magazines…Websites…
Associations & other organizations

Helpful Books

1001 Ways to Market Your Books, John Kremer, Open Horizons.

The American Directory of Writer's Guidelines: Morre than 1,600 Magazine Editors and Book Publishers Explain What They Are Looking for from Freelancers, edited by Stephen Blake Mettee, Quill Driver Books.

The Complete Guide to Self-Publishing, Marilyn and Tom Ross, Writer's Digest Books.

Creative Nonfiction: Researching and Crafting Stories of Real Life, Philip Gerard, Writer's Digest Books.

The Elements of Style, William Strunk, Jr. and E. B. White, MacMillan Publishing.

The Fast-Track Course on How to Write a Nonfiction Book Proposal, Stephen Blake Mettee, Quill Driver Books A short, simple guide on writing a successful book proposal by a seasoned book editor.

Feminine Wiles: Creative Techniques for Writing Women's Features Stories That Sell, Donna Boetig, Quill Driver Books.

Find it Fast: How to Uncover Expert Information on Any Subject, Robert Berkman, HarperPerennial.

Getting the Words Right: How to Rewrite, Edit and Revise, Theodore Cheney, Writer's Digest Books.

How to Be Your Own Literary Agent: The Business of Getting a Book Published, Richard Curtis, Houghton Mifflin.

How to Write a Book Proposal, Michael Larsen, Writer's Digest Books.

How to Write Irresistible Query Letters, Lisa Collier Cool, Writer's Digest Books.

How to Write the Story of Your Life, Frank Thomas, Writer's Digest Books.

The Internet for Dummies, John Levine, IDG Books.

Jeff Herman's Guide to Publishers, Editors and Literary Agents, Jeff Herman, Prima Publishing.

Jump Start Your Book Sales: A Money-Making Guide for Authors, Independent Publishers and Small Presses, Marilyn and Tom Ross, Communication Creativity.

Kirsch's Handbook of Publishing Law, Jonathan Kirsch, Acrobat Books.

A Manual of Writer's Tricks, David Carrol, Paragon House.

National Writers Union Guide to Freelance Rates and Standard Practices, National Writers Union. Provides information on royalties, advances, print runs, and more.

Literary Market Place and *International Literary Market Place,* Bowker Publishing. A comprehensive directory of the publishing marketplace, including the names of specific editors at publishing houses.

Mastering the Business of Writing: A Leading Literary Agent Reveals the Secrets of Success, Richard Curtis, Allworth Press.

Negotiating a Book Contract, Mark Levine, Moyer Bell Ltd.

The Portable Writers' Conference: Your Guide to Getting and Staying Published, Stephen Blake Mettee, Quill Driver Books.

The Self-Publishing Manual, Dan Poynter, Para Publishing

Writer's Market, Writer's Digest Books. The must-have annual directory of large and small publishers.

Writing From Personal Experience: How to Turn Your Life into Salable Prose, Nancy Kelton, Writer's Digest Books.

Writing Life Stories, Bill Roorbach, Writer's Digest Books.

Writing Successful Self-Help and How-to Books, Jean Stine, Writer's Digest Books.

Helpful Magazines

Byline
P.O. Box 5204
Edmond, OK 73083
Monthly magazine offering many tips for writers.

Publishers Weekly
360 Park Avenue South
New York, NY 10010
Infomation on the book publishing business. Lots of extremely useful facts and figures, new book imprints, author profiles, reviews, and more.

The Writer
21027 Crossroads Circle
P.O. Box 1612
Waukesha, WI 53187-1612
A monthly magazine for writers with how-tos and market updates.

Writer's Journal
P.O. Box 394
Perham, MN 56573
Bi-monthly publication covering fiction and nonfiction.

Writer's Digest Magazine
4700 E. Galbraith Road
Cincinnati, OH 45236
Monthly magazine for writers. Wide range of how-tos, market updates, publisher profiles, and more.

Helpful Websites

Agentquery.com
A database of agents.

Association of Authors Representatives—AAR-online.org
A great source for information on literary agents, including a database of member agents currently accepting new clients.

Go-publish-yourself.com
Everything you need to know about publishing your book yourself.

Howstuffworks.com
Learn how virtually anything works, a great reference resource.

Julieduffy.com
Print on demand publishing and marketing and promoting your work.

Publishersweekly.com

The online site for the magazine of the same name. Subscription basis. Great publishing news and articles, including lots of archived material.

Questia.com

Online access to books, magazines, newspapers, journals and encyclopedias.

QuillDriverBooks.com

Free articles on writing and getting published, books for writers. Sign up for a free e-mail newsletter on writing and publishing.

Society of Children's Book Writers and Illustrators—scbwi.org

Market information and much more.

United States Copyright Office—copyright.gov

How much does it cost to copyright your work? Where do you get the proper forms? How much of another author's work can you "borrow" without being charged with plagiarism? Can you copyright a book title? For all of your questions on United States copyright law, check out this website.

Wordpreneur.com

Tips to help you make more money as a writer.

Writefromhome.com

How to write at home while caring for a busy family.

WritersDigest.com

The online version of the magazine by the same name.

Writergazette.com

Offers a free weekly newsletter, information on paying jobs, contest listings, and other resources.

Writersmarket.com

The online version of their massive directory. Instant access to thousands of editors and agents. A subscription to this site is available by the year or by the month.

Organizations

American Medical Writers Association—AMWA.Org

American Society of Journalists and Authors—asja.org

The Authors Guild—authorsguild.org

Canadian Authors Association—Canauthors.org

International Women Writers Guild—IWWG.org

National Association of Science Writers—NASW.org

National Writers Association—nationalwriters.org

National Writers Union—NWU.org

Society of American Business Editors and Writers—SABEW.org

Society of American Travel Writers—SATW.org

Glossary

Advance — The amount a publisher pays an author before a book is published. The advance is deducted from the royalties earned. Often an advance is paid in two or three parts: at the time the contract is signed, upon delivery of an acceptable manuscript, and, if in three parts, upon publication of the book.

All rights — See The Author's Bundle of Rights, page 230.

Auction — Conducted—usually by an agent—when more than one publisher is interested in buying a book manuscript. Often conducted by a series of phone calls over a number of hours or days.

Back matter — The material at the end of a book, usually consisting of one or more of the following: appendixes, notes, glossary, bibliography, index. See also Front matter.

Backlist — A publisher's list of books still in print. See also Front list; Midlist.

Book packager — A company that puts together a book, working with writers, editors, graphic artists, and printers but does not sell the book to the public, instead selling the package to a publisher.

Book proposal — Specific written information on a proposed book. Includes an outline, sample chapter or two, markets, and other such information.

Clips — Samples of an author's published work, usually photocopies of newspaper or magazine stories or articles.

Copyediting — Editing a manuscript for grammar, punctuation, sentence structure, etc., not content.

Copyright — Legal protection of an author's work. Under U.S. law, copyright is automatically secured when the piece is written.

Conventional publisher — Contracts with an author for the right to publish his or her book, then edits, designs, prints, and markets the book at the publisher's expense. Pays the author royalties based on the book's sales. See also: Self-publishing; Subsidy publisher; Vanity publisher.

Copublishing — See Subsidy publisher.

Cover letter — Short letter introducing a manuscript or proposal. Not always necessary. See also Query/Query letter.

Derivative work — A work produced by altering another work.

Electronic submission — Submitting a story, article, or book on disk or via a modem. Most publishers now require this and a hardcopy.

El-Hi — Elementary school to high school market.

Fair use — Copyright law allows a small portion of copyrighted material to be quoted without infringing on the copyright owner's rights. The exact amount that qualifies is debatable. See also Plagiarism.

First serial rights — See The Author's Bundle of Rights, page 230.

Frontlist — Books published in the current season. See also Backlist, Midlist.

Front matter — Also called "preliminaries," this is the material at the front of a book, usually consisting of one or more of the following: title page, copyright page, dedication, epigraph, table of contents, list of illustrations, list of tables, foreword, preface, acknowledgments, introduction. See also Back matter.

Galleys — The first typeset proofs of a manuscript, used for proofreading and error correcting. A number of respected publications require galley copies of a book be sent to them three to four months prior to the publication date in order to be eligible for review in the publication.

Hard copy — Computer printout of material.

High Concept — A short statement that summarizes the essence of a book, often just one or two sentences.

ISBN — International Standard Book Number, the number on books used for ordering, sales, and catalogue information, usually used with a bar code that includes pricing.

Libel — A published accusation that exposes someone to contempt or ridicule, loss of income, or damage to reputation. Defenses include truth, consent and fair comment. The publisher and the author can both be held liable.

List royalty — Royalty payment based on a book's list (also called retail or cover) price. Figured as a percentage. See also Net royalty; Royalties.

Mass-market book — Books appealing to a wider market; these are the smaller-sized paperbacks sold in drugstores and supermarkets as well as bookstores. See also Trade book.

Midlist — Books that may make up the greater part of a publisher's list. Titles not expected to be blockbusters. See also Backlist; Frontlist.

Multiple submissions — Sending a book proposal to more than one publisher or agent at a time. Same as simultaneous submission.

Net royalty — Royalty figured as a percentage of the amount a publisher receives for a book after various wholesale discounts have been granted. See also List royalty.

Onetime rights — See The Author's Bundle of Rights, page 230.

Outline — A skeleton version of a book, often included as a part of a book proposal.

Over-the-transom — Term for unsolicited material sent by a writer to a publisher; comes from the times when authors would toss manuscripts through an open window above a publisher's door in hopes of attracting an editor's attention.

Pen name — A name used on a work instead of the author's real name.

Plagiarism — Stealing another writer's work and claiming it as your own.

Proposal — See Book proposal.

Public domain — Denotes material not protected by copyright laws. It may have never been copyrighted or the copyright has expired.

Query/Query letter — A one-page letter to an editor or agent to propose an article, story, or book. Should be an example of the author's best writing.

Remainders — Copies of a book sold at a greatly reduced price. Often the author receives no royalty, depending on the terms of the contract.

Reporting time — The time it takes an editor or agent to contact the writer regarding a query, proposal, or manuscript.

Royalties — Payment from a publisher to a book author based on the book's sales. For hardcover books, royalties generally range from 4-15 percent of the retail cover price; on paperbacks from 4-10 percent.

SASE — self-addressed, stamped envelope, required with all manuscripts for return or (if you don't need the manuscript back) the editor's reply.

Self-publishing — When the writer arranges for all the production and marketing for his or her book. Now seen as a legitimate alternative to traditional publishing. See also Conventional publisher; Subsidy publisher; Vanity publisher.

Sidebar — A companion piece supplying extra details or complementary information. Sidebars are included separate from the text of a book and are often set off by rule lines or boxes.

Simultaneous submission — See Multiple submissions.

Slant — The emphasis or direction given to a book.

Slush pile — The often large stack of unsolicited manuscripts in an agent's or editor's office. Usually the last task in an editor's list of priorities.

Subsidiary rights — See The Author's Bundle of Rights, page 230.

Subsidy publisher — A publisher who charges the author to typeset and print the book but markets the book at the publisher's expense, usually along with the publisher's own titles. The publisher and the author share in any profits to the degree and by the method agreed upon in advance. This is often done with associations like historical societies. Comes dangerously close to vanity publishing and one should check out a subsidy publisher thoroughly before signing a contract. See also: Conventional publisher; Self-publisher; Vanity publisher.

Tearsheet — The pages removed from a magazine or newspaper showing an author's work. So called because the author tears the pages out of the publication to save for a clip file. See also Clips.

Trade book — Hardcover or larger-size paperback book. Generally denotes a book that is published to sell in bookstores and to libraries. See also Mass-market book.

Unsolicited manuscript — Any manuscript that an editor did not specifically ask to see. See also Slush pile.

Vanity publisher — A vanity publisher charges an author to print and bind his or her book. Often this can be done for much less by going directly to a book manufacturer. (Book manufacturers are listed in *Literary Market Place*, available at your library.) Vanity publishers often run adds in magazines and newspapers that say something like "Publisher in need of Manuscripts." Vanity publishers rarely offer editing assistance and a vanity publisher's imprint on a book is the kiss of death with most potential reviewers. Often a vanity press masquerades as a subsidy publisher offering a very limited amount of promotion and marketing. See also: Conventional publisher; Self-publisher; Subsidy publisher.

Word count — The number of words in a book or manuscript. Generally, a double-spaced, typed document with one inch margins will have about 250 words per page. Nonfiction books usually contain about 50,000 to 100,000 words.

YA — Abbreviation for young adult. Books written for teenagers are called YA books.

Index

About the Author

Former literary agent and best-selling author Marc McCutcheon has thirteen books currently in print, including *Descriptionary*, *The Compass in Your Nose & Other Astonishing Facts About Humans*, and *Roget's Super Thesaurus*, all Book-of-the-Month Club selections.

The editors at Amazon.com recently voted *Roget's Super Thesaurus* one of the "Ten Best" reference books published in the last several years.

Marc doesn't hide the fact that he is a high school dropout. "I almost invariably get unpublished authors' complete attention when I tell them I dropped out of high school. Something about being an autodidact fascinates people and gives them hope that 'if he can do it, I can do it.'"

He lives with his wife, Deanna, and two children, Kara and Macky, in South Portland, Maine.

To sign up for a free e-mail newsletter on writing and getting published, go to QuillDriverBooks.com

The American Directory of
Writer's Guidelines

*More than 1,600 Magazine Editors and Book Publishers
Explain What They Are Looking for from Freelancers*

Compiled and Edited by Stephen Blake Mettee,
Michelle Doland and Doris Hall

$29.95 • 816 pp. • 8.5" x 11" • Indexed by topics
ISBN 1-884956-51-3

Perhaps the best-kept secret in the publishing industry is that many publishers—both periodical publishers and book publishers—make available writer's guidelines to assist would-be contributors. Written by the staff at each publishing house, these guidelines help writers target their submissions to the exact needs of the individual publisher. *The American Directory of Writer's Guidelines* is a compilation of the actual writer's guidelines for more than 1,600 publishers.

A one-of-a-kind source to browse for article, short story, poetry and book ideas.

Both Are
Writer's Digest
Book Club
Selections

Feminine Wiles
Creative Techniques for Writing Women's
Feature Stories That *Sell*

by Donna Elizabeth Boetig

$14.95 • 191pp • ISBN 1-884956-02-5

"More valuable than a dozen writer's workshops or journalism courses. If you're interested in developing a successful career as a freelance writer for women's magazines, read Feminine Wiles—*and get to work."*
—Jane Farrell, Senior Editor, *McCall's*

...commit yourself. You are going to write stories of women's struggles and joys. You are going to discover information that changes the lives of readers. You are going to predict trends and you may even create a few of your own. You are going to look out into the world to see what's happening and take what you find deep within yourself to figure out what it all means—for you, and your readers.

*Available at bookstores or order your copy
today...toll free: 1-800-497-4909*

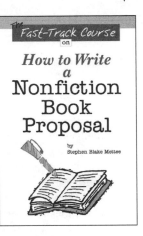